Political Economy and Global Capitalism

Other titles of interest:

Reddy, Y. V. *India and the Global Financial Crisis* (2010)
Felipe, Jesus *Inclusive Growth, Full Employment, and Structural Change* (2009)
Andersen, Esben Sloth *Schumpeter's Evolutionary Economics* (2009)
Nolan, Peter *Capitalism and Freedom* (2008)
Chang, Ha-Joon (ed.) *Institutional Change and Economic Development* (2007)
Fullbrook, Edward (ed.) *Real World Economics* (2007)
Rangaswamy, Vedavalli *Energy for Development* (2007)
Ringmar, Erik *Surviving Capitalism* (2005)
Ritzen, Jozef *A Chance for the World Bank* (2004)
Fullbrook, Edward (ed.) *A Guide to What's Wrong with Economics* (2004)
Chang, Ha-Joon *Kicking Away the Ladder* (2003)

Political Economy and Global Capitalism
The 21st Century, Present and Future

Edited by

Robert Albritton, Bob Jessop and Richard Westra

ANTHEM PRESS
LONDON · NEW YORK · DELHI

Anthem Press
An imprint of Wimbledon Publishing Company
www.anthempress.com

This edition first published in UK and USA 2010
by ANTHEM PRESS
75-76 Blackfriars Road, London SE1 8HA, UK
or PO Box 9779, London SW19 7ZG, UK
and
244 Madison Ave. #116, New York, NY 10016, USA

Editorial matter and selection;
Robert Albritton, Bob Jessop and Richard Westra © 2010
individual chapters © individual contributors

The moral right of the authors has been asserted.
All rights reserved. Without limiting the rights under copyright reserved above, no part of this publication may be reproduced, stored or introduced into a retrieval system, or transmitted, in any form or by any means (electronic, mechanical, photocopying, recording or otherwise), without the prior written permission of both the copyright owner and the above publisher of this book.

British Library Cataloguing in Publication Data
A catalogue record for this book is available from the British Library.

Library of Congress Cataloging in Publication Data
A catalog record for this book has been requested.

ISBN-13: 978 1 84331 279 6 (Hbk)
ISBN-10: 1 84331 279 4 (Hbk)

ISBN-13: 978 1 84331 875 0 (Pbk)
ISBN-10: 1 84331 875 X (Pbk)

ISBN-13: 978 1 84331 888 0 (eBook)
ISBN-10: 1 84331 888 1 (eBook)

1 3 5 7 9 10 8 6 4 2

CONTENTS

List of Abbreviations vii
Notes on Contributors ix

Introduction: Political Economy and Global Capitalism xiii
Robert Albritton, Bob Jessop and *Richard Westra*

Part 1: Political Economy of the Present
Introduction 3

1. Theorizing the Contemporary World: Robert Brenner, Giovanni Arrighi, David Harvey 7
   Moishe Postone

2. Technological Dynamism and the Normative Justification of Global Capitalism 25
   Tony Smith

3. Eating the Future: Capitalism Out of Joint 43
   Robert Albritton

4. What follows Neo-liberalism? The Deepening Contradictions of US Domination and the Struggle for a New Global Order 67
   Bob Jessop

5. Monetary Policy in the Neo-liberal Transition: A Political Economy Critique of Keynesianism, Monetarism and Inflation Targeting 89
   Alfredo Saad Filho

Part 2: Political Economy of a Progressive Global Future
Introduction 123

6. Volatile, Uneven and Combined Capitalism 127
   Patrick Bond

7.	The Erosion of Non-Capitalist Institutions and the Reproduction of Capitalism *David M Kotz*	159
8.	The Transformative Moment *Julie Matthaei* and *Barbara Brandt*	177
9.	Frontiers of Cadre Radicalization in Contemporary Capitalism *Kees van der Pijl*	201
10.	*Green* Marxism and the Institutional Structure of a Global Socialist Future *Richard Westra*	219
	Index	237

LIST OF ABBREVIATIONS

AIDS	Acquired Immune Deficiency Syndrome
ATTAC	Association for the Taxation of Financial Transactions to Aid Citizens
BIS	Bank for International Settlements
CBI	Central Bank Independence
CEO	Chief Executive Officer
CFC	Chloroflurocarbon
CO_2	Carbon Dioxide
DAWN	Development Alternatives with Women for a New Era
ERP	Enterprise Resource Planning
EU	European Union
FAO	Food and Agricultural Organization
FDI	Foreign Direct Investment
GATS	General Agreement on Trade in Services
GATT/WTO	General Agreement on Tariffs and Trade/World Trade Organization
GCAP	Global Call for Action Against Poverty
GDP	Gross Domestic Product
GLBT	Gay Lesbian Bisexual Transsexual
GM	Genetically Modified
GMO	Genetically Modified Organism
HIV	Human Immunodeficiency Virus
IBM	International Business Machines
IFI	International Financial Institutions
ILO	International Labour Organization
IMF	International Monetary Fund
IR	Industrial Revolution
IRS	Internal Revenue Service
IT	Inflation Targeting
IT	Information Technology
ITR	Inflation Targeting Regime
KFC	Kentucky Fried Chicken

LETS	Local Exchange and Trading Systems
LTCM	Long Term Capital Management
MAI	Multilateral Agreement on Investment
MBA	Master of Business Administration
MDGs	Millennium Development Goals
MSF	Médecins Sans Frontières
NAM	Non-Aligned Movement
NCDs	Newly Created Democracies
NGO	Non-Governmental Organization
NICs	Newly Industrialized Countries
NIEO	New International Economic Order
NMPC	New Monetary Policy Consensus
NNEs	Nonviable National Economies
OECD	Organization for Economic Cooperation and Development
OPT	Outward Processing Traffic
PFLAG	Parents, Families and Friends of Lesbians and Gays
PPP	Purchasing Power Parity
PR	Public Relations
QTM	Quantity Theory of Money
R&D	Research and Development
SARS	Severe Acute Respiratory Syndrome
TPCS	Theory of a Purely Capitalist Society
TRIPS	Trade Related Intellectual Property Rights
UCEs	Ungovernable Chaotic Entities
UN	United Nations
UNCTAD	United Nations Conference on Trade and Development
UNDP	United Nations Development Programme
UNHCR	United Nations High Commissioner for Refugees
UNICEF	United Nations Children's (Emergency) Fund
UNSC	United Nations Security Council
WB	World Bank
WEO	World Environment Organization

NOTES ON THE CONTRIBUTORS

Robert Albritton is Professor Emeritus in the Department of Political Science, York University, Toronto, Canada. He is the author of the volumes: *Economics Transformed: Discovering the Brilliance of Marx*, Pluto Press, 2007; *A Japanese Approach to Stages of Capitalist Development*, Macmillan, 1991 (translated into Japanese); and *Dialectics and Deconstruction in Political Economy*, Macmillan, 1999. His recent articles include: 'Theorising Capital's Deep Structure and the Transformation of Capitalism', *Historical Materialism*, Vol. 12, No. 3; 'Returning to Marx's *Capital*: A Critique of Lebowitz's *Beyond Capital*', *History of Economic Ideas*, Vol. XI, No. 3; and 'How Dialectics Runs Aground: The Antinomies of Arthur's Dialectic of Capital', *Historical Materialism*, 13.2, 2005.

Patrick Bond is a political economist and Research Professor at the University of KwaZulu-Natal, School of Development Studies in Durban where he also directs the Centre for Civil Society (http://www.ukzn.ac.za/ccs). His recent books include *Climate Change, Carbon Trading and Civil Society* (co-edited), Rozenberg Publishers, 2007; *The Accumulation of Capital in Southern Africa* (co-edited), Rosa Luxemburg Foundation, 2007; *Looting Africa: The Economics of Exploitation*, Zed Books and University of KwaZulu-Natal (UKZN) Press, 2006; *Talk Left, Walk Right: South Africa's Frustrated Global Reforms*, UKZN Press, 2006; *Elite Transition: From Apartheid to Neoliberalism in South Africa*, UKZN Press, 2005; *Fanon's Warning: A Civil Society Reader on the New Partnership for Africa's Development*, Africa World Press, 2005; and *Against Global Apartheid: South Africa meets the World Bank, IMF and International Finance*, Zed Books and University of Cape Town Press, 2003.

Barbara Brandt is a social change activist, independent scholar, who has been active in the ecology, shorter-work-time, and alternative economics movements (TOES). She is the author of *Whole Life Economics: Revaluing Daily Life*, New Society, 1995, about the theories, values, relationships and institutions of a now-emerging more democratic, feminist-oriented, personally-fulfilling and environmentally sustainable economy.

Bob Jessop is Director of the Institute for Advanced Studies and Professor of Sociology at Lancaster University, UK. He is best known for his contributions to social and political theory and to the critique of political economy. He is currently working on a systematic integration of critical semiotic analysis into the investigation of the economic and political domains and, in addition, the contradictions of the knowledge-based economy. His overall approach is pre-disciplinary in inspiration (notably Marx, Schumpeter and Polanyi) and post-disciplinary in practice. He has published 13 books, more than 80 refereed journal articles and 130 contributions to edited collections of various kinds. His work appears in *Actuel Marx, Antipode, Capital and Class, Competition and Change, Critical Discourse Studies, Das Argument, Economy and Society, Historical Materialism, International Journal of Urban and Regional Studies, New Left Review, New Political Economy, Political Geography, Prokla, Rethinking Marxism, Review of International Political Economy, Studies in Political Economy, Urban Studies* and other journals. His most important books comprise: *The Capitalist State*, Oxford: Martin Robertson, 1982; *Nicos Poulantzas*, London: Macmillan, 1985; *Thatcherism: a Tale of Two Nations* (co-authored with Kevin Bonnett, Simon Bromley and Tom Ling) Cambridge: Polity 1988; *State Theory*, Cambridge: Polity, 1990; *The Politics of Flexibility* (co-edited with Hans Kastendiek, Klaus Nielsen and Ove K Pedersen) Cheltenham: Edward Elgar, 1991; *Strategic Choice and Path-Dependency in Post-Socialism* (co-edited with Jerzy Hausner and Klaus Nielsen) Cheltenham: Edward Elgar, 1995; *The Future of the Capitalist State*, Cambridge: Polity, 2002; *State/Space* (co-edited with Neil Brenner, Martin Jones, and Gordon McLeod) Oxford: Blackwell, 2003; *Beyond the Regulation Approach* (co-authored with Ngai-Ling Sum), Cheltenham: Edward Elgar, 2006; *State Power*, Cambridge: Polity, 2007; and *Towards a Cultural Political Economy* (co-authored with Ngai-Ling Sum) Cheltenham: Edward Elgar, 2007.

David M Kotz is Professor of Economics at the University of Massachusetts Amherst and Research Associate at the Political Economy Research Institute at that university. His co-authored book with Fred Weir, *Russia's Path from Gorbachev to Putin: The Demise of the Soviet System and the New Russia*, is forthcoming with Routledge in 2007. It is a revised and updated version of *Revolution from Above: The Demise of the Soviet System*, with Fred Weir, Routledge, 1997. His recent work has been on the evolution of formerly centrally planned economies, analysis and critique of neo-liberalism, institutional change in capitalist systems and models of participatory socialism. His articles have appeared in *Monthly Review, Science and Society, The Review of Radical Political Economics, Rethinking Marxism* and in several Russian and Chinese journals. He is the Vice President of the World Association for Political Economy.

Julie Matthaei is a social change activist who teaches feminist and radical economics at Wellesley College. She is the author of *An Economic History of Women in America*, Sussex: Harvester Press, 1982 and, with Teresa Amott, of *Race, Gender & Work: A Multicultural Economic History of Women in the United States*, Boston: Southend Press, 1991. Julie is President of Guramylay: Growing the Green Economy, Inc., and is part of the planning group for the Economic Alternatives/Social & Solidarity Economy sessions at the 2007 US Social Forum in Atlanta.

Moishe Postone is Professor of History at the University of Chicago. His recent books include the monograph, *Time, Labor and Social Domination: A Reinterpretation of Marx's Critical Theory*, Cambridge University Press, 1993 and the co-edited volume, *Bourdieu: Critical Perspectives*, University of Chicago Press and Polity Press, 1993. His list of article publications is vast and includes: 'History and Helplessness: Mass Mobilization and Contemporary Forms of Anti-capitalism', *Public Culture*, Vol. 18, No. 1, 2006; 'Critique and Historical Transformation', *Historical Materialism*, Vol. 12, No. 3; 2004; 'Contemporary Historical Transformations: Beyond Postindustrial and Neo-Marxist Theories', *Current Perspectives in Social Theory*, Vol. 19, 1999; 'Deconstruction as Social Critique: Derrida on Marx and the New World Order', *History and Theory*, Vol. 37, No. 3, 1998. And, among the many book chapters he has written the following may be noted: 'Lukács and the Dialectical Critique of Capitalism' in Albritton, R. and Simoulidis, J. (eds.), *New Dialectics and Political Economy*, Palgrave, 2003; 'Rethinking Marx in a Postmarxist World', in Camic, C. (ed.), *Reclaiming the Sociological Classics*, Blackwell Publishers, 1998.

Alfredo Saad-Filho is Senior Lecturer in Political Economy of Development and Head of the Department of Development Studies at the School of Oriental and African Studies, University of London. He is the author of *The Value of Marx: Political Economy for Contemporary Capitalism*, Routledge, 2002; *Marx's Capital*, 4th (ed.), Pluto Press, 2004, with Ben Fine; and the editor of *Anti-Capitalism: A Marxist Introduction*, Pluto Press, 2003 and *Neoliberalism: A Critical Reader*, Pluto Press, 2005, with Deborah Johnston. He has also written numerous articles on value theory, political economy of development and industrial policy.

Tony Smith is Professor and Chair of the Department of Philosophy and Religious Studies at Iowa State University. He is the author of *Globalization: A Systematic Marxian Account*, Brill, 2005; *Technology and Capital in the Age of Lean Production: A Marxian Critique of the "New Economy"*, State University of New York Press, 2000; *Dialectical Social Theory and Its Critics: From Hegel to Analytical Marxism and Postmodernism*, State University of New York Press, 1993; *The Role* *of Ethics in Social Theory*, State University of New York Press, 1991; and *The Logic of Marx's Capital: Replies to Hegelian Criticisms*, State University of New York Press, 1990.

Kees van der Pijl teaches International Relations at the University of Sussex in Brighton, UK. His work deals with transnational classes and international theory. His recent books include: *Global Rivalries from the Cold War to Iraq*, Pluto, 2006; *Global Regulation* (eds.), Palgrave, 2005; and *Global Norms in the Twentieth Century* (eds.), Cambridge Scholars Press, 2006. His articles have appeared in numerous scholarly refereed journals including: *New Left Review*, 37, 2006; *Etudes Internationales*, 37, 2, 2006. He is currently finalizing *Nomads, Empires, States. Beyond International Relations*, Pluto forthcoming 2007.

Richard Westra has taught at universities and colleges around the world: The Royal Military College of Canada; Queen's University, Kingston; the International Study Centre, East Sussex, UK and the College of the Bahamas, Nassau. Currently, he is Associate Professor in the Division of International and Area Studies, Pukyong National University, Pusan, South Korea. His work has been published in numerous international scholarly refereed journals including: *Journal of Contemporary Asia, Capital and Class, Review of International Political Economy* and *Review of Radical Political Economics*. He has also co-edited and contributed to the volumes: *Phases of Capitalist Development: Booms, Crises and Globalizations*, Palgrave, 2001 (translated into Chinese and published by Economic Science Press, Beijing, 2003); *Value and the World Economy Today: Production, Finance and Globalization*, Palgrave, 2003; *New Socialisms: Futures beyond Globalization*, Routledge, 2004; and *Marxist Perspectives on South Korea in the Global Economy*, Ashgate, 2007.

INTRODUCTION: POLITICAL ECONOMY AND GLOBAL CAPITALISM

Robert Albritton, Bob Jessop and Richard Westra

The intellectual impetus for this volume is the abiding interest of its editors in promoting in-depth, cutting-edge analysis of the current global political economy in order to advance a political economy of more equitable, humane, eco-sensitive global futures. In meeting this challenge, the contributors of this book develop distinctive and original theoretical frameworks and propose new mediations between theory and history, which is a deeply problematic relationship in the social sciences. Put differently, this volume offers theory-informed writing which contextualizes empirical research on current world-historic events and trends with an eye towards realizing a future of human socio-economic betterment. We view this project as a sequel to an earlier collection, edited by Albritton, Itoh, Westra, and Zuege, *Phases of Capitalist Development: Booms, Crises, and Globalizations*. Like with that well-received volume, we have gathered internationally recognized contributors who are based in diverse countries and write from different conceptual perspectives within the critical political economy tradition broadly understood. The key difference between the earlier and current volumes, however, is their respective orientations *to* time and location *in* time. While the previous work focused on periodizing capitalism and theorizing its successive world-historic phases to understand the present, the current project focuses on the present in order to better inform our reflections on possible or likely global futures. Moreover, whereas all the essays in the previous volume were written during or prior to the year 2000, this collection captures the momentous transformations of the global political economy, and its leading economies, in the intervening years.

9/11 is probably the most dramatic (and subsequently dramatized) event to have happened in the intervening years on the global political stage and possibly the most significant in terms of future global politics. It is too soon to judge whether the recent publication (in February 2007) of the United Nations (UN) report on climate change may dislodge the neocon American concern with 9/11 and the 'war on terrorism' (and its associated economic and political interests in the energy-military complex) in favour of more concerted global action for a 'war on climate change' (and its associated anthropocentric concerns about global political ecology and the future of humanity). In the intervening five years or so, however, following an initial wave of widespread popular and governmental sympathy with the people and political leadership of the US, the rapid bellicose shift in American foreign policy in line with neoconservative aspirations turned world opinion dramatically against the increasingly militarized and unilateral character of attempts to maintain and reinforce American global hegemony. And while the US brazen violation of international law and human rights and environmental disdain has deeply angered people everywhere, global neo-liberal economic policies are coming under attack as their nakedly exploitative and predatory substance is increasingly revealed. For example, instead of the advertised world of newly industrialized countries (NICs) and newly created democracies (NCDs), neo-liberalism has bequeathed a world of nonviable national economies (NNEs) and ungovernable chaotic entities (UCE's) (De Rivero, 2001). A recent study cited in the conservative weekly magazine *The Economist* names 46 such potentially 'failed states' (2005). Attendant to this, the UN estimates that there exists a steadily rising stream of over 20 million largely 'stateless' refugees the world over (United Nation High Commissioner for Refugees (UNHCR), 2007). Instead of realizing a middle-class dream for humanity, neo-liberalism portends a nightmare scenario where it is estimated half of the world's urban population will be living in slums and shanty-towns by 2020 (Davis, 2004, p.17). Neo-liberalism also holds out a bleak future for today's youth with 50 per cent of the 1 billion young people between 15 and 24 years of age are already living in poverty (Worldwatch Institute, 2004, p. 153).

Nor is all well on the home front in the US, the heralded capitalist 'model' of neo-liberal success. With deepening economic and political divisions throughout the country, wages and salaries form the lowest share of US gross domestic product (GDP) since the government began recording the data in 1947. Yet, corporate profits have climbed to their highest share since the 1960s leading a major US investment bank to describe the current period as 'the golden era of profitability' (*The New York Times*, 2006). In 2005, the US budget (minus Social Security) amounted to $2.5 trillion. Of this enormous sum, it is estimated that 50 per cent goes toward military spending both direct and indirect (Chretien, 2006). Yet, the US manifests shocking increases in poverty with 25 per cent of children born into poverty (Grossberg, 2005, p. 60) and

100,000 children living on the streets at the close of the twentieth century (Anelauskas, 1999, p. 209). Statistics gathered in 1995 show that 49.7 per cent of Hispanic households had annual incomes below $25,000 as did 54.3 per cent of African–American households (Anelauskas, 1999, p. 78). And this is occurring as the cost of living is increasing every year.

When President George Bush Sr. responded to the Rio Earth Summit call for global environmental responsibility that 'our way of life is non-negotiable' (quoted in Lipietz, 2004), it was probably the trinity of rampant militarization, gaping world economic inequality and profaning of the globe's ecosystems that he had in mind. Continuing reductions in the quality of life for the majority of his country's population have also been non-negotiable – but to their detriment, not their benefit as the costs of tax-cuts and corporate welfare have advantaged a tiny minority of the wealthiest and most powerful families and the top corporate and financial enterprises.

Pushed along by oil interests, President George W Bush Jr. not only refuses to go along with the Kyoto Accord, but also steadfastly denies that global warming is even a problem; though the evidence that it *is* a problem is increasingly becoming overwhelming. Today, the earth faces immense problems associated with climate change, with pollution, and with the increasing scarcity of non-renewable resources such as oil, fertile land, fresh water and non-polluted air. So far the response of the richest and most powerful capitalist power in the world has been to drag its feet rather than to take the lead. As would be expected, it is particularly slow to act when the radical changes required might diminish the profits in the oil, auto, food and other key industries.

The capitalist triumphalism at the end of the Cold War that energized neo-liberal economic policies has now been deservedly put on the defensive as it fails to deal with looming human and ecological problems of great scope and seriousness. Has neo-liberal self-confidence begun to unravel? Does the rather belated recantation of neoconservatism by Francis Fukuyama presage the shift from an offensive to defensive step in neo-liberal and neoconservative domination? Has a previously ascendant American global hegemony begun to fall? Are the uprisings of the youth in the Paris suburbs in 2006 harbingers of a more general resistance in a world where neo-liberal economics are depriving the youth of a future? How should we evaluate the signs that indicate a potentially hard and rocky road for neo-liberalism and capitalism itself in the immediate future? What new modes of political economic thought and action are required to deal effectively with problems that neo-liberalism far from solving only makes worse? These are some of the pressing questions that contributors of this book attempt to address.

References

Anelauskas, V. 1999. *Discovering American as It Is*. Atlanta: Clarity Press.

Chretien, T. 2006. 'An Alternative to Endless War and Perpetual Poverty', http://www.counterpunch.org/chretien04072006.html.

Davis, M. 2004. 'Planet of Slums', *New Left Review*, 26.

De Rivero, O. 2001. *The Myth of Development: Non-viable Economies of the 21st Century*. London: Zed Books.

Grossberg, L. 2005. *Caught in the Crossfire: Kids, Politics, and America's Future*. London: Paradigm.

Lipietz, A. 2004. 'Kyoto, Johannesburg, Baghdad', *International Journal of Political Economy*, 34, 1.

The Economist (2005) 'Rebuilding Failed States: From Chaos to Order', March 5.

The New York Times (2006) 'Real Wages Fail to Match Rise in Productivity', August 28.

United Nations High Commissioner for Refugees (2007).

http://www.unhcr.org/basics.html.

Worldwatch Institute. 2004. *State of the World*.

Part I: Political Economy of the Present

INTRODUCTION

David Harvey, Giovanni Arrighi and Robert Brenner have offered three of the most provocative and widely read macro-theorizations of the present global political economy. In the first chapter of this volume, Moishe Postone examines the theoretical presuppositions about capitalism that underpin the different attempts by David Harvey, Giovanni Arrighi, and Robert Brenner to grapple with the large-scale global transformations of the past three decades. Postone's contribution, 'Theorizing the Contemporary World', assesses the theoretical strengths and weaknesses of these important analyses as well as their use of empirical evidence. He concludes by contrasting the perspective of each theorist against key aspects of Marx's critique of political economy in order to advance a more adequate critique of contemporary global capitalism.

In Chapter Two – 'Technological Dynamism and the Normative Justification of Global Capitalism' – Tony Smith first presents what he takes to be the strongest contemporary justification for the normative legitimacy of global capitalism. This combines the normative principle articulated by leading theorists of global justice (the 'moral equality principle') and the theory of endogenous technological change in capitalism developed by the so-called 'new growth theorists'. Specifically, the argument proposes that the technological dynamism of global capitalism in principle enables all individuals to obtain access to the material preconditions of human flourishing and human autonomy. Next, Smith undertakes a critical assessment of this position from a Marxian standpoint. Even when workers' consumption of use-values increases, Smith argues, human flourishing and human autonomy are systematically subordinated to the flourishing and autonomy of *capital*. Smith then demonstrates that a systematic tendency to uneven development can be derived from new growth theory, undermining the claim that in global capitalism 'all persons are equal, so far as the importance of their basic interests is concerned'. His chapter ends with some reflections on the future course of global capitalism. The roles of the state and the financial system in fostering innovation have become so well understood, and effective national innovation systems have become so widely institutionalized, that it is unlikely in the foreseeable future that large surplus profits from innovation will be enjoyed by any region for a whole historical epoch. Problems with overaccumulation, financial bubbles in one category of capital assets after another, pressures to inflict the costs of devaluation on others, and 'accumulation through dispossession' are likely to persist indefinitely. This would make the suggestion that, in principle, global capitalism enables all individuals to gain access to the material preconditions of human flourishing and human autonomy even more ludicrous than it is today.

In Chapter Three – 'Eating the Future: Capitalism Out of Joint' – Robert Albritton argues that the American food regime typifies the extreme emerging contradictions of the current conjuncture of global capitalist development. Utilizing a conceptual framework derived from Marx's *Capital*, Albritton maintains that the US food regime – particularly the fast foods industry – dramatically demonstrate that capitalism is becoming highly destructive of both human and environmental health. The severity of these contradictions suggests that a phase of transition has begun away from capitalism insofar as markets are becoming ideological facades behind which profit-making increasingly relies on forms of coercion that utilize markets and 'neutral' government legislation to camouflage this fact. Because capitalism jeopardizes the very biology of humans and their environment, an unprecedented international mobilization is required to meet these challenges and to democratize all areas of economic life.

Chapter Four – 'What follows Neo-liberalism? The Deepening Contradictions of US Domination and the Struggle for a New Global Order' – by Robert Jessop explores neo-liberalism, its forms, its periodization, and its future in the context of the changing dynamic of the capitalist world market. It focuses particularly on American neo-liberalism and foreign economic policy because the US remains the dominant neo-liberal power. Jessop argues that, notwithstanding the loss of American economic hegemony and the growing challenge to its domination across a number of fields, US economic and political power retains disproportionate significance because the new forms of financial domination promoted by the federal government, its associated international economic apparatuses, and transnational financial capital are still 'ecologically dominant' in shaping the world economy, and the global order more generally. The chapter has five parts. It first addresses issues of periodization that bear on the capitalist world market and neo-liberalism, then defines neo-liberalism and distinguishes its four main forms, proceeds to discuss four forms of economic determination broadly considered, argues that the logic of US neo-liberalism is ecologically dominant in the world market, and concludes with some general remarks on the contradictions and limits of American domination.

Chapter Five – 'Monetary Policy in the Neo-liberal Transition: A Political Economy Critique of Keynesiansim, Monetarism and Inflation Targeting' – by Alfredo Saad-Filho – reviews the transition from Keynesianism to neo-liberalism in terms of changes in the theory and practice of monetary policy. He argues, first, that monetary policy and exchange rate regimes are irreducibly political. They do not just offer alternative approaches to macroeconomic management; they also discipline nation states and social actors. Second, the demise of Keynesianism was due, according to Saad-Filho, to the breakdown of its modes of imposition of discipline, reflected in the development of intractable socio-economic and political problems. Third, the neo-liberal transition was the contingent outcome of the search for solutions to these problems as they affected accumulation. Finally, he argues that the monetary and exchange rate policy regime appropriate for the current phase of mature neo-liberalism is finally in place. This comprises the 'new monetary policy consensus' (NMPC), including inflation targeting (IT), central bank independence (CBI) and floating exchange rates. This consensus is explained in detail and also criticized from a critical political economy angle.

Chapter 1

THEORIZING THE CONTEMPORARY WORLD: ROBERT BRENNER, GIOVANNI ARRIGHI, DAVID HARVEY

Moishe Postone

It is widely recognized that the past three decades mark a significant break with the social, political, economic and cultural order that characterized the decades following World War II. Basic changes include the weakening and transformation of welfare states in the capitalist West, the collapse or fundamental metamorphosis of bureaucratic party-states in the communist East, and the undermining of developmental states in what had been called the Third World. More generally, recent decades have seen the weakening of national, state-centred economic sovereignty and the emergence and consolidation of a neo-liberal global order. Social, political and cultural life has become increasingly global, on the one hand; on the other hand, they have become increasingly de-centred and fragmented.

These changes have occurred against the background of a lengthy period of stagnation and crisis: since the early 1970s, the growth of real wages has decreased dramatically, real wages have remained generally flat, profit rates have stagnated, and labour productivity rates have declined. Yet, these crisis phenomena have not led to a resurgence of working class movements. On the contrary, the past decades have seen the decline of classical labour movements and the rise of new social movements, often characterized by the politics of identity, including nationalist movements, movements of sexual politics and various forms of religious 'fundamentalism'. Trying to come to terms with the large-scale transformations of the past three decades, then, entails addressing not only the long-term economic downturn since the early 1970s, but also important changes in the character of social and cultural life.

It is against the background of this problematic that I wish to discuss three very important works – by Robert Brenner, Giovanni Arrighi and David Harvey[1] – that attempt to grapple with current transformations. This paper is intended as preliminary. It does not attempt to provide a definitive critical analysis of these three authors' works, but rather approaches specific works by these authors on a meta-theoretical level, focusing on their theoretical assumptions, in order to problematize the nature and characteristics of an adequate critical theory of capitalism today.

Why a theory of capitalism – or better – a theory of capital? Let me begin with a point that Harvey and others have made in considering the period of post-war prosperity: During the period 1949–73, Western states engineered stable economic growth and living standards similarly – through a mix of welfare statism, Keynesian management, and control of wage relations – although very different political parties were in power (Harvey, 1989, p. 135). One could add that in all Western states the welfare state synthesis unravelled and was rolled back in the 1970s and 1980s regardless of which party was in power.

These large-scale historical developments can themselves be seen with reference to a still larger historical pattern: the rise and decline of the state-centred organization of socio-economic life, of the apparent primacy of the political over the economic. The beginnings of this period can be located roughly in World War I and the Russian Revolution; its demise can be seen in the crisis of the 1970s and the subsequent emergence of a neo-liberal global order. This general trajectory was global. It encompassed Western capitalist countries and the Soviet Union, as well as colonized lands and decolonized countries. When viewed with reference to this general trajectory, differences in development appear as different inflections of a common pattern rather than as fundamentally different developments. The general character of the large-scale historical pattern that structured much of the twentieth century suggests the existence of overarching structural imperatives and constraints that cannot adequately be explained in local and contingent terms.

Consideration of the general historical patterns that characterize the twentieth century, then, calls into question post-structuralist understandings of history as essentially contingent. This does not, however, necessarily involve ignoring the critical insight that attempts to deal with history contingently – namely, that history, understood as the unfolding of an immanent necessity, should be understood as marking a form of un-freedom.

This form of 'un-freedom' is the object of Marx's critical theory of capitalism, which first and foremost is concerned with delineating and grounding the imperatives and constraints that are generative of the historical dynamics and structural changes of the modern world. The critique of capital does not deny the existence of historical un-freedom by focusing on contingency. Rather, it seeks to analyse that un-freedom socially and historically, uncover its basis, and point to the possibility of its overcoming. In other words, an adequate critical theory of capital seeks to elucidate the dynamics of the modern world, and does so from the immanent standpoint of its transformability. Such a critical theory of capitalism, of the historical dynamics of modernity, I would argue, can provide the best basis for a rigorous approach to the global transformations of the past three decades. It can do so, however, only to the extent that it adequately can deal with the deep social and cultural, as well as economic, changes of recent decades.

All three authors I am discussing attempt to come to grips with these recent transformations within the framework of a critical theory of capitalism. In *The Economics of Global Turbulence*, Robert Brenner marshals a great deal of evidence (data on real wages, profit rates, labour productivity rates and growth rates) to demonstrate that the world economy has been basically stagnant for 30 years (1989, pp. 1–7). Writing in the late 1990s, Brenner argues against the illusion, widespread in that period (actually, a recurrent capitalist illusion) that the problem of business cycles had been solved, that they had been left behind. His main concern is not only to explain the economic downturn of the early 1970s, but also why it persisted for such a long time. The fall in profitability, heralding the end of the post-war boom, began in the mid 1960s, according to Brenner and not, as many have argued, between 1969 and 1972 (p. 36). This, according to Brenner, contravenes what he calls 'supply-side' theories that attribute the downturn as well as its duration to increased pressure on profits exerted by workers, in as much as it indicates that the downturn antedates such pressure (p. 8, p. 18). Moreover, approaches that focus on labour necessarily look at the specific situation in each country. They cannot explain the most salient characteristics of the late twentieth century downturn: that its onset and various phases were universal and simultaneous – encompassing weak economies with strong labour movements (UK) and strong economies with weak labour movements (Japan) – and that the downturn has lasted so long (pp. 18–24). On the basis of such considerations, Brenner argues that an explanation of the downturn and subsequent failure of economies to adjust must be on the level of the international system as a whole (p. 23ff). The fall in the rate of profit was not the result of technological factors, or labour pressures, or political controls, according to Brenner, but, more fundamentally, was the result of international market competition and uneven development (pp. 8–11).

Central to Brenner's analysis is the general argument that capital in a particular industry cannot easily be diverted elsewhere when much of it is tied up in the form of fixed capital. Consequently, in such a situation, increased competition, resulting in lower margins of profit, does not lead to the diversion of capital to other areas as predicted by mainstream economic theory, but to systemic overproduction. Hence, the downturn resulting from overproduction does not result in the predicted shakeout, which then is followed by a recovery, but by a long-term fall in the rate of profit.

Specifically, Brenner argues that, as a result of the devastation wrought by World War II, there was basically only one workshop in the world in the immediate post-war period – the US. By the 1960s, however, the US began to be challenged economically by Germany and Japan. Because of the investment by American firms in fixed capital – for example in the automobile industry – those firms continued to produce at their previous levels, even though the Germans and the Japanese were expanding (automobile) production. The result was endemic, global overproduction (p. 91ff).

Brenner's argument relates crises of overproduction in capitalism to the contingencies of competition. Were it not for these contingencies, firms would know how much they should be investing in fixed capital. But they do not and cannot have this knowledge; therefore they will be subject to unforeseen pressures. Because of their fixed capital investments, however, they cannot afford to cut back and invest elsewhere. Instead they are impelled to fight for market share. Consequently, profits fall. Firms try to counteract this tendency for profits to fall by squeezing labour, destroying unions, and cutting social welfare and pensions (p. 27ff).

Brenner's account of boom and bust successfully addresses important features of the long downturn, especially its global character. It clearly shows that capitalism constitutes a global order – one, however, that is dysfunctional. His account is a useful corrective to mainstream economic discourse. It demonstrates the inadequacy of mainstream understandings of capital flows resulting from competition, and the illusory character of the recurrent notion that business cycles are a thing of the past. Brenner's approach also contravenes the widespread idea that the long downturn of the late twentieth century emerged as a result of and response to working class successes between 1968 and 1972, and provides him with the basis for a critique of the Regulation School's account of the decline of Fordism and the emergence of a post-Fordist regime.[2]

In spite of Brenner's in-depth examination of the long downturn of the late twentieth century, however, he does not adequately address other important dimensions of the transformations of recent decades. In that sense, his approach does not really provide an adequate account of historical change. His analysis of the long downturn with reference to international competition and systemic overproduction does illuminate important dimensions of that crisis. Nevertheless, there is no indication in Brenner's account of a shift in the social, cultural and political dimensions of life that could be related to the economic processes he discusses. Brenner's focus on economy is such that there is little sense that the general historical context of the late twentieth century is in any way different from earlier periods of downturn and inter-capitalist rivalry. That is, Brenner does not thematize the question of qualitative historical changes in capitalist society. Hence, when he criticizes the Regulation School, he does not provide an alternate approach to a central dimension of that theoretical approach – the concern with fundamental social and cultural changes that occur with what Regulation theorists call a new 'mode of regulation'.

If a critical theory of capitalism is to adequately deal with the historical transformations of the past three decades, however, it cannot only elucidate economic developments, understood narrowly, but must be able to illuminate changes in the nature of social and cultural life within the framework of capitalism. Only then can a critical theory of capitalism claim to be a critical theory of the modern world; that is, of a historically specific objective/subjective form of social life, rather than a theory of a determinate economic organization – narrowly understood – of modern society. Related to this (and this is crucially important), a critical theory of capitalism must be capable of elucidating qualitative, interrelated changes in social objectivity and subjectivity if it is to address large-scale cultural changes and social movements. Only then can it be, at least potentially, a theory of capitalism's possible overcoming.

The question in this regard is not whether Brenner, or any other theorist, explicitly deals with such issues, but whether their approach is intrinsically capable of elucidating historical transformations of politics, culture and society. Whatever its strengths, Brenner's approach does not deal adequately with the historical development and structure of capitalism as a form of social life: changes in culture and subjectivity seem to be outside of its purview.

These limitations of Brenner's approach are related to his basic understanding of capitalism. The issue here is not simply one of analytic range – whether a critical account of capitalism should focus on economic processes alone, rather than also addressing other dimensions of social life. Rather, it is whether the basic categories of that account can intrinsically relate different dimensions of life as interrelated aspects of a determinate form of social life. Brenner's analytic point of departure is a traditional Marxist emphasis on the unplanned, uncoordinated and competitive nature of capitalist production (Brenner 1998, p. 8). That is, at the core of his analysis of the long downturn are the notions of uneven development and competition. These notions are centrally defining of capitalism in Brenner's approach, and implicitly point to rational planning as the most salient characteristic of the post-capitalist world. The focus of such a critique of capitalism, in other words, is essentially the mode of *distribution*. Issues of the form of production, of work, and, more fundamentally, of social mediation are outside of its framework. Notions such as competition and uneven development, along with categories central to Brenner's analysis, such as profit, fixed and circulating capital, however, are categories of economy; that is, they are categories of the surface that do not adequately grasp the fundamental nature and historical dynamic of capitalism as a historically specific form of social life.

In this chapter I can only touch upon the theoretical significance of the distinction between surface and deep structure (as marking the distinction between critical political economy and the critique of political economy), and why it would make sense to revisit the category of value. At this point I simply wish to note that to characterize a notion, such as that of uneven development, as one of the surface does not mean that it is illusory, but rather signifies that it does not grasp what is most essential to capitalism.

Characterizing notions, such as competition and uneven development, and categories such as profit as surface phenomena, expresses a position that regards categories such as commodity, value and capital as those of deep structure. Brenner, however, rejects the latter categories, characterizing approaches based on them as 'Fundamentalist Marxism' (Brenner, 1998, p. 11). Differences regarding value theory frequently express different understandings of the categories. For example, value usually has been interpreted essentially as an economic category – a category of distribution that grounds prices, demonstrates exploitation (the category of surplus value), and explains the crisis-ridden character of capitalism (as a result of the growing organic composition of capital). The significance of value, so understood, often has been called into question on the basis of arguments that claim prices, exploitation and crises can be explained without reference to such a category.

I would argue for another understanding of Marx's category of value. It is not simply a refinement of that category as it was developed by Smith and Ricardo. Rather, it is a category that purports to grasp determinate abstract forms of social mediation, social wealth, and temporality that structure production, distribution, consumption and, more generally, social life in capitalist society. The temporal dimension of the categories of deep structure grounds the dynamics of capitalism; it helps explain, in historically specific terms, the existence of a historical dynamic that characterizes capitalism. Those categories, then, seek to grasp the general contours of that dynamic while indicating that an immanent historical dynamic does not characterize human histories and societies per se. Moreover, the categories of value and capital are not merely economic and are not even categories of social objectivity alone – but are categories that are at once social and cultural. Finally, the dynamic grounded in value is such that value becomes less and less adequate to the reality it generates. That is, the dynamic gives rise to the objective and subjective conditions of possibility of a social order beyond capitalism.[3] (I shall begin to further elaborate these contentions when I later discuss the notion of the falling rate of profit, as understood by Brenner and Arrighi). Far from being categories of economic and social life in general, the underlying categories of the critique of political economy purport to grasp the essential core of a historically determinate form of social life – capitalism – in ways that indicate its historically specific and possibly transient character. The abolition of what the categories purportedly grasp would entail the abolition of capitalism.

Engaging this fundamental difficulty/problem fully requires interrogating the nature of temporality in capitalism, an issue that I cannot elaborate extensively in this chapter.[4] I would, nevertheless, like to pursue these considerations further with reference to Giovanni Arrighi's – *The Long Twentieth Century*. Arrighi is among those theorists who conceptualize the period since 1973 as one of qualitative change, which he characterizes in terms of the 'financialization' of capital as its predominant feature (1994, p. xi). Arguing against positions like Rudolf Hilferding's that the increased importance of finance capital marks an entirely new stage of capitalist development, Arrighi maintains that the primacy of financialization is a recurrent phenomenon, a phase of larger cycles of capitalist development that began in late medieval and early modern Europe (p. xi).

Arrighi's study of the crisis of the late twentieth century is embedded in a much larger framework – an analysis of 'the structures and processes of the capitalist world system as a whole at different stages of its development' (p. xi). The latter, in turn, is deeply informed by Arrighi's ambitious attempt to think together what Charles Tilly characterized as 'the two interdependent master processes of the [modern] era: the creation of a system of national states and the formation of a worldwide capitalist system'.[5] In order to relate these two international systems, Arrighi has recourse to the theories of Fernand Braudel and Karl Polanyi. He adopts Braudel's understanding of capitalism as the top layer of a three-tiered structure consisting of a bottom layer of what Braudel calls 'material life', the stratum of the non-economy that can never be moulded by capitalism, a middle layer of the market economy, and a top layer of the 'anti-market', the zone of the giant predators. For Braudel, according to Arrighi, this upper level is the real locus of capitalism (Arrighi, 1994, p. 10). On the basis of Braudel's understanding, Arrighi claims that, historically, capitalist development has not been simply the unintended outcome of innumerable actions undertaken by individuals and the multiple communities of the world economy, but that the 'expansion and restructuring of the capitalist world economy have occurred under the leadership of particular communities and blocs of governmental and business agencies' (p. 9). That is, Arrighi seeks to relate state system and capitalism on the basis of Braudel's uncoupling of everyday economic activity from the upper strata of economically powerful groups.

He reinforces this approach by appropriating Karl Polanyi's critique of the nineteenth century idea of a self-regulating economy. For Polanyi, the latter depended on transforming all elements of industry into commodities, including land, labour and money. The commodity nature of the latter three, however, is completely fictitious, according to Polanyi. A system based on such a fiction is tremendously disruptive socially. Consequently, it generates a counter-movement to restrict its operations. This implies that, for capitalism to function long-term, market mechanisms have to be socially and politically controlled (Arrighi, 1994, pp. 255–8).

On the basis of his appropriation of Braudel and Polanyi, Arrighi outlines the development of the capitalist world system in terms of four systemic cycles of accumulation, each dominated by a capitalist hegemonic state – (i) a Genoese cycle, from the fifteenth to the early seventeenth century, (ii) a Dutch cycle, from the late sixteenth through most of the eighteenth century, (iii) a British cycle from the late eighteenth century to the early twentieth century, and (iv) a US cycle, which began in the late nineteenth century. Each of these cycles refers to the processes of the capitalist world system as a whole, according to Arrighi. He focuses on the strategies and structures of the governmental and business agencies of each of these states because of what he claims was their successive centrality in the formation of these stages (p. xi, p. 6).

Each cycle, according to Arrighi, is characterized by the same phases, from an initial one of financial expansion, through a phase of material expansion, followed by another financial expansion. Financialization plays a crucial role in the supersession of one hegemon by another, according to Arrighi. As he describes it, the upward trajectory of each hegemon is based on the expansion of production and trade. At a point in each cycle, however, a 'signal crisis' occurs as a result of the overaccumulation of capital. Another state then provides the outlet for this accumulated capital. Within this schema, growing financialization entails transferring capital from the current hegemon to a rising new hegemon (p. x, pp. 5–6, pp. 214–38). This developmental pattern is, however, not completely cyclical. It has directionality. Each new cycle is shorter; each new hegemon is larger, more complex, and more powerful. Each hegemon succeeds in internalizing costs its predecessor did not. The Netherlands internalized protection costs, the UK also internalized production costs, and the US adds the internalization of transaction costs (pp. 214–38). By establishing this pattern, Arrighi then argues that the current phase of financialization is a sign of the decline of US hegemony, the beginning of the end of the fourth cycle.

The pattern of development Arrighi outlines is very elegant and frequently illuminating. Nevertheless, there are problematic aspects of his account that, in my view, indicate its limits. So, for example, when Arrighi turns to more contemporary developments, his account of the rise and fall of US hegemony since 1939 is much more eclectic than one would expect from his description of the larger cycles of capitalist development. In discussing the crisis of the

1970s, he refers to the increasing competition internationally, a rise in real wages between 1968 and 1972 that outpaced growth in productivity, as well as a decision by American policymakers in the late 1970s to form an alliance with private high finance in order to discipline what were regarded as Third World threats following decolonization.

It is difficult to see how this account fits within the framework of cyclical development Arrighi presents. Although he characterizes the US cycle as anomalous, he does not explain its anomalous character. Consequently, a gap exists between his eclectic account of the 1970s and his larger framework, which suggests that the developmental pattern he outlines is essentially descriptive. He does not really present an analysis of what drives the developmental patterns he describes.

This issue also emerges implicitly when Arrighi discusses the decline of US hegemony. He argues that it can lead to the rise of a truly global world empire, based on the superiority of force of the West, or to a world market economy without a hegemon, centred in East Asia, or to systematic chaos. The first two possibilities are post-capitalist, according to Arrighi. They would signal the end of capitalism (p. 23, pp. 355–6).

This is a remarkable statement because it makes clear that Arrighi considers the essence of capitalism in terms of a world system organized by a capitalist hegemon. This problematic position has its roots in Arrighi's appropriation of Braudel's distinction between market economy and capitalism. The latter, according to Braudel, cannot be explained on the basis of ongoing market relations, in as much as a world market economy antedated capitalism. What generated the latter was a fusion of capital and the state that was unique to the West (Arrighi, 1994, pp. 10–11). The limits of this attempt to distinguish markets and capitalism by placing states at the very centre of analysis becomes manifest, however, in Arrighi's reflections on the current phase of decline of the US hegemony. However important states may have been in capitalism's development, to define capitalism essentially with reference to the state becomes a conceptual straitjacket when Arrighi attempts to analyse the contemporary world.

Neither Braudel nor Arrighi seem to take cognizance of the very different way Marx and Weber distinguish modern capitalism from markets and trade, as they might exist in other forms of society. For all their differences, both Marx and Weber see modern capitalism as unique because it is based on a process of ongoing, endless accumulation, a process that cannot be grounded in trade or in the state and, indeed, transforms both. In Marx's work, capitalism's historical dynamics is its most salient characteristic. It entails ongoing transformations of social life that are driven by the essential core of capitalism – a core that is both unchanging and, yet, is generative of change. Marx's category of capital attempts to grasp this core and the dynamics it generates.

In Arrighi's treatment of the cycles of capitalism, the category of capital remains fundamentally under-theorized. Consequently, his approach brackets any analysis of what constitutes the unique character of capitalism, its historical dynamics. Instead, as his conception of the end of capitalism indicates, Arrighi conflates this dynamics with the rise and fall of hegemons. His approach substitutes a description of a pattern for an analysis of what grounds the dynamics, and does so in a way that also brackets consideration of the ongoing structuring and restructuring of labour and more generally, of social life in capitalism.

Although, then, the theories of Braudel and Polanyi provide Arrighi with a framework for thinking together the development of the state system and that of worldwide capitalism, they also give rise to serious theoretical problems. Braudel's tripartite division of modern society into the levels of material life, the market economy, and capitalism does not allow consideration of the relation of forms of everyday social life and capitalism, while Polanyi's insistence on the fictitious character of labour, land and money as commodities obscures Marx's analysis of the commodity as a form of social relations. Within the latter framework, nothing is 'naturally' a commodity. Conversely no ontological ground exists on the basis of which 'real' and 'fictitious' commodities could be distinguished. Neither Braudel nor Polanyi allows for an adequate conception of capital and, hence, of the nature of the intrinsic dynamics of capitalist society as well as of the possibility of its overcoming.

These critical considerations are further reinforced when we look more closely at Arrighi's treatment of the crisis of the 1970s. In addressing that crisis, he has recourse to the notion that, in capitalism, there is a tendency for the rate of profit to fall. Like Brenner, Arrighi roots that tendency in competition.

The theorem of the tendency of the rate of profit to fall has been frequently identified with Marx. It commonly has been understood as Marx's attempt to demonstrate the crisis-ridden nature and limits of capitalism. This theorem, however, was not first developed by Marx, but by political economists such as Adam Smith, Thomas Malthus and David Ricardo. It is the case that Marx addresses this theorem of classical political economy. Far from positing an inexorable fall in the rate of profit, however, he treats this theorem as a surface tendency, which, therefore, is subject to many countervailing factors and tendencies (Marx, 1981, pp. 317–75). To the degree to which the rate of profit does fall, according to Marx, it does so as a surface economic manifestation of a more fundamental historical development, the tendency of the organic composition of capital – that is, the ratio of constant capital (machinery, raw materials, etc.) to variable capital (wage labour) – to rise.

The idea of a decline in variable capital relative to constant capital is central for understanding the thrust of value theory in Marx. Marx argues, as is well known, that value is constituted only by the socially necessary expenditure of direct human labour time. Unlike Adam Smith, however, Marx does not regard value as a transhistorical form of wealth but as the form of wealth historically specific to capitalism. The distinctions he makes between the production of value and that of use-value are not to be understood transhistorically and ontologically, but as constitutive of the growing contradiction of capitalism between value production as the structurally defining feature of capitalism and the enormous use-value production capabilities generated by capitalism. The potential embedded in capitalism's contradiction points to a possible fundamental transformation of the nature and social distribution of work. The realization of that possibility, however, is constantly constrained by the systemic reproduction of value-determined labour, even as that labour becomes increasingly anachronistic in terms of the productive potential of the whole.

The changing composition of capital, therefore, is *not* important in Marx's critique mainly to provide a better explanation for the tendency of the rate of profit to fall, thereby placing a theorem of classical political economy on a more solid foundation. Rather it is important first and foremost because, beneath the surface level of prices and profits, it expresses a transformation of work and production that points eventually to the possibility of a post-capitalist society. Far from being primarily a means of explaining crises, then, the theorem of the tendency of the rate of profit to fall, as reworked by Marx, expresses, indirectly, a process of the ongoing structuring and restructuring of social life, one marked by a growing gap between the actual structuring of labour and of social life and the way they could be structured in the absence of capital. Marx transforms a political-economic theorem – which many have taken as an indication of the economic limits of capital – into the surface expression of a more fundamental historical dynamic. The thrust of his critique is less to 'prove' the inevitable economic collapse of capitalism than it is to uncover a growing disparity between what is and what could be, one that constitutes the objective/subjective conditions of possibility of a different ordering of social life. The idea of such a disparity as a lived disparity would allow for an investigation of the historical generation of sensibilities, needs and imaginaries that go beyond considerations of distribution, of direct material interests. Expressed differently, the growing contradiction of capitalism so (non-economistically) understood generates the possibility of a qualitatively different future as an immanent dimension of the present.

This level of consideration, however, is absent in Arrighi, as it is in Brenner. Hence, the categories that are essential to Marx's critique – value, commodity, capital – are also basically absent, or implicitly are understood in narrowly economic terms. So, for example, when Brenner addresses Marx's treatment of the tendency of the rate of profit to fall, he claims that, according to Marx, the rise in the organic composition of capital leads to an increase in the output/labour ratio, which is insufficient to counteract the parallel fall in the output/capital ratio that it also brings about. Therefore, the rate of profit falls because overall productivity can be expected to fall (Brenner, 1998, p. 11). This interpretation completely conflates value and use-value in Marx, obscuring Marx's point that an *increase* in productivity can lead to a *decrease* in surplus value. This, however, means, more fundamentally that it fails to recognize Marx's analysis of value as an analysis of a historically specific, possibly transitory, form of wealth and social life. Consequently, the historical trajectory of capitalism leading to a possible qualitative transformation, as analysed by Marx, becomes reduced to an economic analysis of crises.

Arrighi, for his part, claims that what he calls 'Marx's version of the "law" of the tendency of the rate of to fall' was identical to Adam Smith's thesis regarding the rate of profit. Both Ricardo and Marx accepted Smith's thesis in full, according to Arrighi. The only difference was that Marx criticized Smith's version of that 'law' as too pessimistic regarding the long-term potential of capitalism to promote the development of the productive forces of society (Arrighi, 1994, pp. 222–3). This equation of Smith and Marx, however, means that Arrighi also conflates political economy and its critique, that is, a transhistorical understanding of value as wealth and an understanding of value as a form of wealth historically specific to capitalism.

Arrighi's approach does introduce a very important dimension to the analysis of capitalism – that of the state or, better, the state system. It does so, however, at the cost of central dimensions of a critical theory of capitalism that point to the possibility of another form of life. Arrighi himself notes that his book has a narrow focus, excluding consideration of issues such as class struggle (Arrighi, 1994, p. xii). But the narrowness to which he alludes is not simply empirical. Given his framework, even if Arrighi did introduce such themes, he could not treat them as integrally related to his theoretical account.

The issue is not whether Arrighi and Brenner are faithful to a revealed ('fundamentalist') dogma, but whether their approaches are fully adequate to the object of their investigations – the dynamics of contemporary capitalism. The considerations, I have outlined, seek to illuminate the differences between such critical political-economic perspectives focused on economic issues, and the project of the critique of political economy.

David Harvey in *The Condition of Postmodernity* also emphasizes the predominance of financialization in discussing the period since 1973.[6] Harvey's treatment of financialization, however, is less state-centric than that of Arrighi, which is tied to the question of rising and declining hegemons. Indeed, Harvey emphasizes that in the contemporary world, capital has no determinate locus or site, but is pervasive and global (Harvey, 1989, p. 163). As a result of the universal competition for capital, marginal differences in profit rates become increasingly important, with significant consequences for wage levels in metropolitan countries, for the uneven global extension of wage labour, and for the direction and volume of global capital flows. These flows, according to Harvey, effect a form of discipline that is much more pervasive and effective than any governmental institutions could be (pp. 164–5).

Unlike Arrighi and Brenner, Harvey has recourse to a theory of capital in order to elucidate what he regards as a sea change in culture as well as political-economic practices (Harvey, 1989, p.vii). He tries to deal with the period since 1973 not only in political-economic terms but also in terms of a changed configuration of life. By doing so, with reference to a theory of capital, moreover, with its distinctions between surface and deep structure, and between valorization and labour processes, Harvey is able to critically counter post-industrial approaches, arguing that what they understand as a new epoch is only one strand of a more complex dynamic of constraint, continuity and change. So, for example, in considering the transformation of capitalism in recent decades, Harvey focuses on the demands of valorization as mediating production, rather than on the nature of the labour process in an unmediated manner. Hence, he characterizes the newer configuration of capitalism in terms of 'flexible accumulation' rather than the more labour-process-oriented term, 'flexible specialization'.[7] In this way, Harvey is able to show that this latest phase of capitalist development is generative of a whole range of production practices – from the resurgence of sweatshops to robotics – that on the surface appear opposed, and that cannot adequately be apprehended by post-industrial theories with their one-sided focus on the labour process. This approach distinguishes the critical theory of capitalism from any theory of linear technological development and, certainly, from any theory of technological determinism.

Similarly, by focusing on capital, Harvey is able to show that this new phase of capitalism entails a complex dialectic of decentralization and centralization, heterogeneity and homogeneity. On this basis Harvey unleashes a scathing critique of postmodern approaches as hypostatizing one side of this dialectic, thereby misrecognizing current developments as marking an epochal, liberating break with the past. Because they critically grasp the existing order only in terms of centralization and homogeneity, such approaches celebrate the decentralization and heterogeneity also generated by contemporary capitalism. Far from being critical, postmodernist approaches, according to Harvey, are expressions of a new configuration of capital they do not apprehend. As such they serve to veil and affirm capital in its newest manifestation (Harvey, 1989, p. vii, p. 39ff, p. 113ff, p. 336ff, p. 350ff).

By seeking to relate postmodernist cultural changes to a new configuration of capital, Harvey moves beyond positions that understand capitalism in economic terms alone. His approach to the relation of culture and capitalism also moves beyond that of regulation theory, which does attempt to take cognizance of culture as a constitutive moment of any given epoch of capitalism, but, by positing a completely contingent relation of culture, and capitalism, does so on the basis of an understanding of culture that is essentially empty. Whereas the latter approach provides a functionalist account of the relation of cultural forms and any given large-scale configuration of capitalism, Harvey attempts to relate them intrinsically (1989, p. 201ff).

Harvey's approach explicitly raises the question of historical dynamics. His argument that the past decades have involved the emergence of a new configuration of capitalism, reminds us that this emergence involves both a process of change (a new configuration) and continuity (capitalism). By distinguishing surface from the underlying forms of capitalism, he also indicates that what remains unchanged is a core feature of capitalism.

These considerations help clarify some features of capitalism and the significance of the analysis of capital. Viewed retrospectively, the domination of capital has existed in various historical configurations, ranging from more mercantile forms through nineteenth century liberal forms, twentieth century state-centric forms, and, now, neo-liberal global forms. These changing configurations indicate that capitalism cannot be identified completely with any of its configurations. At the same time, to refer to these various configurations as forms of capitalism implies that a characterizing core – capital – underlies all of them.

This, however, suggests that the core of capitalism is generative of its various historical configurations. Although a full discussion of the issue of the historically dynamic character of capitalism is not possible within the space of this essay,[8] it should be noted that what is involved is a complex dialectic of change and reproduction, whereby the core features of capitalism both generate change and, at the same time, reproduce themselves. This dialectical dynamic is based on the distinction between surface and deep structure in capitalism, and opens up the possibility of a future, beyond capital, even as it reproduces the underlying core of the present, thereby hindering the realization of that future.

The approach I am outlining, then, does not presuppose the existence of a historical dynamic, as a characteristic of human social life, but analyses the form of social domination intrinsic to modern, capitalist society as generative of a historical dynamic. That is, it grounds that dynamic in the historically specific social forms at the heart of capitalism – such as commodity and capital. By grounding the historical dynamic of modern, capitalist society in historically specific social forms, this approach seeks to overcome the opposition between the notion of a transhistorical logic of history and its related complement – a transhistorical notion of historical fortuity. I would argue that such a non-linear, dialectical approach allows for a more sophisticated theory of capitalist development than those that remain within the framework of the traditional, dualistic, essentially metaphysical, opposition of determinism and contingency.

Harvey's approach points to these issues. Yet his elaboration of the core of capitalism is such that important aspects of a critical theory of capital remain bracketed or, at the very least, underdeveloped. For Harvey, there are three core elements of capitalism: it is growth-oriented, based on the exploitation of living labour in production, and necessarily is technologically and organizationally dynamic. These three core factors, however, are inconsistent. Consequently, capitalist development is characterized by a crisis-ridden tendency towards overaccumulation. The problem for capitalism historically, then, has been the management of overaccumulation (Harvey, 1989, pp. 180–3). On the basis of this analysis, Harvey then proceeds to analyse the transition from Fordism to post-Fordism (p. 184).

This understanding of the core of capitalism allows Harvey to distinguish deep structure from surface, on the basis of which he formulates his critique of postmodern approaches, and to analyse constraints and imperatives that have characterized the development of capitalism from one mode of regulation to another. Nevertheless, his focus on the crisis-ridden character of capitalism does not address the growing gap between the form social life has under capitalism and the form it could have, were it is not for capitalism. An approach that more explicitly would problematize and place at its centre the category of capital could focus more rigorously on this gap.

The differences between the two approaches become clearer with regard to the issue of the relation of forms of subjectivity and objectivity in capitalism. Harvey treats changing conceptions of space and time, for example, as reactions to changes in capitalism. Capitalism effects what Harvey calls space-time compressions. These change peoples' experiences of space and time, which are then expressed culturally and reflected upon theoretically (Harvey, 1989, p. viii, pp. 201–325). As illuminating as Harvey's account might be, his emphasis on experience as mediating capitalism and culture remains basically extrinsic to the social forms expressed by the Marxian categories. As such, it lacks the epistemological/subjective dimension of those categories, which allows them to address a wider range of issues pertaining to forms of knowledge and subjectivity. For example, the categorial approach can address other theories of economy or history, as expressing misrecognitions that are rooted as possibilities in the social forms themselves. Such an approach not only purports to explain perceptions and theories of the world, such as those of Smith and Ricardo, or Hegel, as not being fully adequate to their objects;[9] it also seeks to ground the possibility of critique itself. The latter, of course, is related to the question of the historical generation by capitalism of needs and sensibilities that point beyond capitalism. Such a categorial approach, then, treat forms of subjectivity as intrinsic to the categories themselves.

The differences between these two approaches become more evident when one considers Harvey's discussion of postmodernism and capitalism. When he relates the two, he does so in ways that implicitly treat capitalism as one-dimensional. Harvey does not, in other words, treat capital as pointing beyond itself even as it reconstitutes itself. That is, he does not raise the question of whether postmodernism also has an emancipatory moment, even if very different from that expressed by postmodernist self-understandings. Within the framework I am outlining, postmodernism could be understood as a sort of premature post-capitalism, one that points to possibilities generated, but unrealized, in capitalism. At the same time, because postmodernism misrecognizes its context, it can serve as an ideology of legitimation for the new configuration of capitalism, of which it is a part.

This raises a more general issue with which critical theories of capitalism have to grapple. In an earlier global transition of capitalism, Marxists frequently opposed general rational planning to the anarchic irrationality of the market. Instead of necessarily pointing beyond capitalism, however, such critiques frequently helped legitimate a subsequent state-centric capitalism. Similarly, the contemporary hypostatization of difference, heterogeneity and hybridity, doesn't necessarily point beyond capitalism, but can serve to veil and legitimate a new global form that combines decentralization and heterogeneity of production and consumption with increasing centralization of control and underlying homogeneity.

Each of these positions, however, has also had an emancipatory moment. The difficult task is to conceptually separate out the emancipatory dimension of the possibilities generated by capitalism from the non- or anti-emancipatory forms in which they have been generated. A critical theory of capitalism should be able to elucidate, as forms of misrecognition, approaches that take a dimension of social life generated by capitalism to be the whole. By obscuring the underlying core of capitalism as a form of social life, such approaches are only apparently emancipatory. Their critical orientations end up promoting and legitimating the domination of capital in new forms, such as state-centric capitalism and postmodern capitalism. This does not mean that the emancipatory potential of general social coordination or of the recognition of difference should be dismissed: but that potential can only be realized when it is associated with the historical overcoming of capital, the core of our form of social life.

For all of their strengths, the different approaches formulated by Brenner, Arrighi and Harvey do not succeed in fully elucidating the historical core of capital in a way that points to the possibility of its historical overcoming. Without such an analysis of capital, however, one that is not restricted to the mode of distribution, but that can, nevertheless, address the emancipatory impulses expressed by traditional Marxism, on the one hand, and postmodernism, on the other, our conceptions of emancipation will continue to oscillate between a homogenizing general (whether effected via the market or the state) and particularism, an oscillation that replicates the dualistic forms of commodity and capital themselves.

Notes

1. See Brenner (1998); Arrighi (1994); and, Harvey (1989).
2. Brenner characterizes the Regulation School as 'left-wing Malthusianism', which locates the source of the economy's falling profitability in the declining productive dynamism of the Fordist technological paradigm. See Brenner (1999, p. 62).
3. For an extensive elaboration of these arguments, see Postone (2003).
4. Though, one more extended treatment of temporality in capitalist society may be found in Chapter Three of this volume.
5. Tilley (1984, p. 147) as cited in Arrighi (1994, p. xi).
6. See Harvey (1989, p. 160 ff). As an aside it should be noted that both Harvey and Arrighi have a non-romantic, non-reactionary critique of finance. Both treat finance as generated by capital, not as something that is separable from and imposed upon capitalist production.
7. Harvey (1989, p. 124, p. 147, p. 186 ff). For the notion of 'flexible specialization', see Piore and Sabel (1984).
8. For a fuller discussion, see (Postone, 2003).
9. This approach is not limited to analysing theories, but also serves as a point of departure for an analysis of widespread world views, of ideologies. It could, for example, begin to relate the increasing diremption globally of capitalist society into post-industrial sectors and increasingly marginalized sectors to the rise of identity politics within a postmodern frame, on the one hand, and various forms of 'fundamentalism', on the other.

References

Arrighi, G. 1994. *The Long Twentieth Century: Money, Power, and the Origins of Our Times*. London: Verso.
Brenner, R. 1998. 'The Economics of Global Turbulence: A Special Report on the World Economy, 1950-98', *New Left Review*, 229.
—. 1999. 'Reply to Critics', *Comparative Studies of South Asia, Africa, and the Middle East*, XIX, 2.
Harvey, D. 1989. *The Conditions of Postmodernity: An Enquiry into the Origins of Cultural Change*. Oxford: Basil Blackwell.
Marx, K. 1981. *Capital*, vol. 3, translated by D. Fernbach, Harmondsworth: Penguin Books.
Piore, M and Sabel, C. 1984. *The Second Industrial Divide*. New York: Basic Books.
Postone, M. 2003. *Time, Labor, and Social Domination*. Cambridge: Cambridge University Press.
Tilly, C. 1984. *Big Structures, Large Processes, Huge Comparisons*. New York: Russell Sage.

Chapter 2

TECHNOLOGICAL DYNAMISM AND THE NORMATIVE JUSTIFICATION OF GLOBAL CAPITALISM

Tony Smith

It is certainly possible to overestimate the practical importance of arguments for the normative legitimacy of global capitalism. But normative arguments continue to circulate in the social world, and it would be foolish to think that they do so without significant social effects. As long as ideological defences of capitalism continue to be produced, there will be a need for ideology critiques.

Arguments – for the normative legitimacy of global capitalism – unfold in three main stages. A normative principle (or set of principles) must be proposed and defended. Then, it must be established that a global capitalist order is compatible with, or even necessary for, the adequate institutionalization of that principle. If the global economy is at present flawed from the standpoint of the given principle, this must be shown to be a contingent matter, capable of being reversed through appropriate reforms.

In the first section I shall present what I take to be the strongest contemporary version of this argument, combining the normative principle articulated by the leading contemporary theorists of global justice with the most significant recent development in mainstream economics – 'new growth theory'.[1] In the second section, I shall present a critical assessment of this position from a Marxian standpoint. In the third section it will be shown that the position is internally incoherent. The paper concludes with a speculation regarding the future course of global capitalism.

Global Justice and New Growth Theory

Normative assessments presuppose normative principles. A striking feature of contemporary political philosophy is the extent of consensus regarding the principle that ought to govern assessments of the global order. A typical formulation of what may be termed *the moral equality principle* is found in Alan Buchanan's recent *Justice, Legitimacy, and Self-Determination: Moral Foundations for International Law*, 'justice requires respect for the inherent dignity of all persons ... this notion of dignity includes the idea that all persons are equal, so far as the importance of their basic interests are concerned' (Buchanan, 2004, p. 42). Another version is expressed in the principle of autonomy defended by David Held:

> [P]ersons ... should be free and equal in the determination of the conditions of their own lives, so long as they do not deploy this framework to negate the rights of others (Held, 1995, p. 147).

Jürgen Habermas calls for 'equal respect for the human worth of each individual', a view he terms 'egalitarian universalism' (Habermas, 2001, p. 94, p. 103). Slightly different formulations can be found in the work of Thomas Pogge,[2] Martha Nussbaum,[3] and many others.

In another context it would be important to examine the different versions of this principle, the various arguments that have been proposed in its favour, and the responses that are given to criticisms of these arguments. Here, however, I shall simply take the moral equality principle as given.[4] The next step is to attempt to establish that global capitalism is compatible with the adequate institutionalization of this principle. If we take the so-called 'new growth theory' as the cutting-edge of mainstream economics, then it is this theory that must provide the required account.[5]

In the 'old growth theory' of Robert Solow, growth resulted from increased investments in 'capital' (physical inputs) and/or labour, the increased productivity of capital and/or labour, and increases in 'total factor productivity' above and beyond increases in capital and labour productivity. Econometric studies trace most economic growth to the increases in total factor productivity that result from advances in scientific-technological knowledge. In Solow's models these advances (and the innovations based upon them) are treated as freely available public goods exogenous to the economy ('manna from heaven', so to speak).

Neoclassical economists found this framework useful for explaining persisting divergences in the global economy, which were taken to be caused by different levels of investment in capital.[6] But the framework suffered from an obvious shortcoming. The single most important variable of growth, technological change, was treated as a 'residue', a 'black box'. Economic historians were never satisfied with this treatment. New growth theory was developed by similarly dissatisfied mathematical economists.

Paul Romer — the leading new growth theorist — agrees with Solow that many forms of scientific-technical knowledge are *non-rivalrous* and *non-excludable*, the two essential characteristics of public goods. Unlike the pie you cannot consume after I have eaten it, my intellectual appropriation of $e=mc^2$ does not prevent you from fully appropriating the formula as well. The pie is a rivalrous good, the formula is not. And while I can keep the pie locked away until I am ready to eat it, once Einstein published the formula there was no way to exclude anybody from using it. Romer notes, however, that many forms of innovation and scientific-technical knowledge are not true public goods. Many are *excludable*, at least for an extended period of time. This insight made it possible to open the 'black box' and treat technological change as endogenous to the economic system. Romer's models include terms representing investments in Research and Development (R&D), innovations embodying advances in scientific-technological knowledge, the education and training of a workforce capable of employing these innovations efficiently, intellectual property rights, and so on. This then led Romer to break from the assumptions of declining returns and perfect competition that have always been at the heart of neoclassical economics. Firms able to exclude others from innovations and scientific-technical knowledge are in principle able to appropriate *increasing* returns from their investment. Such a state of affairs cannot be conceptualized in terms of a 'perfect competition' in which all firms are price-takers appropriating identical rates of return. At the heart of the technological change process we find the drive to *avoid* being a mere price-taker, a drive to attain (temporary) monopolies on product and process innovations in order to win above average returns.

For some observers, at least, new growth theory is a revolutionary breakthrough in the history of economics.[7] Be that as it may, it is of undoubted importance to any contemporary argument for the normative justification of global capitalism. Anyone seeking a state-of-the-art defence of the thesis that global capitalism is consistent with the adequate institutionalization of 'egalitarian universalism' must look here. And such a defence can be found. Models in which technological change is treated as endogenous to capitalism have been taken to show that *the technological dynamism of global capitalism in principle enables all individuals to obtain access to the material preconditions of human flourishing and human autonomy to the greatest feasible degree.*

Growth may be endogenous to capitalism, but it does not necessarily occur. One of the most interesting implications of new growth theory from the standpoint of capitalist ideology is its undermining of neo-liberal dogma. Neo-liberals hold that free trade, the free flow of investment capital across borders, and governments that protect property rights and maintain monetary stability, more or less automatically generate economic growth and improved living standards. New growth theorists reject this assertion, replacing it with a quite different claim: global capitalism provides access to the material preconditions for human flourishing and autonomy, only when a fairly extensive institutional background is in place. In specific, governments throughout the globe need to institute effective technology policies, including:

- State support of R&D.
- Legislation encouraging private research labs, corporate/university collaboration and entrepreneurial activity, and
- The effective promotion of foreign direct investment (FDI) by corporations operating on (or close to) the scientific-technological frontier, which results in technology transfers and higher skill levels in the domestic workforce.

Government corruption must also be avoided, and state spending must shift from unproductive military expenditures to educational and health programmes.

Domestic policies alone may not be sufficient. The stringency with which intellectual property rights are enforced globally may have to be adjusted (so that, for example, the costs of patented acquired immune deficiency syndrome (AIDS) drugs falls in regions where AIDS threatens to ravage the labour force). Subsidies and trade barriers in wealthy regions hampering imports from poor countries need to be reduced or, better yet, eliminated. And it no doubt would be a good thing if (carefully targeted) aid from wealthy nations were increased. But the main point is clear enough: no regions of the global economy are in principle condemned to remain in disadvantageous circumstances. As long as the proper background conditions are in place, any region anywhere can in principle obtain capital from domestic savings, FDI, or borrowings on global capital markets, and then invest that capital to generate technological advance, economic growth and improved living standards. The great success stories of globalization appear to spectacularly corroborate this claim. In East Asia, after all, more people have been lifted out of poverty at a faster rate than ever before in human history.

Leading contemporary theorists of global justice also reject neo-liberalism, insisting that in the absence of proper background conditions global capitalism does not automatically tend to function in a normatively acceptable manner. And they too regard the shortcomings of the present global order as a contingent matter to be addressed through reforms. Their proposals, however, tend to be more far-reaching, for example:

- A global progressive tax redistributing income to the poorest regions in the global economy (Barry, 1998).
- A 'global resources dividend' based on the idea that natural resources are the common property of all humanity, and so all individuals are owed a 'dividend' from those who use them (Beitz, 1979; Pogge, 2002, Chapter 8) and,
- A new international agency charged with ensuring high levels of basic income, full employment in the global economy, rights to access to decision-making power in industrial and financial sectors, the oversight of social investment funds targeted to the poorest regions in the global economy, global regulations regarding capital inflows and outflows, and so on (Held, 1995).

This is not the place to examine particular reform proposals in detail (see Smith, 2003; 2005, Chapters 4, 7). In the present context the fundamental question is whether new growth theory does in fact establish that global capitalism enables the principle of moral equality to be adequately institutionalized. A closer examination of this theory is clearly in order.

A Marxian Assessment of New Growth Theory

Perhaps, the best way to introduce this section is to note how Marx is evaluated by advocates of new growth theory. Marx receives his due as someone who appreciated capitalism's unprecedented technological dynamism. But his writings are also dismissed as merely 'literary', completely lacking in the mathematical sophistication displayed in contemporary growth models. Given his historical period, this could hardly be otherwise. The truly fatal flaw is that his position is internally incoherent. Marx juxtaposed an account of endogenous technological change in capitalism with a call to class struggle, oblivious to the fact that the former undermines the latter. Capitalism is 'a kind of perpetual cornucopia machine forever spilling out new goods' (Warsh, 2006, p. 224). Over time productivity advances reduce the unit costs of what had previously been luxury goods, lowering prices to the point where ordinary workers have opportunities to incorporate them in their consumption baskets. In the face of the unprecedented material prosperity generated by endogenous technological change, Marx's call to the barricades was doomed to historical irrelevance.

> Technology was far and away its [the economy's] most important source of growth. Labor unions could forget [Marx's] warnings against new machinery. They could stop worrying and learn to love the cornucopia of new innovations (Warsh, 2006, p.147).[8]

The first point to make in response is that Marx's theory is not a mere 'literary' anticipation of new growth theory. Unlike Romer, Marx did not develop a political economy to stand alongside other political economies. His project was the *critique* of political economy, a critique based on the concept of capital. In both old and new growth theories, 'capital' refers primarily to things used as inputs in production processes. For Marx, in contrast, 'capital' is a totalizing force whose various moments – investment capital, commodity capital, production capital, inventory capital and realized capital (or M-C-P-C′-M′, respectively) – reflect a historically specific social relation: the relation between a class that owns and controls investment funds, and one that does not; a class that purchases labour-power, and one that is forced to sell its labour power as a commodity; a class claiming the authority to structure the labour process, and one whose activity is an object of control; and a class that at the conclusion of a M-C-P-C′-M′ circuit retains a monopoly of investment funds (now augmented by realized profits), and one that is once again forced to sell its labour-power, having spent its wages to gain access to means of subsistence.

Within this framework productivity advances are not solely a matter of increasing the output of use-values, as in Romer's endogenous growth framework. Technological change in capitalism occurs in the context of a valorization process revolving around the production of surplus value, the difference between the money capital initially invested (M) and that realized at the conclusion of a capital circuit (M′). Surplus value in turn is a function of the difference between the time workers spend producing an amount of value equivalent to what they receive back in the form of wages, and the time they spend engaged in surplus labour, producing a value beyond what they receive back in the form of wages. Assuming a fixed length of the working day, surplus labour is increased by decreasing the portion of the day devoted to necessary labour. Investments in advanced technologies are generally required for this to occur. However, these investments are generally *not* made with the explicit goal of lowering necessary labour. Productivity gains are instead sought in the hope that the *individual value* of the produced commodities will be below their *selling price*, with this in turn less than their *social value* (expressed in the average market price of the given category of commodity). This can enable the innovating firm to expand its market share while attaining above average profits. In effect, more productive (higher-order) labour is then paid as if it were labour of average productivity, raising the rate of surplus value for the given unit of production.

Eventually, the above average profits are lost as other capitals duplicate or surpass the innovations responsible for the productivity gains. But the imperative to seek productivity-enhancing innovations is found in industries producing wage goods no less than in other sectors, and so there is a tendency for the unit costs and prices of wage goods to decline. Everything else being equal, a decline in the prices of wage goods enables the surplus labour/necessary labour ratio to increase, raising the rate of surplus value (Marx, 1976, Chapter 12; Mandel, 1975, Chapter 3; Smith, 2004).

This account of the endogenous technological dynamism of capitalism explicitly refers to the manner in which innovations can be at least temporarily excludable. This is what enables surplus profits to be appropriated. It explicitly refers as well to the manner in which the scientific-technological knowledge underlying innovations is non-rivalrous, which accounts for the temporary nature of the surplus profits. Marx also explicitly refers to the increasing importance of scientific-technological knowledge in capitalism (Marx, 1976, pp. 1053–5). As far as these central ideas are concerned, there is nothing new about 'new growth theory'. Finally, Marx was well aware that productivity advances tend to expand the consumption of use-values by workers over time. His emphatic reference to the 'historical and moral' component of the value of labour-power explicitly refers to this tendency (Marx, 1976, p. 275). On this crucial point too there is nothing new about 'new growth theory'.

Marx, however, would insist that the technological dynamism of capital does *not* establish that capitalism is in principle compatible with the institutionalization of 'egalitarian universalism'. Even when workers' consumption of use-values increases the activities of human agents are still subsumed under a non-human imperative, the accumulation of capital as an end in itself. As long as this is the case human flourishing and human autonomy are systematically subordinated to the flourishing and autonomy of capital. Working men and women continue to be alienated from their own collective powers, as well as the powers of nature, machinery, and science, all of which appear to be powers of capital.[9] Further, a higher level of consumption still leaves exploitative social relations in place.[10] When one class owns and controls the means of investment, it is able to purchase the labour-power of others as a commodity. It also has the power to structure the labour process without being accountable to those over whom this authority is exercised, and benefits from the systematic reproduction of these advantages over time, what possible case could be made that even in principle 'all persons are equal, so far as the importance of their basic interests are concerned'? Or that even in principle 'persons [are] free and equal in the determination of the conditions of their own lives'?

Putting these (decisive) considerations aside, gains in use-value consumption by wage labourers resulting from endogenous technological change are also *precarious* and *partial*.[11] They are *precarious* in that even relatively privileged workers necessarily remain subject to generalized economic insecurity:

- As innovations diffuse, competitive pressures tend to erode the wage gains of workers in no-longer-leading firms.
- If a given unit of capital does maintain its advantages, it will usually do so through further innovations that threaten to displace wage labourers.
- Technological change may enable the implementation of effective 'divide and conquer' strategies, in which the threat of employing less privileged categories of workers is used to reduce wages and worsen work conditions.
- Machinery regularly 'deskills' categories of workers, making previously won gains difficult to maintain.[12]
- In some contexts machinery can be used to replace striking workers, lessening the chances of strikes being successful (or even undertaken at all).

The gains to workers from technological change in capitalism are *partial* as well. Most obviously, these gains do not generally extend to those laid off due to the introduction of labour-saving machinery, or to those employed by less productive firms. They also:

- Do not eliminate the physical and psychological harms associated with the intensification of work, a phenomenon that necessarily tends to accompany technological changes in a capitalist workplace.
- Do not eliminate the pressure to lengthen the work day in order to compensate for the risks of the 'moral depreciation' (technological obsolescence) of machinery, and
- Do not address the environmental costs associated with technological change in capitalism, a wildly disproportionate share of which is borne by those who do not own and control capital.

There is undoubtedly much in Marx's work that is outdated. The cross-border production chains that have proven so effective at dividing sections of the labour force, lowering wages and breaking strikes, are not discussed in *Capital* (Moody, 1998). The technologies and forms of social organization in which the labour process is subject to the control of capital are now those of flexible ('lean') production, rather than the mass production of the nineteenth century (Smith, 2000a). Marx also did not foresee the emergence of 'the spectacle' bestowing on each new generation of commodities an all but irresistible allure (Debord, 1995; Retort, 2006, pp. 178–88). None of these or other developments, however, refutes Marx's essential claim that global capitalism is not, and in principle cannot be, a system in which 'the free development of each is the condition for the free development of all'. This is not due to a lack of consumption of commodities, and cannot be overcome by an expansion of consumption in the wake of endogenous technological change. It is due to the subsumption of men and women under capital as an alien social form, and can only be overcome through a world historical rupture from that form.

There are, then, many reasons to deny that global capitalism functions in a manner consistent with the principle of moral equality. A further one that has not yet been mentioned deserves separate consideration.

New Growth Theory and The Systematic Tendency to Uneven Development

Within the framework of new growth theory there are no guarantees that any particular region of the capitalist global economy will enjoy success. But most of the authors in this movement apparently believe that any region anywhere can enjoy productivity gains, economic growth, and living standards converging with those of advanced regions, if only the right sorts of policies are consistently instituted (see Jones, 2002, Chapter 7; Warsh, 2006, pp. 207–8). *This belief does not follow from the inner logic of the theory.*

New growth theory implies that units of capital with access to advanced R&D are best positioned to enjoy increasing returns from innovations. These capitals are thus also best positioned to establish a virtuous circle in which increasing returns provide the funds necessary to operate at or near the scientific-technical frontier in the future – an essential precondition for being able to successfully introduce the next generation of the innovations and thereby, appropriate the next generation of increasing returns. In contrast, units of capital without initial access to advanced R&D necessarily tend to be trapped in a vicious circle. Their resulting inability to introduce significant innovations prevents them from enjoying above average returns, which limits their ability to participate in advanced R&D in the succeeding period. This in turn limits future innovations and thus future profit opportunities.

In this context one fact about the global economy warrants emphasis before all others: *More than 95 per cent of all research and development is undertaken in the wealthy regions of the global economy* (Helpman, 2004, p. 64). Units of capital without access to advanced R&D are clustered in the poorer regions, where over three quarters of the global population lives. Units of capital from the so-called North are thus in a far better position to maintain the virtuous circle described above, while those elsewhere have tremendous difficulty avoiding the vicious circle. Within the framework of new growth theory, then, the dialectical unity of the virtuous and vicious circles described in the previous paragraph is the defining structure of the global economy. To put the point provocatively, mainstream theories of endogenous technological change in effect confirm Marx's thesis that the drive to obtain surplus profits through innovations tends to systematically reproduce uneven development in the world market (Marx, 1981, pp. 344–5).

Consider what happens when units of capital enjoying temporary monopolies due to innovations interact with other units in the global economy. The latter necessarily tend to suffer disadvantageous terms of trade. When hegemonic capitals from the North operating at or near the frontier of scientific-technical knowledge sell inputs to, and purchase the outputs of, small-scale producers from the South operating far from that frontier, the prices these producers must pay for their inputs tend to rise, while the prices they receive for their outputs tend to stagnate or decline over time. In this manner, the capitals of the North are able to appropriate a disproportionate share of the value produced in global production and distribution chains. They are also able to displace an increasing share of economic risks elsewhere in these chains (Freeman, 2001; Kaplinsky, 2005, Part III). Numerous investors and managers in the South may prosper as junior partners in this arrangement. But the pressure on work conditions, wage levels, and worker communities in these regions will be unrelenting. And this pressure will inevitably be transferred to working men and women and their communities in the North. This certainly does not imply that it is impossible for particular national economies to rise or fall in the hierarchy of the world system. But that possibility hardly establishes the irrelevance of the tendency to uneven development in the world market as a whole.[13] If we want to understand why the population of global slums is expected to exceed 2 billion human beings in the next 25 years, the tendency to uneven development in the capitalist world market may not be the entire story. But it is surely the place to start (Davis, 2004).[14]

The tendency to uneven development is not a subsidiary matter only contingently linked to the essential determinations of the capital form. The tendency is inextricably tied to the drive to innovation, and this drive is utterly fundamental ('endogenous') to the capital form. The most honest of new growth theorists explicitly admit that a systematic tendency to uneven development does indeed directly follow from their position:

> [I]nvestment in innovation widens the gap between rich and poor countries. The output gains of the industrial countries exceed the output gains of the less-developed countries. We therefore conclude that investment in innovation in the industrial countries leads to divergence of income between the North and the South (Helpman, 2004, p. 85).

This is an astounding statement. Given the manner in which advanced research and development is concentrated in certain regions, it is impossible even in principle to assert that in global capitalism 'all persons are equal, so far as the importance of their basic interests are concerned'. The interests of those owning and controlling the firms having access to advanced research and development are systematically privileged at the cost of the interests of the vast majority of the globe's population, who can hardly be said to be 'equal in the determination of the conditions of their own lives'. In other words, any attempt to construct a normative defence of global capitalism based on the principle defended by today's leading normative theorists cannot appeal to the results of contemporary mainstream economics, which imply that the dominant tendencies in the global economy point in a quite different direction. This is, I believe, a new and significant development in the history of legitimating ideologies.[15]

It would be extremely difficult to argue that the sorts of proposals recommended by global justice theorists (a significant global redistribution of income, a global resource dividend, etc.) are likely to be implemented as long as capitalist property and production relations are in place, given the furious and unrelenting hostility with which they would be met by the owners and controllers of capital and the political and media elites allied with them. The majority of such proposals could realistically hope for is to improve the conditions of the worst off in the global economy at the margins. That would be a profound accomplishment. But it would not reverse the fundamental unfairness at the heart of the global order, as judged by the normative standard proclaimed by theorists of global justice themselves.[16] Just as there can be more or less humane slave systems, and more or less humane forms of feudalism, there can be more or less humane forms of capitalism. But no master-slave relation, no lord-serf relation, is compatible with 'egalitarian universalism'. And no global order that systematically reproduces uneven development is either.

A Closing Conjecture

In this final section I shall first discuss another tendency implicit in the process of endogenous technological change in capitalism, the tendency to overaccumulation crises. Recognition of this tendency is impossible in the new growth framework due to a set of arbitrary and unacceptable presuppositions. The paper then concludes with a conjecture regarding the future development of global capitalism. Both themes strongly reinforce the thesis that the global capitalist order is not compatible with, let alone necessary for, an adequate institutionalization of the moral equality principle.

The break from the notion of perfect competition undertaken by new growth theory is drastically incomplete. In Romer's models temporary monopolies and increasing returns are found only in an intermediate sector dedicated to the production of goods embodying innovations, which are then sold to a sector producing final products. Perfect competition is assumed to hold in the sale of these final products. The first obvious difficulty is that it is completely arbitrary to restrict the drive to appropriate surplus profits to some sectors and not others. Other problems arise from the mechanism supposedly underlying the perfect competition that is retained in the models: when more efficient plants or firms enter an industry producing final products, other plants and firms are assumed to leave that industry at a rate that maintains an equilibrium of supply and demand.

Suppose the drive to appropriate surplus profits from innovations leads to the entry of a more efficient plants or firm in a given industry. There is no reason to assume that a sufficient number of established firms and plants will automatically shut down to maintain a balance of supply and demand. Their fixed capital costs are already 'sunk', and so they may be happy to receive the average rate of profit on their circulating capital. They also may have established relations with suppliers and customers impossible (or prohibitively expensive) to duplicate elsewhere in any relevant time frame. Further, their management and labour force may have industry-specific skills. And governments may provide subsidies for training, infrastructure, or R&D that would not be available if they were to shift sectors. When sufficient number of firms and plants do not withdraw when more efficient competitors enter the given industry, the result is an overaccumulation of capital, manifested in excess capacity and declining rates of profit. When this dynamic unfolds simultaneously in leading industries, an economy-wide fall in profit rates results for an extended historical period (Reuten, 1991; Brenner, 1998; 2002; Smith, 2000b).[17]

When overaccumulation crises break out, previous investments in fixed capital must be devalued. At this point each unit, network and region of capital attempts to shift the costs of devaluation onto other units, networks and regions. And those who control capital mobilize their vast economic, political, and ideological weapons in the attempt to shift as many of the costs of devaluation as possible onto wage labourers, through increased unemployment, lower wages, and worsened work conditions. The dynamic David Harvey terms 'accumulation by dispossession' intensifies as well, as attempts are made to withdraw more and more aspects of society and nature from the global commons in order to commodify and monetarize them within new circuits of capital (Harvey, 2003). As the concentration and centralization of capital proceeds in the course of capitalist development, overaccumulation, devaluation, and dispossession necessarily tend to occur on an ever-more massive scale.

Global turbulence and generalized economic insecurity increasingly become the normal state of affairs. And the tendency to uneven development is greatly exacerbated, since the poorest regions of the global economy are especially vulnerable to predatory forms of capitalism.

Needless to say (one hopes), the connection between endogenous technological change and the tendency to overaccumulation crises makes talk of the compatibility of the moral equality principle and the social relations of capitalism even more hollow. But that is not all. The very institutional arrangements furthering the 'perpetual cornucopia machine' of capitalism may ironically be bringing about a new epoch in which periods of dynamic growth shorten and periods of overaccumulation, devaluation and dispossession are prolonged. Before elaborating this conjecture a brief historical digression must be undertaken.

Building on clues in Marx and Braudel, Giovanni Arrighi has developed a theory of 'systematic cycles of accumulation' in which surplus profits through innovation play a central role (Arrighi, 1994). The first part of a cycle is a phase of material expansion in the world market, pushed forward by capitals clustered in a particular region able to appropriate surplus profits for an extended period. The privileged place of these capitals is essentially connected to the privileged place of the state with which they are associated in the hierarchical inter-state system. Eventually, these units of capital confront serious overaccumulation difficulties. The phase of material expansion then gives way to the second phase of a systematic cycle, in which the primary form of profit-seeking in the hegemonic region shifts to financial speculation. Alongside financial investments, however, increasing amounts of capital begin to flow to a different region, where a new type of state with new sorts of capacities nurtures new units of capital, capable of attaining surplus profits from new innovations. According to Marx and Arrighi, over the past 500 years Venice, Holland, England, and the US have alternated as the hegemonic region at the centre of a systematic cycle of accumulation in the world market.[18]

Predicting the course of history is a fool's game. Nonetheless, I believe that there are good reasons to think that the above pattern may not continue. The role of the state and the financial system in fostering innovation has become so well understood, and effective national innovation systems have become so widely institutionalized, that it is unlikely in the foreseeable future that any region will again enjoy extensive surplus profits from innovation for an extended historical epoch.[19]

Suppose some form of scientific-technical advance shows promise of leading to commercializable products capable of generating surplus profits. Some states will be quicker than others to support this advance, and some financial sectors will be more effective than others at mobilizing credit to new units of capital dedicated to commercialization. Certain units of capital will then enjoy 'first mover' advantages, which can be considerable. But other states with effective national innovation systems and financial systems capable of allocating credit on a large scale will quickly target the sector in question. There are now enough states with effective national innovation systems, and enough financial sectors capable of allocating massive amounts of credit to units of capital starting up (or moving into) industries where high future profits are anticipated, that the period in which initial innovators enjoy surplus profits from their quasi-monopoly on innovations necessarily tends to shrink.

From this standpoint the extension of intellectual property rights is more than a privatization of types of scientific-technical knowledge previously considered public goods. It is a desperate attempt to use state law and inter-state agreements to change the rules of the game in order to enable surplus profits to be appropriated for extended periods in the radically changed historical circumstances. I believe the attempt is doomed to fail. Units of capital with intellectual property rights to one part of complex technology systems will find themselves having to purchase licenses or enter into cross-licensing agreements with other units with intellectual rights to other parts of the same complex technology systems. This will most likely prevent any significant subset of them from enjoying surplus profits over an extended historical epoch.

I am not arguing that the dynamism of capitalism is eroding in use-value terms. Nor am I suggesting that surplus profits from innovation will no longer play a role in reproducing uneven development in the world market. The relative brevity of the period in which surplus profits can be won in comparison to earlier epochs will probably motivate state officials in the wealthiest regions to increase their efforts to foster the next generation of innovations. Poorer regions will in general have great difficulty matching these efforts, although successes in niche areas cannot be ruled out. The general convergence of the national innovation systems of the North is completely consistent with a continued gap between the innovation systems of the North and the innovation systems of the South, and the continuing importance of this gap in reproducing uneven development.

What I am arguing is that the dynamism of the capitalist world market may be eroding in value terms. In previous periods, the surplus profits from innovation enjoyed by capitals in hegemonic regions have pushed forward phases of material expansion in the world market. I do not expect that non-financial sectors of the US economy will play this role in the twenty-first century the way they did in much of the twentieth, despite the high number of patents that continue to be granted to corporations based in the US. The horrifically low wages of China's workforce, and the strategic intelligence of China's political elites, probably ensure that China will continue to receive a disproportionate share of the world's new investment funds in coming decades. But I also do not foresee Chinese firms dominating the world market in the twenty-first century the way US firms did during their 'golden age'. I do not expect *any* region to take a place in the historical chain extending from Venice to Holland to England to the US. I expect instead that individual firms, or networks of individual firms, based mostly in the North, will introduce innovations, enjoy surplus profits from those innovations for relatively brief periods, and then watch their surplus profits erode as national innovation systems and financial sectors operating elsewhere funnel massive amounts of state subsidies and private credit to competitors. I am predicting, in brief, that the overaccumulation difficulties that erode surplus profits will arise in the emerging sectors of the twenty-first century at an ever-faster rate.

Even if this speculation is correct, it does not imply that capitalism has at long last entered its terminal crisis. It does mean, however, that the period of global turbulence that has characterized the capitalist world market since the mid 1970's may persist indefinitely, punctuated by financial bubbles in one category of capital assets after another. Since overaccumulation difficulties are inevitably connected to devaluation and 'accumulation through dispossession', these too can be expected to persist. If they do, then the suggestion that global capitalism enables all individuals to obtain access to the material preconditions of human flourishing and human autonomy will become even more ludicrous than it is today.

Notes

1. This, at least, is the thesis of Warsh, 2006, endorsed by two Nobel Prize winners in economics.
2. Pogge calls for principles that 'assign the same fundamental moral benefits (e.g. claims, liberties, powers, and immunities) and burdens (e.g. duties and liabilities) to all', such that 'these fundamental moral benefits and burdens are formulated in general terms so as not to privilege or disadvantage certain persons or groups arbitrarily' (Pogge, 2002, p. 92).
3. 'If we agree that citizens are all worthy of concern and respect . . . then we ought to conclude that policies should not treat people as agents or supporters of other people, whose mission in the world is to execute someone else's plan of life. It should treat each of them as ends, as sources of agency and worth in their own right, with their own plans to make and their own lives to live, therefore as deserving of all necessary support for the equal opportunity to be such agents' (Nussbaum, 2001, p. 58).
4. See Callinicos, 2000, for a sympathetic Marxian assessment of this principle, which can also be expressed in the affirmation that 'the free development of each is the condition for the free development of all' (Marx and Engels, 1969, p. 127).
5. The following paragraphs are based upon Jones, 2002; Helpman, 2004; Warsh, 2006, and, ultimately, Romer, 1990, 1994.

6. This explanation, however, does not remove an anomaly in the neoclassical framework. According to standard neoclassical assumptions the marginal contribution of each additional unit of capital should be higher in areas of capital scarcity. And so returns on investments in capital should be higher there. Everything else being equal, capital investments should flow to capital-poor regions of the global economy, eventually leading to a convergence in which all regions of the globe enjoy the same per capita income and the same rate of steady state growth. As leading neoclassical economists have noted, there is no evidence that global capitalism in fact functions in this manner (Baumol, 1986). Whether new growth theorists can better account for the persisting divergences in the global economy remains to be seen.

7. 'In Buffalo [where Romer first presented his 1990 paper] ... participants had witnessed the entry into the macroeconomics literature of the first successful account of the aggregate economics of knowledge... The excitement was unmistakable, but it was ill-defined. Only gradually did it become a conviction shared by many that the world had changed once and for all that day' (Warsh, 2006, p. 299).

8. I have taken the liberty of substituting 'Marx' for 'Ricardo' in this passage. From Warsh's perspective, Marx simply magnifies Ricardo's mistake of treating momentary labour disputes as manifestations of A fundamental social antagonism.

9. 'The division of labour and the combination of labour within the production process is a machinery which costs the capitalist nothing. He pays for the individual labour capacities, not for their combination not for the social power of labour. Another productive force which costs him nothing is SCIENTIFIC POWER. The growth of the population is a further productive force which costs nothing. But is only through the possession of capital – in particular in its form as machinery – that he can appropriate for himself these free productive forces; the latent wealth and powers of nature just as much as all the social powers of labour which develop with the growth of the population and the historical development of society'. (Marx, 1994, p. 18).

10. In fact, the rate of increase in worker consumption can be less than the rate of increase of productivity, implying a *higher* rate of exploitation: 'It is possible for wages to stand e.g. higher in England than on the Continent, and yet be lower *relatively*, in proportion to the productivity of labour' (Marx, 1994, p. 40).

11. The issues mentioned in this paragraph and the following are discussed in depth in Marx's chapters on 'Machinery' in the *1861–63 Manuscripts* and Volume 1 of *Capital*.

12. 'Deskills' is not the correct general term. A *generalization* of previously above average skills may also lead to a fall in wages.

13. Many of the supposed 'success stories' of globalization rested on contingent geopolitical considerations that do not generally hold. For example, the Cold War motivated the US government to accept high levels of exports from East Asian countries, despite the fact that they greatly restricted both imports from US manufacturers and portfolio capital investments from the US With the end of the Cold War this arrangement ceased being acceptable to US political and economic elites. Another important issue concerns the fallacy of composition. From the fact that some regions are able to win a higher place in the hierarchy of the world market it does not follow that all can. For a comprehensive critical assessment of the so-called East Asian miracle, see Burkett and Hart-Landsberg, 2000.

14. Many other dimensions of the world market reinforce and exacerbate the tendency to uneven development. A partial list includes the remission of profits resulting from foreign direct investment in poorer regions, the ability of multinational firms to manipulate the 'prices' of commodities 'exchanged' in intra-firm transactions, the capital flight of local elites, the ever-present dangers of the 'debt trap', the structural adjustment programmes imposing austerity on debtor countries in order to safeguard investors' interests, the refusal to enforce or even acknowledge labour rights, the stampedes of speculative capital inflows and outflows that most harm the groups that benefit least from financial bubbles; and so on. New growth theorists are conspicuously silent about such matters, despite the fact that they are all 'endogenous' to global capitalism.
15. In contrast, the normative defence of capitalist welfare states developed in the most important work of political philosophy of the twentieth century, Rawls' *A Theory of Justice*, did not conflict with the Keynesian economics of Rawls' day.
16. In the writings of liberal egalitarians there is always a point where the moral equality principle is abandoned and replaced with the much weaker imperative to institute a global order in which all individuals enjoy an acceptable minimal level of subsistence. When a shift of this magnitude occurs, it is a fairly clear sign that ideological considerations are at work.
17. Brenner has provided considerable empirical evidence that the lower rates of growth that afflicted the world economy after the so-called 'golden age' ended in the late 1960s and early 1970s was due in large part to excess capacity in the leading sectors of the global economy.
18. '(T)he villainies of the Venetian system of robbery formed one of the secret foundations of Holland's wealth in capital, for Venice in her years of decadence lent large sums of money to Holland. There is a similar relationship between Holland and England . . . The same thing is going on today between England and the United States' (Marx, 1976, p. 920). Exactly when in this process the world market became a *capitalist* world market is a disputed issue I shall not address here (see Wood, 2002).
19. See Nelson, 1993 and Kantor, 1995. This presentation is based on Smith, 2005, pp. 253–5.

References

Arrighi, G. 1994. *The Long Twentieth Century*, New York: Verso Press.
Barry, B. 1998. 'International Society from a Cosmopolitan Perspective', in Mapel, D. and Nardin T. (eds.), *International Society: Diverse Ethical Perspectives*, Princeton: Princeton University Press.
Baumol, W. 1986. 'Productivity Growth, Convergence and Welfare: What the Long-Run Data Show', *American Economic Review*, 76.
Beitz, C. 1979. *Political Theory and International Relations*. Princeton: Princeton University Press.
Brenner, R. 1998. 'The Economics of Global Turbulence', *New Left Review*, 229.
—. 2002. *The Boom and the Bust: The US in the World Economy*, New York: Verso.
Buchanan, A. 2004. Justice, Legitimacy, and Self-Determination, New York: Oxford University Press.

Burkett, P. and Hart-Landsberg, M. 2000. *Development, Crises and Class Struggle: Learning from Japan and East Asia,* New York: St. Martin's Press.

Callinicos, A. 2000. *Equality*, Malden: Polity Press.

Davis, M. 2004. 'Planet of Slums', *New Left Review*, 26.

Debord, G. 1995. *The Society of the Spectacle*, Cambridge: Zone Books.

Freeman, A. 2001. 'Has the Empire Struck Back?' in Albritton, R., Itoh, M., Westra, R., and Zuege, A. (eds.), *Phases of Capitalist Development: Booms, Crises and Globalizations*, New York: Palgrave/Macmillan.

Habermas, J. 2001. *The Postnational Constellation.* Cambridge: MIT Press.

Harvey, D. 2003. 'The "New" Imperialism: Accumulation by Dispossession', in Panitch, L. and Leys, C. (eds.), *The New Imperial Challenge: Socialist Register 2004.* New York: Monthly Review Press.

Held, D. 1995. *Democracy and the Global Order: From the Modern State to Cosmopolitan Governance.* Stanford: Stanford University Press.

Helpman, E. 2004. *The Mystery of Economic Growth.* Cambridge: Belknap Press.

Jones, C. 2002. *Introduction to Economic Growth.* New York: W W Norton.

Kantor, R. 1995. *World Class: Thriving Locally in the Global Economy.* New York: Touchstone.

Kaplinsky, R. 2005. *Globalization, Poverty and Inequality.* Malden: Polity Press.

Mandel, E. 1975. *Late Capitalism.* London: Verso.

Marx, K. 1976. *Capital, vol 1,* New York: Penguin Books.

—. 1981. *Capital, vol 3,* New York: Penguin Books.

—. 1994. *Economic Manuscript of 1861–63,* in Marx, K. and Engels, F. *Collected Works:* vol 34, New York: International Publishers.

Marx, K and Engels, F. 1969. 'The Communist Manifesto', in *Selected Works*, vol 1, Moscow: Progress Publishers.

Moody, K. 1998. *Workers in a Lean World.* New York: Verso Press.

Nelson, R. (ed.), 1993. *National Innovation Systems.* New York: Oxford University Press.

Nussbaum, M. 2001. *Women and Human Development.* New York: Cambridge University Press.

Pogge, T. 2002. *World Poverty and Human Rights.* Malden: Polity Press.

Retort. 2005. *Afflicted Powers: Capital and Spectacle in a New Age of War.* New York: Verso.

Reuten, G. 1991. 'Accumulation of Capital and the Foundation of the Tendency of the Rate of Profit to Fall', *Cambridge Journal of Economics*, 15, 1.

Romer, P. 1990. 'Endogenous Technological Change', *Journal of Political Economy*, 98.

—. 1994. 'The Origins of Endogenous Growth', *Journal of Economic Perspectives*, 8.

Smith, T. 2000a. *Technology and Capital in the Age of Lean Production: A Marxian Critique of the "New Economy".* Albany: State University of New York Press.

—. 2000b. 'Brenner and Crisis Theory: Issues in Systematic and Historical Dialectics', *Historical Materialism 5.*

—. 2003 'Globalisation and Capitalist Property Relations: A Critical Assessment of Held's Cosmopolitan Theory', *Historical Materialism*, 11, 2.

—. 2004 'Technology and History in Capitalism: Marxian and Neo-Schumpeterian Perspectives', in Bellofiore, R. and Taylor, N. (eds.), *The Constitution of Capital: Essays on Volume One of Marx's Capital.* New York: Palgrave/Macmillan.

—. 2005. *Globalisation: A Systematic Marxian Account.* Leiden: Brill.

Warsh, D. 2006. *Knowledge and the Wealth of Nations: A Story of Economic Discovery.* New York: W W Norton.

Wood, E. 2002. *The Origin of Capitalism: A Longer View.* New York: Verso Press.

Chapter 3

EATING THE FUTURE: CAPITALISM OUT OF JOINT

Robert Albritton

In this essay I want to utilize a particular interpretation of Marx's *Capital* to explore the extreme contradictions of the contemporary fast food system as it manifests in a particular sector (food) and in acute forms the general contradictions that Marx discussed in his brilliant three volume study of capital's inner logic.[1] My approach features two levels of analysis proceeding from a theory of capital's deep structures to an analysis of some central features of the production and consumption of food in the US currently. The abstract level develops seven crucial themes extracted from capital's inner logic, and the historical level illustrates some ways in which these themes are played out in the current fast food sector of the increasingly globalized American economy.

Following the remarkable work of Japanese political economist Thomas Sekine, I have come to see that Marx's *Capital* can be reconstructed as a rigorous dialectical logic making it potentially the most powerful theory in modern social science.[2] While the commodity-form never rules us completely, in developed capitalist societies, it does so to such an extent that it is possible to complete its rule in theory. By doing this we convert social power relations into economic structures that can be theorized as forming necessary inner connections that interrelate through quantities (essentially price signals) that are manifested in markets. As a result, we can know precisely and clearly exactly what a capitalist commodity is and what a society will look like when such an entity takes charge of its economic life.

Of course, in concrete history structures are never so reified that power relations are totally absorbed into the movement of prices. And it is for this reason that levels of analysis are required to mediate the theory of capital's inner logic with capitalist history.[3] 'Value' that reduces social relations to quantitative relations can only become 'self-valorizing value' (this is the basic definition of capital used by Marx throughout the three volumes of *Capital*) by subsuming the use-value obstacles (or qualitative properties) presented by the basic economic categories of capitalism.[4] If we think of value as essentially quantity and use-value as essentially quality, this means that by the end of the dialectic of capital, such qualitatively different commodities as land and labour-power must be subsumed to a logic of short-term profit-making that takes no interest in differences of quality except as they effect profit-making itself. In other words, capital never takes an interest in qualitative difference in itself, but only as it affects quantity. But in actual history use-values (including human practices) often cannot be so neatly subsumed to the commodity form. This may mean that they remain only partially commodified and even this only with political and ideological supports. It is fundamentally the different configurations of use-value obstacles (including obstacles like class struggle) relative to time and place, and how value manages or mismanages these obstacles that give rise to the theoretical requirement of levels of analysis.

Themes from Capital's Inner Logic

Indifference to Use-Value

With Marx's (1976, Chapter 4) formula C-M-C (C=commodity, M=money), one is exchanging a commodity that one does not want for money with which to buy a qualitatively different commodity that one does want. Here what matters are the material properties of the two commodities, and presumably, once one has what one wants, there is no reason to repeat the exchange. In Marxian language, what is prominent in the exchange is 'use-value' or the qualitative and material characteristics of the two commodities. The shift to the exchange relation M-C-M′ (buying cheap and selling dear) radically alters the nature of exchange. Because M and M′ are qualitatively the same, the only reason for carrying out the exchange is the quantitative one that M′ is larger than M. Moreover, there is now no limit to M-C-M′, such that the greater the difference between M′ and M (i.e. the profit), the greater the motivation for pursuing the exchange. Marx (1978, p.109, p.185; 1985, pp. 241–2, p. 275) shows that in the theory of capital's deep structure M-C-M′ can expand itself through a commodity-economic logic by subsuming a capitalistically organized production process and by subsuming the major economic variables, labour, land and capital itself. To the extent that M-C-M′ can subsume the basics of economic life to a set of competitive interlocking markets, capitalists can be indifferent to use-value and the qualitative except as it enhances profit and the quantitative. For example, capital will only take an interest in the qualitative differences between cigarettes and broccoli, if producing one is more profitable than the other.

In concrete situations there are usually costs in switching production from one commodity to another, yet in principle, capital will not remain 'loyal' to a particular qualitative use-value, when shifting more resources to producing another one is likely to bring substantially greater profits. Under the given legal, human, technical and natural constraints, capital in general will always be indifferent or opportunistic towards use-value, producing whatever it hopes will be most profitable no matter how socially costly and even destructive the 'externalities' may be. Indeed, were they not illegal, opium or cocaine would be ideal commodities for capital since inelasticity of demand in the case of such addictive drugs would mean that little advertising would be required and profits could be counted on even in the deepest depression. In its purest form capital is absolutely indifferent to use-value in and of itself, and this frees up capital to focus single-mindedly on profit. From the point of view of capital, the social costs or benefits of profit-making are all 'externalities'. This raises enormous problems for consumers, who have had to devise political controls to protect themselves from commodities of poor quality or that have negative externalities (short - or long-term harmful consequences to social life or nature). In *Capital,* for example, Marx (1976, p.358) documents the measures taken against the adulteration of bread in nineteenth century England. And, as we shall see, the battle for safe and nutritious food continues.

Arguably, the history of capitalism has been primarily the history of struggle against capital's indifference to use-value (including indifference to class exploitation). Such indifference is truly callous since it implies that in the case of conflict, short-term profit considerations will prevail over all other human values. Thus, while typically human's spend most of their waking hours in a workplace, workers have had to continually fight against ugliness, filth, noise, heat, dangerous chemicals and machinery, bad air, too long hours, too intense work, job insecurity, low wages, and authoritarian supervisors and rules. Why? Because in most cases the alleviation of these problems would reduce profits and profits come first. Unless constrained by outside regulation (by a relatively autonomous state) capital will pollute the environment, desertify the land and squander scarce resources. Caring only for profits, capital ignores disabled people or other oppressed groups unless a profit can be made from them. This means that the oppressed must always organize and fight against capital's indifference. Likewise all forms of oppression are of no interest to capital unless a profit can be made from them, as for example, in utilizing divide and rule tactics to undermine solidarity amongst those who might otherwise resist capital.

The dominance of value means the dominance of those things that can be capitalistically produced and priced in markets. Costs or benefits relating to things like health, happiness, beauty, democracy, equality, a sense of community, goodness, and truth that do not register in markets are 'externalities' to be ignored. This means that capitalist economic logic excludes ways of thinking that would enable us to integrate thought about the qualitative dimensions of life into economic thought. For example, given that many people spend a great deal of time in factories, consider what might be gained in making them beautiful places, the work as pleasurable as possible, and organized democratically, even if, heaven help us, such changes reduced short-term profits for the owners or in the case of democratic socialism ended profits accruing to private property altogether.

Speeding up The Pace of Life

In Volume Two of *Capital* (Part II), Marx argues that anything that will reduce the turnover time of M-C...P...C-M′ (money buys inputs of production M-C, ...P...a production process of variable time, C′-M′ a newly produced commodity of increased value is sold for a profit M + M) will increase profits.[5] Turnover time is the time from the initial purchase of commodity inputs for a production process to the time that the newly produced commodity outputs are sold. A particular capital may turnover once in a year or a hundred times in a year. Increasing the speed of turnover time is an important means of increasing profits. Turnover time can be increased by insuring that sufficient money is immediately available to buy and combine labour-power and means of production in the technical ratio required for a particular production process to take place. Not only must the money be available, but also labour-power and means of production at the right price. Advances in finance as well as in transportation and communication technologies can facilitate this. The amount of production in a given day can be increased by lengthening the work day, increasing the pace of work, or introducing newer and more productive technology. Selling time can also be reduced by advances in both finance and transportation and communications technology. In the buying of inputs and the selling of outputs, ease of debt expansion plays a key role (e.g. interest rate). Since decreasing the turnover time of capital, increases the speed of production and consumption, one would expect that this might also impact on the pace of life, at the limit exhausting both the human and natural substrate of economic life.[6] Further, except for the small number of cases where waste is profitable, capital considers waste an externality. Other things being equal, one would expect that speeding up the rate of production and consumption would also increase waste, pollution, and dangerous by-products like carbon dioxide.[7]

In pure capitalism, time is primarily time for profit-making so that wasting time is profits forever lost. Consistent with this impulse, it is not surprising then, that in history, time and motion studies would be developed and aimed at getting the most productivity out of a unit of time and at finding ways of preventing workers from resisting the intensification of work. Further, it is not surprising that idleness has always been a cardinal sin of capitalism.[8] The loss of time is the loss of profit. Indeed, time and the quantity of money are so closely connected in capitalism, that we have coined the term 'quality time' to refer to those brief periods set aside from monetized quantitative time for human contact as an end in itself. But this only demonstrates the degree to which quality tends to be absorbed into quantity in capitalism.

Homogenization of Space

For capital in the abstract, space is simply stuff for profit-making, or it is distance that must be traversed faster and faster in order to decrease the turnover time. Space (mainly the earth and its atmosphere), then, is something to be altered at will in order to maximize profit, and it is to be shrunk for the same reason. Space is a potential or actual source of raw materials or is a built environment. In both cases there is potential for homogenization and degradation as in deforestation, strip mining, or suburbanization. This can in some ways be profitable since the more homogenized and degraded space becomes, the more capital can charge for access to 'unspoiled' parts of the globe or to artificially created 'heterogeneous' space such as Disneyland.

The material, qualitative, use-value characteristics of space can be quite resistant to being totally subsumed to the valorization of value. A major result of this is that capital has always developed unevenly in space. Yes, it has always had an expansive and globalizing thrust, but this has run up against the limits of technology, against political policies, and against social formations that are in varying degrees resistant to capitalism. Indeed capital, has only managed to gain as much global hegemony as it has by often compromising its own inner principles, when popular movements have forced upon it the concern for quality that it would prefer to ignore.

Often it is said that capitalism subordinates time to space by making time as linear-sequential as space. Time, then, would become the fourth dimension of space. This perspective is particularly developed by those who think that time is essentially something qualitative.[9] I believe, however, that capitalism makes time so fundamental and so fundamentally linear-sequential, that it might be more accurate to say that capitalism converts space into the second, third and fourth dimension of time. Or, in other words, I believe that space maintains more connectedness with the qualitative in capitalism than does time, contrary to the romanticism of thinkers like Bergson and Sorel. Perhaps Brennan's (2003) use of 'space-time compression' is a good usage that summarizes the connections between space and time in capitalism.

Resistances of C-M-C

A basic problem of capital is how to expand the rate of personal consumption commodity-money-commodity (C-M-C) to just keep pace with M-C-M′. The problem is exacerbated by the fact the C-M-C ends with the satisfaction of a want, whereas M-C-M′ lacks any determinant point of satisfaction, and can in this sense be considered insatiable. Arguably, for Keynes, this was *the* crucial question ('marginal propensity to consume'). At the level of pure capitalism, where we do not have things like state intervention or advertising, there are only a few ways of expanding C-M-C: increase consumption by increasing consumer income, increase the number of consumers, or lower the prices of the commodities to be consumed. Because capital is prone to periodic crises[10], those who produce commodities for which there is little demand elasticity will have the advantage.

In history, this has meant efforts to increase personal consumption through debt expansion, keeping prices down by sourcing the world for cheap resources and labour, planned obsolescence and psychological manipulation. Psychological manipulation refers to all those efforts to make demand inelastic by getting consumers to continue to buy because of brand loyalty, frequent changes in fashion, or, in the most successful cases, a sort of addiction (psychological or physiological) to the commodity.

Legal Subjectivity

In order to operate as self-expanding value, capital must recognize only one kind of subjectivity and that is legal subjectivity.[11] A legal subject or legal person in this instance is an autonomous individual or entity that can own property, buy or sell property, or make contracts with regard to property. Class subjectivities are not recognized by capital and, in the case of the working class, they must be created in the face of capital's hostility. In a purely capitalist society individuals are absolutely sovereign within the world of their own private property, but in sharp contrast can command the outside world only through a cash nexus. Quite literally, only money speaks. The seeming absolute sovereignty within each legal person's private property, fuels all theories that celebrate negative freedom (non-interference); and, however attractive such freedom may seem, even in the purest capitalism, there is another side to the story. For even the richest individual can fall into penury as the result of an economic crisis. Moreover, the steep gradient between absolute control within one's private property and little control outside, makes the continual expansion of private property seem to be the surest path to some control: hence, the 'rat race' amongst capitalists. And of course, for the vast majority, the notion that only 'money speaks' essentially means that they have no voice, and the notion that negative freedom varies with the size of one's private property means that they have very little freedom at all. For legal subjects in a purely capitalist society, freedom is essentially Hobbesian freedom, the absence of external impediments to motion. For capitalists this implies the freedom to move anywhere in order to maximize profits, the freedom to switch production between diverse commodities, the freedom to organize the labour and production process, and the freedom to structure personal consumption. For the working class, freedom is the right to exit from any job, the right to move in search of a job, and the freedom to structure personal consumption. If we want to ignore class, we can say that everyone in a capitalist society has the freedom of movement and the freedom to buy and sell. And if we want to be blatant apologists for capitalism, we can go further and claim that these two freedoms are fundamental to all other freedoms.[12]

Legal subjects as legal entities with a will are essentially externalized selves with identity based on their external positioning and packaging. In a purely capitalist society this packaging can only consist of accumulated private property, and in any particular time and place there are always conspicuous commodities that signal status. But what is important at this level of analysis is the simple condition that one's property accoutrement is the only basis for establishing a distinct identity. One's identity simply is one's commodities. Thus, for legal subjects consumption is crucial to identity formation.

The only purpose in life that capital can give legal subjects is the making and spending of money. Further, since identity can only be based on commodified status, the capitalist self tends to be a hollowed out, externalized self. Such selves must be considered extremely vulnerable to social forces that might fill their emptiness by giving meaning and purpose to their lives whether it is the consumption of commodities, religion, crime, or various forms of dependency or addiction.

While in a purely capitalist society there is an abstract possibility of forming a class identity, nothing determinate can be said about this at this level of abstraction because the class relation is essentially structural and class identity would only emerge with the dawning of class solidarity from class struggle. It is at more concrete levels of analysis that we can address issues having to do with types of class struggle and class consciousness. Strictly from the point of view of capital in a purely capitalist society, only legal subjects exist.

The Commodification of Labour-power

The total commodification of labour-power that accompanies pure capitalism implies unregulated competitive labour markets. Working class legal subjects must sell their labour-power every working day or forever lose the income that they could have earned. But on any given day, the supply of workers may considerably exceed demand, leaving large numbers unemployed. Moreover, even if employed, any worker can be suddenly fired without notice (there are no trade unions, nor state regulations in pure capitalism). As a result, legal subjects who must contract with employers for a wage or salary, face extreme insecurity, particularly when they have little private property to fall back on. Arguably, from Marx to Polyani, it is the radical insecurity that workers face everyday in pure capitalism that makes the commodification of labour-power and its employment in machine-based factories the most intolerable dimension of capital. This insecurity is multiplied by periodic crises which give rise to high levels of unemployment. Finally, even when workers make enough to buy their daily bread, *caveat emptor* (buyer beware) rules between legal subjects, such that the bread may be intentionally or unintentionally adulterated in ways that are not readily detectable by the buyer.

Furthermore, being reduced to a commodity input to a privately owned factory means that within the factory, the owners have control. Thus in history workers enter an authoritarian workplace, where their only real freedom is the right to exit – not much of a right when other factories are also authoritarian and an industrial reserve army awaits with the threat of unemployment. Because of the insecurity and objectification associated with the commodification of labour-power, in history, workers have always struggled against being treated as simply one more commodity input. As a result, class struggle is endemic to capitalism as it unfolds in history. Also being treated as simply one more commodity input in the production process, must be considered yet another dimension to the hollowing out of the subject.

The Centralization of Capital

In pure capitalism the centralization or merging of capital into larger and larger units is facilitated by interest-bearing capital and periodic crises. And while at this abstract level of analysis, we cannot say anything determinant about the rate of centralization, it is clear that corporations in oligopolistic or monopolistic sectors have significant advantages over those in competitive sectors. By exercising more control over prices of both inputs and outputs, they can boost their profits by shifting value from workers, the competitive sector, consumers, or the state sector. Further, because of their power and influence, they can often get state contracts or state subsidies.

These seven tendencies characteristic of pure capitalism are closely interconnected, and the most basic is indifference to use-value or quality except as it is implicated in profit-making. The other six can all be considered as specific forms of this indifference. Even legal subjectivity flows from selves considered purely from the point of view of their external calculating capabilities in connection with economic maximizing behaviour. Such externalized or hollow selves are lacking in the qualitative materiality that goes into what we would generally call 'character'. As legal persons they are caught up in a world of economic calculation, where the directions that wills take are determined by purely short-term quantitative forms of calculation. Indeed, it is this feature of subjectivity that makes it so easy for persons to move back and forth from being subjected to the commodity form as in the commodification of labour-power to being legal subjects as consumers.

Historical Analysis, Eating the Future

Food production and consumption in the US has only gradually been transformed from petty commodity production to a highly concentrated form of capitalist industrial production; and as capitalism takes control of something so basic to human well-being as eating, its relative indifference to use-value results in increasingly spectacular threats to the health of humans and their environment. Indeed, eating brings together human biology and the environment at a very fundamental level, so that capitalism's failure at this level is extremely telling and alarming. Because through food we relate directly to the health of the earth, and because food of the right types and right quantities is so central to our health, it ties human health directly to ecology. The way in which we produce food, distribute it, and consume it is crucial to shaping who we are and to shaping the health and sustainability of our societies. Indeed, a minimum of nutritious and safe food is a prerequisite to all other life chances. For these reasons one would like to see an economic system that would in the long run meet the basic food needs of the entire population of the world in ways that are sustainable, that do not exploit or endanger the workers who produce the food, and that advance the health and pleasure of consumers. According to United Nations (UN) studies, in 2000, approximately one half of the people in the world (three billion) suffer from malnutrition; and furthermore, 'hunger, overeating, and micronutrient deficiencies...account for an estimated half or more of the world's burden of disease' (Gardner & Halweil, 2000, pp. 6–8). Each year more than five million children die of hunger-related diseases, and many of the survivors of hunger have ongoing hunger-related health problems (Gardner & Halweil, 2000).

Indifference to Use-Value

Capitalism's general orientation to short-term profit and indifference to use-value has meant that despite immense and continuing efforts for over two centuries on the part of all those with a strong sense of social justice to resist capital's indifference to the human and natural devastation that it has caused, capital is still in the driver's seat. It is not that important reforms have not been won in some parts of the world or for some lengths of time, but despite capitalism's continual promise of prosperity for all, in fact more people live in poverty on a global scale than ever before.[13] And the statistics would be much worse were it not for the development of a middle-class in quasi-capitalist China after unparalleled growth. And with the take off of American fast food corporations in the 1970s, capitalism's indifference to use-value (qualitative considerations) is penetrating like never before the food sector, which is so basic to human health and the health of the planet. For, while there are other causes of obesity, the fast food industry, with its heavy reliance on foods laced with fat, sugar and salt, is a major contributor. We live in a world with so many alarm bells that it is difficult for any one to be heard through the generalized cacophony. But surely the looming global medical crisis that will materialize if the obesity epidemic continues much longer is an alarm worth noting. Fast foods and inactivity (connected to the auto/suburbia/television complex) have contributed enormously to the overweight health crisis now unfolding in the US and across the planet.[14] Since the early 1970s, there has been a five-fold increase in the consumption of corn syrup globally (Manning, 2004, p. 10). And each soft drink averages about ten teaspoonfuls of sugar (Schlosser, 2001, p. 54). From 1985 to 1998 adult onset diabetes has increased five-fold globally, keeping pace exactly with the increased global consumption of corn syrup (Gardner & Halweil, 2000, p. 39). Given the connections between obesity and all sorts of health problems, the US and many other countries face a severe medical crisis in the future.

The global distribution of food is obscenely distorted. Health costs in the US related to being overweight were estimated at $117 billion in 1999, while the cost of the billions of poor suffering from hunger and malnutrition is incalculable. Globally fully one half of the 1 billion young people between the ages of 15 and 24 are living in poverty (*Worldwatch*, 2004, p.153) and 22.4 per cent of US children live in poverty (Hacker, 2004, p. 39). And given that fast foods tend to be the cheapest, it is particularly the poor and often the young in the industrialized countries who ingest them almost on a daily basis.

The fast food system is heavily dependent on petroleum, because most fertilizers and pesticides are petroleum based and because the mechanization and transportation associated with production and distribution are also heavily petroleum dependent. And the trend is such that every year it takes more and more calories of fossil fuel to produce one calorie of food (21 per cent of fossil fuel energy goes to the global food system and this is increasing) (*Worldwatch*, 2004, p. 37). Fossil fuel consumption has increased globally five times in the past 50 years (*Worldwatch*, 2004, p. xviii), and agriculture gobbles up an increasing share of this consumption. It now takes 35 calories of fossil fuel to produce one calorie of beef and 68 calories of fossil fuel to manufacture one calorie of pork (Manning, 2004, p. 12). In light of these statistics, Pimentel (Manning, 2004, p. 8) claims that if the entire world were to have the same food system as the US, all known reserves of fossil fuel would be used up in seven years. This is a rather literal example of 'eating the future'.

Globally an estimated 200,000 agricultural workers die from pesticides each year and over five million suffer from pesticide poisoning (*The New Internationalist*, 2000, p. 10). Of course, the purveyors of genetically modified seeds, claim, for instance, that genetically modified cotton (being agricultural it is like much food production) needs fewer pesticides. Even the evidence supporting this claim is mixed (Nestle, 2003, p. 181), not to mention the many downsides of such genetic engineering (monopolies of seeds, killing good insects, developing resistant insects, monoculture, affecting bird populations, transgenic pollution, etc.). As it turns out the cotton industry, like nearly all agriculture in the US, is highly subsidized ($3.4 billion a year) (*The New Internationalist*, #364, p. 34) even though current American cotton agriculture uses immense amounts of chemical fertilizers that pollute large bodies of water. It also uses large amounts of pesticides (*Worldwatch*, 2004, p. 162) (globally the cotton industry consumes 10 per cent of all pesticides), large amounts of water, and alarming amounts of fossil fuels. The production of a single cotton T-shirt generates ten times its weight in carbon dioxide (*Worldwatch*, 2004, p. 163).

Speeding up the Pace of Life

Fast food got its name because the serving of the food is very fast, but speed and 'economies of scale' characterize the entire capitalist system, including, now more than ever the of provision of food. According to Tim Lang (2003, p. 557), 'by the late 20th century the food sector had replaced the motor industry as the benchmark of efficiency'. And according to Eric Schlosser

(2001, p. 10), 'No other industry offers, both literally and figuratively, so much insight into the nature of mass consumption'. Thus, speeding up affects both production and consumption as the line speed of meatpackers pushes past the limits of human endurance and more and more people 'eat on the run' or 'grab a bite'. Thus, fast food fits well with the general intensification of the pace of life so characteristic of this phase of capitalism.

The fast food industry is 'fast' in many respects. Indeed, the fact that it is prone to change quickly makes it difficult to study. On the positive side, the fast food industry provides inexpensive 'food' quickly. The popularity of fast foods is attested by the fact that every year Americans spend even more on fast foods than on new cars (Schlosser, 2001, p. 3). Fast foods fit in with a faster pace of life, with more demanding jobs and less sleep time. Intensified competition at nearly every level of life means that the average person is attempting to fit more and more into daily life, and work time is increasing with the Americans now working on average 350 hours more per year than the Europeans (*Worldwatch*, 2004, p. 168), while sleep depravation reaches epidemic proportions (The average sleep time in the US is down 20 per cent in the twentieth century). Fast food is almost a necessity in such a system, since many people simply do not have the time and energy to do the shopping and cooking required for home-cooked meals.

Beef production generates the highest revenues of any agricultural product in the US, and it employs nearly half the agricultural workforce (Schlosser, 2001, p. 198). Slaughterhouses have cut costs and increased profits by speeding up the line and by hiring illegal immigrants, who, as vulnerable workers, cannot easily resist speeding up the line, bad working conditions and low pay. In its heyday, the maximum speed of a Chicago meatpacking line was 50 cattle an hour, now this has been increased to 400 (pp.174–5). In this industry, there is widespread use of amphetamines ('speed') by workers in order to keep up with the pace of the line. This has meant among other things that the injury rate in the meatpacking industry is three times the national average, making it the most dangerous work in the US (Schlosser, 2001, pp.174–5). Over 40,000 workers in this industry alone require medical treatment each year for work-related injuries or illnesses (Schlosser, 2001, p.172). Clearly, while the short-term profits stemming from speed up are very high, so are the long-term social and environmental costs.

The Homogenization of Space

The fast food industry fits well with the automobile – suburbia – television complex that tends to homogenize through the standardization of suburbs, strip malls, fashion, advertising and entertainment.

Agricultural practices that degrade the land turn it into a homogenized medium for the reception of chemicals. About two-thirds of the world's agricultural land is degraded to some extent, and this degradation is not helped by the food system's reliance on mechanical and chemical inputs (*The Economist*, 2000, p. 11). In extreme cases, the prodigal use of the land produces degrees of desertification that are extremely difficult to reverse. And heavy reliance on irrigation can dangerously lower water tables, while surface water is polluted by fertilizer and pesticide run off. Of course, it is not only the fast food industry that is at fault here, but it does tend to be more at fault than other sectors of the food industry.

The meatpacking industry affects the health of Americans in other ways. The concentration of meatpacking means that the spread of pathogens from avian flu to E. coli can occur widely and quickly.[15] One might think that this would lead to better inspection, but so far the meatpacking lobby has successfully resisted this, despite a continued high rate of food-borne illness.[16] In the US, the home of the fast food system, an estimated 200,000 people a day are sickened by food-borne illnesses (Schlosser, 2001, p. 195).

The increased global reach of a small number of very large fast food corporations has the effect not only of homogenizing public spaces with similar commercial advertising, but also to some extent of homogenizing agricultural practices, labour practices and diet. And given how poor the diet is, this is a most unfortunate homogenization. The largest fast food restaurant chains are McDonalds, with 30,000 restaurants in 119 countries and Yum! Brands like Taco Bell, Pizza Hut and Kentucky Fried Chicken (KFC), have around 32,500 restaurants in 100 countries (*Worldwatch*, 2004, pp. 145–6).

Globally 2.5 billion people (mostly poor) depend on agriculture for their main income, making it by far the main source of income for most people in the world (*The New Internationalist*, 2003, p. 20). Many of these people are not employed directly by the global food industry, but few are not indirectly affected by it. Thus, food subsidies and protectionism in the advanced industrial countries combined with International Monetary Fund (IMF) structural adjustment policies have a large impact on food production in poorer countries. And where highly oligopolistic processors of food buy from mainly small producers as in the coffee and chocolate industries, very low prices can be imposed on the farmers. Farmers in poorer countries can also be adversely affected by the commodification and privatization of inputs, by unfavourable terms of trade, and by gluts that are sometimes artificially created or exacerbated by the policies of the rich and powerful.

The Resistances of C-M-C or Tendencies towards Underconsumption

So, how does modern day capital keep the consumers' dollar flowing? One way is cheaper commodities, and this is achieved by among other things speeding up turnover time, by paying low wages, cutting costs that have to do with the health of workers or the environment, using monopoly power to force lower costs upon suppliers of inputs, using monopoly power to achieve direct and indirect government subsidies, and 'economies of scale'. Fast food corporations utilize all of these techniques to achieve 'cost-cutting'.

Another way to combat 'underconsumption' is to increase disposable income, but this would seem to fly in the face of the need for lower wages to cut costs. One way out of this dilemma is to cut taxes even though this usually means underfunding the public sector that provides health, education and welfare. And another way is to increase debt expansion by making borrowing easier. Debt expansion is particularly useful because it expands the profits of the financial sector, while disciplining the workforce to work all the harder and faster to shoulder its growing debt burden.

Expanding production into countries where costs are very low, such as China, and where high growth rates generate significant increases in disposable income is an increasingly important way in which the fast food sector (and most other sectors) combats underconsumption. In 2003 when a survey was written for *The Economist*, China already had over 1000 Yum! Brand restaurants with more opening every week (*The Economist*, 2003, p.8). This expansion into China is important, given that there is very little increase in real disposable income amongst the older 'advanced industrial countries'.

Large fast food corporations try to locate food outlets where there are large captive groupings of consumers, such as rest stops along expressways or near transportation arteries, at sports venues, at educational institutions, at governmental institutions, and where there are large population densities. Given the underfunding of most public institutions that has resulted from tax-cuts and from changed governmental priorities, large fast food corporations now offer 'bribes' to public institutions in order to gain exclusive access to their populations. Bribing educational institutions in order to gain access has become particularly important given the importance of eating habits formed when young. It is now common for schools and even universities to receive funding from fast food corporations in return for access to the student body through vending machines, pouring rights, or fast food outlets. Many universities are now exclusively Pepsi universities or Coca-Cola universities.

Legal Subjectivity

In contemporary capitalism, a major way of dealing with the threat of underconsumption is advertising, and it is important to draw some of the connections between the construction of legal subjectivity in pure capitalism and the closely connected kind of subjectivity spawned by advertising. Just as the commodity form itself generates externalized selves, whose recognition and status would depend on their commodity packaging, so does advertising exaggerate this tendency by channelling desire towards commodities. For advertising operates primarily by stimulating and manipulating fundamental desires, whether hunger for novelty, sex, love, recognition, or food, such that heightened desires get attached not only to particular commodities but to the whole array of commodities. The result is the creation of personality structures where happiness is often translated into the attainment of a certain lifestyle or array of commodities. And when the attainment of the lifestyle does not bring happiness, the answer to be sought is yet more commodities. So we have a treadmill, the speed of which, we can never quite catch up to, for as we gather more commodities, we seem to need yet more in order to achieve that elusive happiness.

And fast food advertisers are seeing to it that their messages are reaching the young and impressionable. It is often said that the youth is the future, and fast food corporations have come to realize that the youth is particularly their future. Food corporations spend $30 billion (Nestle, 2002, p. 22) a year on advertising in the US, and over one half of these advertisements are for candy, sweetened cereals, or fast foods, and many of these are aimed at children. Everyday 8.3 million students form a captive audience to Channel One (the school television channel) (Nestle, 2002, p.189), on which they cannot avoid watching food commercials. And the advertising has been successful. For example, in 1997, 50 per cent of the calories consumed by American children were from sugar and fat added ('value-added'?) to their foods (Nestle, 2002, p. 175). Salt (the excessive consumption of which can cause health problems) consumption in the US has increased 20 per cent in ten years (*The New Internationalist*, 2003a, p. 9). And *The Journal of the American Medical Association* has predicted that one of every three boys and two of every five girls born today will develop diabetes (Wellness Letter, 2004, p. 1).

To the extent that consumers can be psychologically conditioned to crave certain food items or become addicted to them, a demand inelasticity is created that may persist even if the price of the food should suddenly increase dramatically. Or, the craving may result in consuming more of the food than is healthy. And since humans tend to crave sugar, fat, and salt, it is particularly these 'empty-caloried' foods that the fast food industry relies on to get people hooked on their products. And given the hollowed out character of legal subjects, fast foods invite individuals to fill their inner emptiness with fat, sugar and salt.

Besides, there is also a sense in which the prominence of legal subjectivity tends to reduce politics to a sort of legalism. Because of capitalism's general deferral to the market, political economic discourses do not often publicly discuss the harmful effects of particular products, especially when large and influential industries are involved. Usually it is only when an individual or group of individuals is both sufficiently harmed and has the necessary finances that a lawsuit is brought. While the lawsuit may bring some recompense to those harmed, usually it is long after the harm is done and the recompense does not necessarily lead to a rational altering of the socio-economic processes that caused the harm.

Big tobacco, traditionally one of the most profitable industries, has bought heavily into the food industry to protect themselves from tobacco liability suits. Now Philip Morris (Nestle, 2002, p. 13) is among the top three food producers in the world, but alas, obesity has now become a greater threat to health than tobacco, and they may in the future face obesity liability suits. Research is discovering ever closer connections between obesity and heart disease, diabetes, cancer, and other chronic conditions. And it is chronic conditions in wealthy countries rather than infectious diseases that are more profitable to pharmaceutical firms.[17] Killers in the Third World like malaria and tuberculosis are of little interest to the pharmaceutical industry because effective drugs would not be profitable.[18]

The Commodification of Labour-power

Early in the modern world, some food production got attached to slavery, plantation production and colonialism. Since food production often involves very hard work, sometimes dangerous work, at times seasonal work, and usually dirty work, its association with the most exploited labour has continued. For example, the 3.5 million workers (not unionized) in fast food restaurants in the US receive the lowest wage of any category of workers except for migrant farm workers (Schlosser, 2001, p. 6). At 1 million workers annually, McDonalds hires more workers than any other US organization (Ibid., p. 4). And the annual turnover of workers in fast food restaurants is 300–400 per cent, making this an almost impossible sector to unionize (Ibid., p. 73). At the same time, these restaurants receive substantial government subsidies for 'training' workers (Ibid., p. 72).

The dangers faced by workers in slaughterhouses have already been mentioned, but field workers often face back-breaking work and exposure to chemicals. The situation is usually worse in the Third World where there are fewer regulations governing the use of chemicals and it is easier to ignore those that do exist. Though the fast food sector is less labour-intensive than more traditional food sectors, it still utilizes a great deal more labour than most other sectors. It follows that low-wages form a significant part of their profit picture. Imagine if McDonald's workers had anything like the wages and benefits of workers in the auto industry.

The Centralization of Capital

'Efficiency' in the fast food context has meant, first and foremost, greater concentration of corporate power. For example, in the soft drinks industry Coca-Cola, Pepsi and Cadbury-Schweppes control over 90 per cent of the US soft drink market (Schlosser, 2001, p. 53). Abroad Coca-Cola sells more than 300 brands in 200 countries with 70 per cent of its income from outside the US (*Worldwatch*, 2004, p. 146). Burger King, McDonald's and Tricon (now renamed 'Yum! Brands') employed 3.7 million people worldwide in 2000 (Schlosser, 2001, p. 71). Many other sectors of the food industry also have high degrees of corporate concentration. For example, over 80 per cent of American beef is slaughtered by the top four firms operating in this sector (Nestle, 2003, p. 44).

The degree of concentration in the fast food industry means that corporations can assert a great deal of control over prices of inputs and outputs and therefore, profits. For example, farmers and ranchers in the US find themselves getting 'Third World' prices for their products. This is because giant food processing companies can impose low prices on the direct producers, because government subsidies keep farmers afloat, and because an increasing share of the total value of the food goes not to primary producers but to middlemen and those who carry out the ever-greater processing of food.[19] Since humans tend to crave sugar, fat and salt, 'value-added' processing essentially means the addition of these inexpensive but semi-addictive inputs. The profits of the food processors increase dramatically as people become addicted to ever-greater quantities of food high in 'empty calories'. The profits of the farmers, however, seem to fall, as the American potato farmer gets only two cents from a $1.50 large order of fries (Schlosser, 2001, p. 117). 50 years ago, North American farmers got between 45 per cent and 60 per cent of the selling price of the final product and now it is 3.5 per cent, approximately the same as for Third World farmers (*The New Internationalist*, 2003, p. 10).

Yet, Americans continue to eat fast foods. Is it because they are unaware of the impact of fast foods on the health of humans and the environment? This is perhaps one reason, but here are some others:

- Food with a lot of fat, sugar, caffeine and salt tastes good and/or alters moods to the point of being mildly addictive.
- Eating habits are formed at a young age and the marketing and advertising of the fast food industry has targeted the young (Schlosser, 2001, p. 122).
- People with low incomes can often only afford fast foods.[20]
- The pace of life requires people to eat on the run.
- Fast food restaurants are everywhere and often monopolize certain spaces such as sports venues, expressway fuel stops, schools, airports, and suburban malls giving one little choice.
- The flow of fast food advertising is relentless.[21]
- Food cravings are heightened by antidepressants, which are now widely used.
- The inner emptiness that accompanies consumerism can be conveniently filled by omnipresent fast food.

It is interesting to note that 'free market ideologues' continually oppose government intervention in the fast food industry that would deal with health-related issues, but they do not oppose massive government subsidies to the entire food industry. As a commentator in *The Economist* (A Survey of Food, 2003, p. 11) wrote, 'People are constantly torn by the battle between their better or worse selves. It's up to them, not to governments, to decide who should win'. This is perhaps a particularly good example of blaming the victims.

Conclusions

I have presented very brief sketches of aspects of capital accumulation at two levels of analysis. As a way of tying together some of the threads presented in the historical analysis of the current American food system, I shall summarize them in point form. It is my belief, though beyond the scope of this paper to demonstrate, that many of the unfortunate tendencies of the food sector can be generalized to many other sectors. For example, Wal-Mart, one of the most successful corporations in the world in recent years, is in many respects the McDonalds of merchandizing.

Though indifference to use-value is characteristic of capital in general, in this case the result is probable immense future costs to the health of humans and the environment. This is because of increasing reliance on petroleum-based chemicalization, mechanization, and high-tech with consequences that are either unsustainable, destructive, or unknown. The 'unknown' may be the long-term impact of Genetically Modified Organisms (GMOs), the environmental impact of a particular chemical, or the health impact of fast foods and eating on the run on future generations. It is the powerful way that food ties together the health of the earth and the health of humans that makes indifference to use-value so devastating in this sector of the economy.

The speeding up of both the production and the consumption of food results in problems associated with the exhaustion of human and natural resources, degraded environments, severe impacts on human health, and increased costs of waste disposal. Arguably, the higher rates of turnover of capital that in most cases first developed with non-food commodities (such as 'just-in-time lean' auto production) is now increasingly characteristic of the food system, which because of the prominence and character of use-value, has much more harmful effects than with most other commodities. In this case, food production is becoming like other kinds of production, and the overall effect is an increasing degradation of human and environmental health.

The homogenization of space including the commercialization of public and private space, as well as the increasing dominance of monocultures of the soil and mind is another disturbing trend associated with the American food regime.[22] More and more public space is given over to the homogenizing food advertising of a small number of large fast food corporations, or to fast food outlets that sometimes gain privileged or monopolistic access to captive consumers.

The young are continually seduced by the creation of new and fashionable commodities with high value added and a high rate of turnover. This trend can be seen in everything from breakfast cereals to information technology (IT) or from new kinds of potato chips to clothing. Furthermore, consumption is expanded by debt-expansion: reliance on debt (all forms of profiting or of consuming in the present at the expense of the future) to maintain profits, money debt, sleep debt, health debt, ecological debt, etc. Of course, some kinds of debt are easier to measure than others. For example, studies show that a long-term health debt accrues to stress in the workplace, but a precise measure of this would be hard to come by. Similarly there are long-term health debts that attach to both lack of nutritious food and to obesity. And, of course, petroleum-based food production contributes significantly to global warming, which could transfer an enormous debt load to future generations.

There is an effort to get consumers psychologically committed to or even relatively addicted to particular commodities. In this regard, it is natural for tobacco corporations to move into the food industry. And while other commodities do not necessarily have the physically addictive qualities of tobacco or the craving that sometimes goes with food, the aim of advertising and fashion is to create a psychological addiction or a status hunger that will maintain demand in the face of rising prices or competition. Further, there is a generalized effort to set consumption patterns at a young age by bombarding vulnerable children with advertising and marketing strategies that they cannot easily resist. One result of this is that preoccupation with consumption tends to fill the psychic space of young people much earlier in life. Thus, the tendency of pure capitalism to create hollowed out, externalized selves is exacerbated by marketing food to today's youth.

The reliance on vulnerable workers who often face dangers and receive little income or benefits for their efforts, is a trend with a long history in food production, but it has been worsened by the global reach of the food system, immigration policies that foster large numbers of 'illegals', circumvention of protective legislation, and multiplication of unorganized workers. For example, evidence from Ivory Coast (grows 50 per cent of the world's cocoa) finds cocoa growers enslaving children in desperate attempts not to go out of business as a result of structural adjustment policies imposed on them (Robbins, 2001–4). Profiting from and perpetuating extreme degrees of inequality is a threat to human health. And, if we remove the special case of China, empirical studies show that inequality on a global scale is increasing at an alarming rate.[23] And, of course, poor people, unless well-organized, tend to be vulnerable workers

Concentration and globalization of food production and consumption as capitalist (petroleum dependent) industrial agriculture and fast food provision is increasing its influence in the global food system. Throughout the American food system there is heavy reliance on public subsidies to maintain profits. This can happen in both direct (e.g., direct subsidies, tax breaks, tariffs to protect a particular sector) and disguised ways (e.g., the public absorbing the cost of training or the cost of pollution or other social costs). In the food industry this reliance is often extreme, with, for instance, more than 50 per cent of US farm income coming from government payments.[24]

I have argued that the inner logic of the theory of capital demonstrates that unless forced by some outside intervention, capital always subsumes qualitative use-value considerations to profit maximization. While the history of capitalism is largely an effort by large numbers of people to resist this indifference, the tendency still persists. I believe that the current American food regime and particularly its fast food sector dramatically illustrate how this indifference can threaten our future. It is food production and consumption that most directly and dramatically exposes capitalism's terrible inability to find healthy ways of connecting production, consumption, biology and the earth.

And, of course, as I write this, various reform movements are afoot trying to counter these threats. However, I would suggest that the depth and persistence of the problems cry out for a new approach to economic theory and practice. Reforms are not to be dismissed, but as is patently clear in the age of neo-liberalism, they can be rolled back. We desperately need to move towards a democratic socialist world. A world that is far more equalitarian and democratic: a world in which qualitative human values have at least as much status in our economic calculations as the quantitative thinking of the market place. The basic question confronting us is: Will capitalism eat the future before humans have a chance to live it?

Notes

1. This version is strongly influenced by the work of Japanese political economists Kozo Uno and Thomas Sekine.
2. See Sekine, 1997; 2003: Albritton, 1991; 1999: Albritton and Simoulidis, 2003b: Bell, 1995; 2003: Kourkoulakos, 2003.
3. Some notion of levels of analysis is at least posited by nearly every important contemporary Marxist theorist, but none have taken it so seriously as this approach. While I would prefer to use three levels of analysis, the theory of capital's deep structure, mid-range theory, and historical analysis, the scope of this paper only permits discussing the theory of capital's deep structure for the light it sheds on historical analysis.
4. In the translation of *Capital* that I am using 'self-valorizing value' is used literally hundreds of times.
5. Marx, 1978, Part II.
6. See Brennan, 2003 and 2004 for an interesting take on capital's tendency to exhaust human and natural resources.
7. Strasser, 1999.
8. For a discussion of capitalism and anti-idleness ideology, see Albritton, 1991, pp. 105–9.
9. One of the more influential thinkers here is Henri Bergson.
10. See Sekine,1997 for a strong argument that periodic crises will necessarily occur in a purely capitalist society.
11. See Albritton, 2003b, for an expanded discussion of value theory and subjectivity.
12. For a discussion of the possible superiorities of socialist freedom see Albritton, 2004.
13. In the 1990s real per capita income decreased in 55 countries and according to Oxfam by the end of the 1990s 1.2 billion people were living on less than $1 a day (Seabrook, 2002, p. 12, p. 131).
14. 'You'd have to run half a marathon to burn off the calories of an average fast food meal' (*Toronto Star*, 25 January 2004).
15. Nestle (2003, p. 27) argues that the estimated 76 million food-borne illnesses a year in the US is an underestimation because most cases are not reported.
16. 'Major food industries oppose pathogen control measures by every means at their disposal' (Nestle, 2003, p. 27).
17. It is estimated that over 100 million Americans have chronic conditions (Brennan, 2003, p. 70).

18. An estimated 1 million Africans die of malaria each year (*The Economist*, 2003, p. 73). An estimated 3,000 children a day die of malaria and 200 million people alive in 1998 will develop tuberculosis, and yet no major pharmaceutical firm has a research programme devoted to drugs that would deal with these diseases (*The New Internationalist*, 2001, p. 24).
19. According to Striffler (2005, p. 3), the federal government subsidizes agriculture to the tune of $20 billion a year.
20. For example the median income for singles in the US is now $16,934 per year (Hacker, 2004).
21. The most advertised commodity in the US at $33 billion a year is food (Gardner & Halweil, 2000, p. 9; Striffler, 2005, p. 2).
22. See the works of Vandana Shiva for extended analysis of how the current food regime is connected to monocultures of the soil and mind.
23. According to the UN in 1960 the ratio of the share of global income going to the richest 20 per cent in relation to the poorest 20 per cent was 30 to 1, and in 1997 it has increased to 74 to 1 (Ellwood, 2001, p. 101).
24. N. E. Harl, 'Converging Forces Afflict Farms', *The New York Times* (Business, p. 5), 29 April, 2001.

References

Albritton, R. 1991. *A Japanese Approach to Stages of Capitalist Development*. London: Macmillan.
—. 1995a. 'Theorizing the Realm of Consumption in Marxian Political Economy' in Albritton, R. and Sekine, T. (eds.), *A Japanese Approach to Political Economy, Unoist Variations*. Basingstoke: Macmillan.
—.1995b. 'Regulation Theory, A Critique' in Albritton, R. and Sekine, T. (eds.), *A Japanese Approach to Political Economy, Unoist Variations*. Basingstoke: Macmillan.
—. 1999. *Dialectics and Deconstruction in Political Economy*. Basingstoke: Palgrave.
—. 2003a. 'Superseding Lukacs, A Contribution to the Theory of Subjectivity', in Albritton, R. and Simoulidis, J. (eds.), *New Dialectics and Political Economy*. Basingstoke: Palgrave.
—. 2003b 'Marx's Value Theory and Subjectivity' in Westra, R. and Zuege, A. (eds.), *Value and the World Economy Today*. Basingstoke: Palgrave.
—. 2004. 'Socialism and Individual Freedom' Albritton et al. (eds.), *New Socialisms, Futures Beyond Globalisation*. London: Routledge.
Albritton, R., Itoh, M., Westra, R. and Zuege, A. (eds.), 2001. *Phases of Capitalist Development*. Basingstoke: Palgrave.
Albritton, R. and Simoulidis, J. (eds.), 2003. *New Dialectics and Political Economy*. Basingstoke: Palgrave.
Albritton, R., Bell, J., Bell, S. and Westra, R. (eds.), 2004. *New Socialisms: Futures Beyond Globalization*. London: Routledge.
Bell, J. 1995. 'Dialectics and Economic Theory', in Albritton, R. and Sekine, T. (eds.), *A Japanese Approach to Political Economy, Unoist Variations*. Basingstoke: Macmillan.
—. 2003. 'From Hegel to Marx to the Dialectic of Capital', in Albritton, R. and Simoulidis, J. (eds.), *New Dialectics and Political Economy*. Houndmills, Basingstoke: Palgrave.

Brennan, T. 2003. *Globalization and Its Terrors*. London: Routledge.
—. 2004. 'From Socialists to Localists' in Albritton, R. et al. (eds.), *New Socialisms: Futures Beyond Globalization*. London: Routledge.
Cross, G. 2000. *All-Consuming Century*, New York: Columbia.
Ellwood, W. 2001. *The No-Nonsense Guide to Globalization*. Toronto: New Internationalist Publications.
Fine, B. 2002. *The World of Consumption*. London: Routledge.
Gardner, G. and Halweil, B. 2000. 'Overfed and Underfed, the Global Epidemic of Malnutrition', Worldwatch Institute, Paper #150, March.
Giroux, H. 2004. *The Terrors of Neoliberalism*. Aurora, Ontario: Garamond Press.
Glickman, L. 1999. *Consumer Society in American History, A Reader*. Ithaca: Cornell University Press.
Goldman, R. and Papson, S. 2000. 'Advertising in the Age of Accelerated Meaning', in Schor, J. and Holt, D. (eds.), *The Consumer Society Reader*. New York: The New Press.
Hacker, A. 2004. 'The Underworld of Work', *New York Review of Books*, February 12.
Kourkoulakos, S. 2003. 'The Specificity of Dialectical Reason', in Albritton, R. and Simoulidis, J. (eds.), *New Dialectics and Political Economy*. Basingstoke: Palgrave.
Lang, T. 2003. 'Food Industrialisation and Food Power, Implications for Food Governance', *Development Policy Review*, 21, (5–6).
Manning, R. 2004. 'The Oil We Eat', *Harpers*, February, p. v 308.
Magdoff, F., Foster, J. B. and Buttel, F. (eds.), 2000. *Hungary For Profit*. New York: Monthly Review.
Marx, K. 1968. *Theories of Surplus Value*, vol. II. Moscow: Progress.
—. 1976. *Capital*, vol. I. New York: Penguin.
—. 1978. *Capital*, vol. II. New York: Penguin.
—. 1981. *Capital*, vol. III. New York: Penguin.
May, E. 1999. 'The Commodity Gap, Consumerism and the Modern Home', in Glickman, Lawrence, *Consumer Society in American History, A Reader*. Ithaca: Cornell University Press.
McMurtry, J. 1999. *The Cancer Stage of Capitalism*. London: Pluto.
Menzies, H. 2005. *No Time, Stress and the Crisis of Modern Life*. Vancouver: Douglas and McIntyre.
Nestle, M. 2002. *Food Politics*. Berkeley: University of California Press.
—. 2003. *Safe Food*. Berkeley: University of California Press.
Polyani, K. 1944. *The Great Transformation*. Boston: Beacon Press.
Postone, M. 1996. *Time, Labor, and Social Domination*. Cambridge: Cambridge University Press.
Robbins, J. 2001–4. 'Is There Slavery in Your Chocolate?' www.foodrevolution.org/slavery_chocolate.htm
Schor, J. and Holt, D. 2000. *The Consumer Society Reader*. New York: The New Press.
Schlosser, E. 2001. *Fast Food Nation*. New York: Harper Collins.
Seabrook, J. 2002. *The No-nonsense Guide to Class, Caste, and Hierarchies*. Toronto: New Internationalist Publications.
Sekine, T. 1997. *An Outline of The Dialectic of Capital*, 2 vols., London: Macmillan.
—. 2003. 'The Dialectic, or Logic that Coincides with Economics', in Albritton, A. and Simoulidis, J. (eds.), *New Dialectics and Political Economy*. Basingstoke: Palgrave.
Shiva, V. 1992. *The Violence of the Green Revolution: Third World Agriculture, Ecology and Politics*. London: Zed Books.

Strasser, S. 1999. *Waste and Want*. New York: Henry Holt.
Striffler, S. 2005. *Chicken: The Dangerous Transformation of America's Favorite Food*. New Haven: Yale University Press.
Taylor, B. and Tilford, D. 2000. 'Why Consumption Matters', in Schor, J. and Holt, D. (eds.), *The Consumer Society Reader*. New York: The New Press.
The Economist (2003) 'A Survey of Food', May 3, p.11.
— (1991) 'A Survey of America', October 26.
— (1993) 'A Survey of the Food Industry', December 4.
— (1994) 'A Survey of Television', February 12.
— (2000) 'A Survey of Agriculture and Technology', March 25.
— (2003) 'A Survey of Food', December 13.
The New Internationalist (2000) May #323.
— (2001) Jan./Feb. #331.
— (2002) March, #343.
— (2003) Jan./Feb. #353.
— (2003a) Dec. #363.
— (2004) Jan.–Feb. #364.
Uno, K. 1980. *Principles of Political Economy*. Sussex: Harvester Press.
Wellness Letter. 2004. Berkeley: University of California, February 20.
Westra, R. and Zuege, A. (eds.), 2003. *Value and The World Economy Today*. Basingstoke: Palgrave.
Worldwatch Institute. 2004. *State of the World*.
Yates, Michael. 2003. *Naming the System, Inequality and Work in the Global Economy*. New York: Monthly Review.

Chapter 4

WHAT FOLLOWS NEO-LIBERALISM? THE DEEPENING CONTRADICTIONS OF US DOMINATION AND THE STRUGGLE FOR A NEW GLOBAL ORDER

Bob Jessop

This chapter explores neo-liberalism, its forms, its periodization, and its future in the context of the changing dynamics of the capitalist world market. It focuses particularly on American neo-liberalism and foreign economy policy because the US remains the dominant neo-liberal power. It argues that, notwithstanding the loss of American economic hegemony and the growing challenge to its domination across a number of fields, US economic and political power retains disproportionate significance. This is because the new forms of financial domination promoted by the federal government, its associated international economic apparatuses, and transnational financial capital are still 'ecologically dominant' in shaping the world economy and global order more generally. The chapter has five parts. It first addresses issues of periodization that bear on the capitalist world market and neo-liberalism, then defines neo-liberalism and distinguishes its four main forms. Subsequently, it proceeds to discuss four forms of economic determination broadly considered, argues that the logic of American neo-liberalism is ecologically dominant in the world market, and concludes with some general remarks on the contradictions and limits of American domination.

Questions of Periodization

To ask what follows neo-liberalism is to pose a problem of periodization. The primary purpose of any periodization is to interpret an otherwise undifferentiated 'flow' of historical time by classifying events and/or processes in terms of their internal affinities and external differences in order to identify successive periods of relative invariance and the transitions between them (cf. Elchardus, 1988, p. 48). It is widely accepted that the rise of neo-liberal regimes marks a major discontinuity in capitalist development in important respects but there is less agreement on the stages of neo-liberalism and what might follow the collapse or decomposition of its continued dominance on a world scale. The key issue in both respects is to identify what lends neo-liberalism a certain structural coherence as the basis for identifying relative continuities across stages of neo-liberalism as well as the radical discontinuity that would mark its decomposition, whether or not a new stable regime replaced it immediately or at all. Relative continuity does not presuppose the stasis of identical self-repetition – only that relevant changes do not disrupt the structural coherence typical of the neo-liberal regimes. Nor need the end of neo-liberalism signify a total rupture with all features of neo-liberalism – only that surviving features operate in a new context that radically transforms their place and function within the prevailing economic, political and ideological order. In short, we must inquire whether there are changes in the structured coherence of neo-liberal regimes that enable us to demarcate specific stages within neo-liberalism and whether there is a clear tipping point that might lead to a period of structured incoherence or even to a new coherent configuration (for a general discussion on periodization and its application to Fordism and post-Fordism, see Jessop, 2001).

A second set of questions concern the issue of when the world market became sufficiently unified that it was both possible and necessary to write a history of world capitalism rather than to focus on the dynamics of a plurality of more or less autonomous space economies distributed across the globe. This poses some interesting issues about the historical specificity of capitalism as a mode of production, about varieties of capitalism and about their integration into a world market tendentially characterized by one 'variegated capitalism', and, finally, about the periodization of this variegated global capitalism. This transition to world capitalism has occurred unevenly over several steps from the late nineteenth century onwards is linked particularly to the development of world money and global finance and was given a major push by the unprecedented neo-liberal high point following the collapse of the Soviet bloc (see below).

The increasing integration of world capitalism makes it especially inappropriate to study it in terms of 'varieties of capitalism'. There are four main grounds for this. First, the latter approach is overly concerned with distinct (families of) *national* models of capitalism, treating them as rivals competing on the same terrain for the same stakes, and ignoring potential complementarities within a wider international or global division of labour. Conversely, a focus on changing divisions of labour in an increasingly integrated world market suggests that there is a tendentially emerging *single variegated* capitalism rather than a more or less enduring set of *national varieties* of capitalism. These supposed varieties of capitalism are often studied in terms of their respective forms of internal coherence on the false assumption that they can be studied in relative isolation from each other. In contrast, focusing on a tendentially emerging variegated global capitalism involves identifying and explaining various zones of relative stability in terms of their changing complementarities, contradictions, and crisis-tendencies in a complex 'ecology' of accumulation regimes, modes of regulation, and spatio-temporal fixes – and paying due attention to their respective capacities to displace and defer contradictions and crisis-tendencies into the future and/or into zones of relative incoherence, instability and even catastrophe. Situating the conventional varieties of capitalism in a globally variegated capitalism highlights the importance of connecting relatively successful performance in certain economic spaces not only to their external as well as internal conditions of existence but also – and crucially – to the various costs imposed by this performance on other spaces and future generations. In this context, neo-liberalism should not be regarded as merely one variety of capitalism among others that has proved more or less productive and progressive (or more or less inefficient and exploitative) than other varieties and that could be adopted elsewhere with the same positive (or negative) results, as if the whole world economy could be organized along neo-liberal lines. Instead, we learn more by locating neo-liberalism within a global ecology of economic regimes (and their economic and extra-economic supports) and asking which, if any, of these regimes has the greatest impact through its distinctive logic on the overall dynamics of accumulation on a world scale.

This argument casts a new light on Marx's claim that the world market is the arena at which all relevant forces interact. For this claim did not entail a singular logic operating with singular directionality at the level of the world market (the mistake made in crude versions of world system theory). Instead the most developed mode of existence of the integration of abstract labour with the value form is the world market, a place in which production is posited as a totality together with all its moments, but within which, at the same time, all contradictions come into play' (Marx, 1973, p. 227). Expressed in the new terminology developed below, this can be read as a call to explore the structural coupling, co-evolution, and mutual complementarities-compossibilities as well as the contradictions and mutual exclusivities among varieties and stages of capitalism and their implications for the future dynamics of capital accumulation on a world scale. In short, the ultimate theoretical and practical horizon of a periodization of capitalism should be 'variegated capitalism' at the level of the world market.

My starting point, then, is the increasing integration of the world market in contemporary capitalism and the claim that this makes Marx's analysis of *Capital* even more relevant today than when Marx wrote it. But how should we understand and elaborate this logic of the world market? To do justice to the complexities of world society, we need to avoid economism and allow for other societal logics. Here, I draw on arguments from my analysis of *The Future of the Capitalist State* (Jessop, 2002), especially those concerning alternative modes of societalization (*Vergesellschaftungsmodi*); the limits of possibility (and compossibility) of different logics of societalization; the ideas of structural coupling and co-evolution among functional systems; institutional orders and organizations; the historical specificity of capitalism and its contradictions; and, especially, the significance of relations of ecological dominance within and among systems. I argue that internationalization and globalization, especially of financial capital, are crucial processes in enabling the logic of capital to operate more completely than ever before on a global scale. This does not exclude uneven development and temporary leads and lags but these should be seen in part as factors driving neo-liberal globalization forward rather than as fundamental obstacles that will sooner or later bring it to a halt. The true limits to capital accumulation reside in the capital relation itself and in its increasing destruction of nature rather than in short-term fluctuations, medium-term cycles and crises, and long-term waves of accumulation.

What is Neo-Liberalism?

For present purposes, we can distinguish four meanings of neo-liberalism. The first, and most radical, is the *neo-liberal system transformation* following the collapse of the Soviet bloc, i.e., a *tabula rasa* approach in which the creative destruction of inherited state socialist institutions was somehow expected to lead to the spontaneous emergence of a fully functioning liberal market society and to the more gradual development of a functioning representative democracy. Second, there are essentially endogenous *neo-liberal regime shifts* such as the turn from post-war settlements based on an institutionalized compromise between capital and labour to economic policies based on liberalization, deregulation, privatization, market proxies in the residual public sector, internationalization, and reduced direct taxation – a set of policies that are intended to alter the balance of forces in favour of capital. The paradigm cases for this are Thatcherism and Reaganism but similar, largely endogenous shifts have occurred elsewhere in the advanced capitalist economies and in some Latin American economies such as Chile and Argentina. Third, there are neo-liberal economic restructuring processes and regime shifts that have been externally imposed on crisis-ridden economies and their states by the leading capitalist powers and/ or their allies in transnational economic institutions and organizations as a condition of receiving financial and other assistance.[1] And, fourth, there are relatively pragmatic and hence potentially reversible neo-liberal policy adjustments. These comprise the minimal changes necessary in the face of growing internationalization and a global shift in the balance of forces to enable alternative economic and social models to be maintained in the face of new conditions. Examples can be seen in the Nordic social democracies, the *Model Deutschland*, and other forms of Rhenish capitalism.

The high point of neo-liberalism occurred in the second half of the 1980s and first half of the 1990s, when there was a largely contingent combination of neo-liberal system transformation, neo-liberal regime shifts and neo-liberal policy adjustments. This conjuncture enabled neo-liberal triumphalists and their neoconservative supporters to claim that the whole world had become neo-liberal or would soon do so (e.g., Fukuyama, 1992). It has subsequently become clear that neo-liberal system transformation has largely failed as a 'grand project', that neo-liberal regime shifts need to be flanked and supplemented by various forms of 'Third Way' and even neo-communitarian policies and that the return to the market must be accompanied by multi-level governance in the shadow of continued hierarchy, and that neo-liberal policy adjustments rarely lead to neo-liberal regime shifts (witness, most recently, the Swedish and German cases, where, once again, conservative governments have chosen to operate within the broad constraints of inherited models rather than to attempt a whole-hearted neo-liberal regime shift).

Does this mean that we can ignore neo-liberalism or treat it as just one trend among many? No. For we must take account of: (i) the path-dependent legacies of the neo-liberal high point and of the failures of neo-liberal system transformation; (ii) the continuing transition from neo-liberal rollback to neo-liberal roll-forward in the case of neo-liberal regime shifts (cf. Peck and Tickell, 2002) and the associated search for flanking and supporting mechanisms and policies to maintain that roll-forward (cf. Jessop, 2003); and (iii) the regular cyclical return to neo-liberal policy adjustments – as part of a cyclical movement of neo-corporatist, neo-statist, and neo-communitarian adjustments – in the case of national and regional economies that did not undertake a neo-liberal regime shift. As indicated above, we must also distinguish points in a continuum that stretches from the 'normal' domestic politics of neo-liberalism in advanced capitalist economies (especially where it is largely limited to policy adjustments) through to the more 'exceptional' imposition of neo-liberal policies and politics (sometimes in 'emergency conditions' and/or under military rule) in the imperialist struggle between rival capitalist and state interests for markets and domination in more dependent (and crisis-ridden) capitalist economies.

In addition, we should consider the contribution of neo-liberal policies to the forms, timing and dynamics of economic crises (broadly understood) in regions where neo-liberalism has not yet been adopted, imposed, or adapted. For the pursuit of neo-liberalism in a world market tends to disrupt the structured coherence of economies based on other modes of regulation and/or governance based on managing medium-to long-term material interdependencies rather than on maximizing short-term financial returns in the name of shareholder value. This point can be elaborated by noting the inherent tensions and potential for contradiction and conflict between the two faces of each of the main forms of the capital relation. Thus, the commodity is both an exchange-value and a use-value; the worker is both an abstract unit of labour-power substitutable by other such units (or, indeed, other factors of production) and a concrete individual with specific skills, knowledge, and creativity; the wage is both a cost of production and a source of demand; money functions both as an international currency and as national money; productive capital is both abstract value in motion (notably in the form of realized profits available for re-investment) and a concrete stock of time-and place-specific assets in the course of being valorized; knowledge can be appropriated as intellectual property or circulate as part of the intellectual commons; and so forth. For each of these social forms, neo-liberalism privileges its exchange-value over its use-value moment, emphasizing cost recovery and cost reduction and subjecting all economic activities to demands to meet or exceed the prevailing world market average rate of profit (cf. Jessop, 2000; 2001).

This privileges hypermobile financial capital at the expense of those capitals that need to be valorized in particular times and places and also encourages the extension of profit-oriented, market-mediated accumulation into spaces where it did not previously obtain. Even after the neo-liberal high point had ended and neo-liberal hegemony had been weakened, the dominant neo-liberal economic, political and ideological forces still resorted to multi-and bi-lateral domination to impose neo-liberalism on recalcitrant economies.

This point can be elaborated by considering how current neo-liberal trends in globalization increase the importance of the first side of each of the contradictions mentioned in the preceding section. These trends reinforce the abstract-formal moment of exchange-value in these structural forms at the expense of the substantive-material moment of use-value (see above). For it is capital in these abstract moments that is most easily dis-embedded from specific places and thereby released to 'flow' freely through space and time.[2] However, in each of its more concrete moments, capital has its own particular productive and reproductive requirements. These can often be materialized only in specific types of spatio-temporal location. This leads to a general tension between neo-liberal demands to accelerate the flow of abstract (money) capital through an increasingly dis-embedded space and the need for the more concrete forms of capital to be 'fixed' in time and place as well as embedded in specific social relations as a condition for their valorization.

Neo-Liberalism and Economic Determination

What does it mean to talk about the dominance of neo-liberalism? Contrary to the received wisdom attributed (often falsely or misleadingly) to orthodox Marxism, there is no 'determination in the last instance' in the relations between the dynamics of the profit-oriented, market-mediated process of accumulation and other institutional orders and associated forms of consciousness. This is ruled out by the inevitable dependence of capital accumulation on extra-economic factors. But this dependence does not exclude other modalities of economic determination. Elsewhere I distinguish economic determination, ecological dominance, economic domination, and bourgeois hegemony. The first principle is a systemic feature of the operation of the economy, the second concerns the institutional and organizational dimensions of structural power in the economy and/or the relation between economic agents and extra-economic forces, the third mechanism operates in the first instance on an ideational or discursive plane – although successful hegemony also tends to become structurally embedded and dispositionally embodied; and the fourth concerns the systemic relations between the economy and other systems:[3]

- Economic determination in the first instance – this is the primary role of the circuits of productive capital within the overall circuit of capital or, if you like, the primacy of production inside the economic system. This involves no more (but certainly no less) than the fact that wealth must first be produced before it can be distributed or, in more Marxist terms, value must first be produced before it can be realized, redistributed and reallocated. Such economic determination will increase to the extent that the logic of commodification extends into areas where profit-oriented, market-mediated exchange was previously absent even if other types of exchange relations previously obtained in these areas.
- Economic domination – the primacy of those who control strategic resources in a given commodity chain and or broader set of economic activities, e.g., oil in the Fordist and, indeed, post-Fordist economy or, more recently, gene patents in the field of bio-capitalism. By extension, economic domination also encompasses the relative 'strike power' or 'blackmail power' of the economy vis-à-vis other systems and institutional orders because of their material dependence on specific economic inputs.

- Economic hegemony – the capacity of a given set of social forces to establish the primacy of their techno-economic paradigm and accumulation strategy as the dominant economic imaginary, leading other forces to adapt their paradigms, business models, and strategies to this hegemony.
- Ecological dominance, i.e., the capacity of the profit-oriented, market-mediated capitalist economic order – including its extra-economic supports – to have a greater impact on the evolution of other social orders than these orders can have on it. Ecological dominance depends on the specific properties of accumulation regimes and modes of regulation, the nature of other systems in its environment, and specific conjunctural features. Other systems and their actors will be more or less able to limit or resist commodification and to steer economic activities by imposing their own systemic priorities and modes of calculation on the economy.

In general terms, ecological dominance refers to the capacity of a given system in a self-organizing ecology of self-organizing systems to imprint its developmental logic on other systems' operations through interpenetration, structural coupling, blind co-evolution, strategic drift, and strategic coordination to a greater extent than other systems can impose their respective logics on that system.[4] This capacity is always mediated in and through the operational logics of other systems and the communicative rationalities of the life-world. Ecological dominance is always differential, relational and contingent. Thus, a given system can be more or less ecologically dominant; its dominance will vary across systems and in different spheres or aspects of the life-world; and its dominance will depend on the development of the entire social ecosystem. This does not mean that the ecologically dominant system is unaffected by the operation of other systems or that specific social forces will not attempt to reverse, brake or guide that dominance. Rather, as its name implies, ecological dominance involves an *ecological relation* where one system acquires dominance in a complex, co-evolving situation; it does not involve a one-sided *relation of domination* where one system unilaterally imposes its logic or will on others (cf. Morin, 1980, p. 44). There is no 'last instance' in relations of ecological dominance – they are always contingent. Thus, we must study the historically specific conditions under which accumulation tends to become the ecologically dominant process in the wider social formation.

The Ecological Dominance of the Economy

There are seven analytically distinct, but empirically interrelated aspects of the social (as opposed to biological) world that affect a system's potential in this regard (see Table 1). In these terms, the profit-oriented, market-mediated capitalist economy, with its distinctive, self-valorizing logic, tends to have just those properties that favour ecological dominance over other types of social relations.

First, as the capitalist economy gets increasingly dis-embedded from other systems, internal competition to reduce both socially necessary labour-time and socially necessary turnover time becomes an ever more powerful driving force in the dynamics of capital accumulation. Extra-economic pressures on the economy are thereby, translated into competition among capitals to find new opportunities for profit in these pressures and/or to exit from particular markets in order to preserve capital by investing elsewhere (including in liquid assets). Different degrees of liquidity, flexibility and fungibility mean that capitals vary in their ability to respond to such pressures and competition. Finance capital controls the most liquid, abstract and generalized resource and therefore, has the most capacity to respond opportunities for profit and external perturbations. Derivatives have developed as the most generalized form of this capacity and, indeed, have an increasing role in the commensuration of all investment opportunities in the world market, serving thereby as a self-generating, self-referential expression of capital in general on a world scale (cf. Bryan and Rafferty, 2006; 2007).

Second, the capitalist economy is internally complex and flexible because of the decentralized, anarchic nature of market forces and the dual role of the price mechanism as a flexible mechanism for allocating capital to different economic activities and as a stimulus to second-order observation, learning and self-reflection. One of the aspects contributing to ecological dominance in the natural world is a given species' superior capacity to tolerate environmental disturbances (Keddy, 1989, pp. 18–9). Arguing by analogy, this capacity is well-developed in the economy because of its greater internal complexity (multiplicity and heterogeneity of elements), the looser coupling among these elements, and the high degree of reflexive capacity (self-monitoring) in the market economy (Baraldi et al., 1998, p. 151). Moreover, as capitalism develops, different organizations, institutions and apparatuses tend to emerge to express different moments of its contradictions, dilemmas and paradoxes and these may then interact to compensate for market failures within the framework of specific spatio-temporal fixes.

Third, capital has developed strong capacities to extend its operations in time and space (time-space distantiation) and/or to compress them in these regards (time-space compression). The mutual reinforcement of these twin processes facilitates real-time integration in the world market and makes it easier to maintain its self-expansionary logic in response to perturbations. These capacities are related to the formal, procedural rationality of the market (the anarchic invisible hand), its reliance on the symbolic medium of money to facilitate economic transactions despite disjunctions in time and place, its highly developed abstract and technical codes (with well-developed mechanisms of capitalist accounting and monetary returns as its easily calculable formal maximand), and the requisite variety of its internal operations (on Marx and capitalist accounting, see especially Bryer, 2006). All of these capacities increase capital's 'resonance capacity' to react to internal and external conditions (Luhmann, 1988, pp. 37–41): The greater this capacity relative to other systems, the greater the scope for capital's ecological dominance.

Table 1: Factors Relevant to Ecological Dominance in the Relations among Functional Systems

Internal	• Scope for continuous self-transformation because internal competitive pressures are more important than external adaptive pressures in the dynamics of a given system
	• Extent of internal structural and operational complexity and the resulting scope for spontaneous self-adaptation in the face of perturbation or disruption (regardless of the external or internal origin of adaptive pressures)
	• Capacity to distantiate and/or compress its operations in time and space (i.e., to engage in time-space distantiation and/or time-space compression) to exploit the widest possible range of opportunities for self-reproduction
Transversal	• Capacity to displace its internal contradictions, paradoxes and dilemmas onto other systems, into the environment, or defer them into the future
	• Capacity to redesign other systems and shape their evolution through context-steering (especially through organizations that have a primary functional orientation and also offer a meeting space for other functional systems)[8] and/or constitutional (re)design
External	• Extent to which other actors accept its operations as central to the reproduction of the wider system and orient their own operations to its reproduction 'needs' (e.g., through their naturalization within system programmes or decision premises as naturalized constrains or imperatives). Organizations also have a key role

| | here through capacity to respond to irritations and expectations of several functional systems |
| | • Extent to which a given system is the biggest source of external adaptive pressure on other systems (perhaps through the implications of recurrent system failures, worsening social exclusion, and positive feedback effects)[9] and/or is more important than their respective internal pressures for system development |

Fourth, through these and other mechanisms, capital develops its chances of avoiding the structural constraints of other systems and their attempts at control, thereby increasing its 'indifference' to the environment (cf. Lohmann, 1991; Luhmann, 1988). This is especially true of the only *sub*system in the capitalist economy that has become more or less fully integrated on a global scale: international finance (Luhmann, 1996). This does not mean that finance (let alone the economy more generally) can escape its overall dependence on the diverse contributions of other functional systems to its operations or, of course, from crisis-tendencies rooted in its own contradictions and dilemmas. Attempts to escape particular constraints and particular attempts at control can nonetheless occur through its own internal operations in time (discounting, insurance, risk management, futures, derivatives, hedge funds, etc.) or space (capital flight, relocation, outsourcing abroad, claims to extra-territoriality, etc.), through the subversion of the logic of other systems owing to the colonization of organizations central to the latter's operation by the logic of exchange-value, or through simple personal corruption.

Fifth, in contrast to natural evolution, where species must adapt to or exit from their environment, social evolution may involve reflexive self-organization and attempts to redesign the environment (cf. Marx on the distinction between bees and architects, *Capital I*, 1965, p. 284). This capacity may even extend to attempts to change the mode of social evolution (Willke, 1997). This does not mean that the evolution of particular functional systems, let alone the evolution of world society, can be fully controlled but nor does it exclude attempts at shaping the path of co-evolution among organizations, systems, and, eventually, world society. Where different organizations and systems seek to adapt to and/or to change their environment, 'the logic of evolutionary progress is toward ecosystems which sustain only the dominant, environment-controlling species, and its symbionts and parasites' (Bateson, 1972, p. 451).[5] This poses the question of the relative capacity of different organizations and systems to change their environment rather than being forced to adapt to changes in their respective environments (see also point seven).

Sixth, the primacy of accumulation over other principles of societalization (e.g., national security, 'racial' supremacy, religious fundamentalism, social solidarity) can be explored in terms of the relative influence of the self-descriptions and associated social values of different functional systems, especially as these are articulated and represented in the mass media and public sphere and the struggle for political, intellectual, and moral leadership. The importance of such self-descriptions and values may vary within generalized societal communication (everyday language and the mass media) in relation to: (i) alternative logics of societal organization; (ii) secondary coding in the programmes of each functional system such that economic considerations play a key role in choosing among alternatives relevant to its primary function, e.g., in designing school curricula, choosing research topics, deciding what is newsworthy, calculating quality of life years in the medical system, timetabling world sporting events; (iii) the decision premises of organizations; (iv) the relative weight of different interests in negative coordination among organizations with different functional primacies (where such coordination aims to ensure that the application of their respective codes does not lead to mutual blockages), and (v) the changing character of public opinion. The mass media also have a crucial role in offering information to functional systems, organizations, and interactions, especially where those who control the means of production also tend to control the means of mental production and thereby shape news values. The struggle for hegemony in this context will be easier where a functional system is internally organized, like the world economy, on the basis of centre-periphery relations and/or stratification rather than in a segmented fashion with essentially similar units (Luhmann, 1996; Simsa, 2002).[6] Hegemonic struggle will also be easier where social forces emerge that cross-cut functional systems and seek to harmonize (through positive or negative coordination) their operations. A power bloc organized through parallel power networks provides an important mechanism of system and social integration in this regard (Poulantzas, 1978; cf. Baecker, 2001; 2006). None of this implies that a hegemonic vision could adequately represent the identity of world society as *repraesentatio identitatis* any more than this would be possible from the viewpoint of a single system. But the function of hegemony is not to represent the whole of society but to represent a set of particular interests as the interests of society (cf. Marx and Engels, 1976; Gramsci, 1971).

Seventh, the ecologically dominant system is the most important source of external adaptive pressure on other systems. In general, any increase in the complexity of one functional system increases the complexity of the environment of other systems and forces them to increase their own internal complexity in order to maintain their capacity for autopoiesis (Baraldi et al., 1998, p. 96). For the first four factors above increasing internal complexity with repercussions for other systems in an emerging world society, is most likely to characterize the international market economy. Indeed, for Wagner (2006), it is the system with the highest tendency to fail with the most significant consequences for other systems that will gain primacy (*Primat*) or, in current terminology, ecological dominance. This is especially likely because the organizations that are so important for the realization of other systems' activities must secure the revenues to support their operations from the economy, either directly or indirectly (cf. Lange, 2003, p. 233). This enhances the capacity of the profit-oriented, market-mediated economy to colonize other functional systems and the life-world through the logic of commodification and the adoption of net revenues as the major secondary code. Pressures on individual territorial states in this regard have been increased through globalization (Stichweh, 2000, p. 195f), leading to permanent irritation by economic problems (Wagner, 2006, p. 7).

This all suggests that 'ecological dominance' could be used productively to reinterpret the classical Marxist idea of 'economic determination in the last instance' and the Gramscian concept of 'historical bloc'. The former idea was always problematic because the capitalist mode of production lacks the autonomy (as a cause without cause) to be fully determinant in the first, medium, or final instance. But retreat from such a notion of determination to a theory of internal relations cannot explain the asymmetry entailed in the primacy of economic relations. An alternative is to suggest that capital is ecologically dominant insofar as the logic of accumulation tends to cause more problems for other systems than they cause for the expanded reproduction of capital. This does not exclude reciprocal influence from other systems insofar as their operations and dynamics disturb, irritate, or disrupt the circuit of capital and thereby influence the course of its profit-oriented, market-mediated evolution. In turn, the resulting co-evolutionary structural drift in the shadow of ecological dominance (especially when reinforced by successful struggles over economic hegemony) can explain the nature of the 'historical bloc' as a pattern of structured coherence between base and superstructure (Gramsci, 1971). Central to the development of any such bloc is the tight coupling between the economic, juridical and political systems as operationally autonomous but materially interdependent societal complexes.

Nonetheless, even when conditions do favour the long-term ecological dominance of the capitalist economy, other systems may gain short-term primacy in response to crises elsewhere. For no individual system represents, or can substitute for, the whole. Each autopoietic system is both operationally autonomous and substantively interdependent with other systems. Even an ecologically dominant system depends on the socially adequate performance of other systems and a normally subordinate system may become dominant in exceptional circumstances. This would occur to the extent that solving a non-economic crisis becomes the most pressing problem for the successful reproduction of all systems – including the capitalist economy. For example, during major wars or preparations for them, states may try to plan or guide the economy in the light of perceived military-political needs. This can also be seen in Cold War national security states in which national security concerns give a distinctive inflection – as well as political legitimacy in the eyes of the American hegemon – to their character as developmental states (for example, Taiwan, South Korea). A different example is the increasing dominance of security concerns associated with the 'War on Terror(ism)' in the US – with the magnitude of these concerns reflecting the construction of 9/11 as a global security threat to American society in a manner that clearly serves specific political and economic interests and is already proving irrational from the viewpoint of the expanded reproduction of the domestic space economy. After genuine or spurious states of emergency have ended, however, the primacy of accumulation is likely to be reasserted. This does not exclude path-dependent traces of such exceptional conditions in the normally dominant system (for example, the legacies of total war on economic trajectories after 1945). But, even given such path-dependency, the 'quasi-transcendental meta-code'[7] of the ecologically dominant system will still impact more on other systems' development in this complex evolutionary process than they can on it (for further discussion, see Jessop, 2002, pp. 24–30).

The Ecological Dominance of Capitalism vis-à-vis World Society

Marx and Engels noted in *The German Ideology* that, during the initial development of capitalism, '[t]he movement of capital, although considerably accelerated, still remained, however, relatively slow. The splitting up of the world market into separate parts, each of which was exploited by a particular nation, the exclusion of competition among themselves on the part of the nations, the clumsiness of production itself and the fact that finance was only evolving from its early stages, greatly impeded circulation' (1976, p. 56n). Moreover, as Marx (1971, p. 253) argued:

> It is only foreign trade, the development of the market to a world market, which causes money to develop into world money and *abstract labour* into social labour. Abstract wealth, value, money, hence *abstract labour*, develop in the measure that concrete labour becomes a totality of different modes of labour embracing the world market. Capitalist production rests on the *value* or the transformation of the labour embodied in the product into

social labour. But this is only [possible] on the basis of foreign trade and of the world market. This is at once the pre-condition and the result of capitalist production.

In this sense, Marx's missing book on the 'world market and crises' would have presented the world market as the ultimate 'concrete synthesis of multiple determinations' because 'the most general abstractions arise only in the midst of the richest possible concrete development, where one thing appears as common to many, to all. Then it ceases to be thinkable in a particular form alone' (Marx, 1973, p. 101, p. 104). Or, as Bonefeld puts it, 'All and everything subsists not only in relation to the world market but, fundamentally, in and through the world market…In short, the world market is the "categorial imperative" of the political economy of capital' (Bonefeld, 2000, p. 36).

Taking these arguments further in the light of the preceding section, one could argue that the ecological dominance of capitalism is closely related to the extent to which its internal competition, internal complexity and loose coupling, capacity for reflexive self-reorganization, scope for time-space distantiation and compression, externalization of problems, and hegemonic capacities can be freed from confinement within limited ecological spaces policed by another system (such as a political system segmented into mutually exclusive sovereign territories). This is where globalization, especially in its neo-liberal form, promotes the relative ecological dominance of the capitalist economic system by expanding the scope for accumulation to escape such political constraints (Jessop, 2000, p. 328–33). Neo-liberalism promotes the opening of the world market and reduces the frictions introduced by national 'power containers'. It reinforces the dominance of the exchange-value moment of the various forms of the capital relation and frees money capital as the most abstract expression of the capital relation to move at will within the world market to maximize opportunities for profit (Jessop, 2002). Liberalization, deregulation, privatization, administrative commodification, internationalization, and the lowering of direct taxes all boost the scope for internal variation and selection in the profit-oriented, market-mediated economy. Combined with an emphasis on shareholder value, this particularly benefits hypermobile financial capital, reinforcing its competitiveness and ratcheting up its ability to displace and defer problems onto other economic actors and interests, other systems, and the natural environment. Yet this will also enhance the scope for the contradictions and dilemmas of a relatively unfettered (or dis-embedded) capitalism to shape the operation of other systems and may thereby undermine crucial extra-economic conditions for accumulation.

The significance of the ecological dominance of the capital relation is well expressed by István Mészáros in the following statement:

> Capital is not a 'material entity' – let alone a rationally controllable 'mechanism' ... – but an *ultimately uncontrollable mode of social metabolic control*. ...One cannot think of a more inexorably all-engulfing – and in that important sense '*totalitarian*' – system of control than the globally dominant capital system. For the latter blindly subjects to the same imperatives health care no less than commerce, education no less than agriculture, art no less than manufacturing industry, ruthless superimposing its own criteria of visibility on everything, from the smallest units of its 'microcosm' to the most gigantic transnational enterprises, and from the most intimate personal relations to the most complex decision-making processes of industry-wide monopolies, favouring always the strong against the weak...the price that must be paid for this incommensurable totalizing dynamism is, paradoxically, the *loss of control* over the decision-making processes (1995, p. 41).

Even though the global neo-liberal high point has passed in terms of elite consensus (let alone popular support), this has not reversed the ecological dominance of the logic of neo-liberalism within the context of capital accumulation on a world scale that is ecological dominance in relation to world society. This reflects the continuing ecological dominance of the American economy within the world market and the ecological dominance of this market within the overall development of world society. In other words, the pursuit of neo-liberalism on a global scale can cause more problems for other urban, regional, national and supra-regional economies than other economic strategies can cause for neo-liberalism in a deregulated global economy; and the overall logic of the world market, organized in the shadow of neo-liberalism, causes more problems for other systems and the life-world than they can cause for the economy.

This changes how we think about the US in the world market and world society. The US is often discussed as a hemispheric or global hegemonic power in world society and/or as the economically dominant power in the world economy. But it no longer enjoys the hegemony that it exercised in the immediate post-war economic order, when it sacrificed immediate economic interests to promote its longer term interests in global economic expansion whilst promoting the economic-corporate interests of other advanced capitalist formations through their integration, directly or indirectly, into the circuits of Atlantic Fordism or the wider international economy. In the immediate post-war period, the US also enjoyed the benefits of economic dominance through its technological supremacy, control over oil reserves and other strategic commodities, gold and foreign currency reserves, possession of the master currency, and 'soft' power exercised through the cultural industries. In the last two decades, the US has been losing this dominance, especially relative to the European Union (EU), Japan, and the BRIC economies (Brazil, Russia, India, and China). The neo-liberal regime shift developed as a response to this crisis in political hegemony and economic dominance. This has not reversed the loss of US political hegemony (despite its appeal in post-socialist economies) or the overall decline of American economic dominance (witness the continuing fiscal, budgetary, and trade deficits in the US economy). But the US still retains the (destructive) power of ecological dominance, i.e., it still causes more problems for other economies than they can cause for it. It is better able to displace and defer the contradictions of neo-liberalism onto other spaces and times than other varieties of capitalism in other spaces can displace their problems into the American economy. This illustrates on a global scale the old aphorism that, if a firm owes a bank $10,000, it has a problem, but if the debt is $10,000,000, the bank has a problem. In other words, the threats posed by current economic imbalances in the neo-liberal US and its relations to other major economic players (especially China and Japan) threaten the stability of the world market and, a fortiori, world society. Indeed, the blowback effects of US policies are more likely to damage the growth dynamic of the US economy than the policies pursued in other varieties of capitalism.

Among the most obvious indicators of the ecological dominance of the US economy are the positive feedback effects of the growing international trade and financial imbalances between the US, China and Japan as well as their implications for environmental destruction through the unsustainable growth of production in China and consumption in the US. It is difficult to foresee how the necessary adjustments can be made without a major global crisis that will forcibly reimpose proportionalities in the global circuit of capital that have proved impossible to resolve politically. The likely consequences of this will be a dramatic bursting of asset bubbles, an intensification of 'competitive austerity' policies, and deepening imperialist rivalries and trade wars.

These positive feedback effects are especially significant in the current period because of the specific neo-liberal and neoconservative policies pursued under the exceptional political regime presided over by George W Bush and its domination by a distinctive set of particular capitalist interests. In contrast to the normal form of the capitalist type of state, a bourgeois democratic republic, in which class power is largely structural and rendered invisible through the normal functioning of free markets and political democracy, the federal state has more and more assumed the form of an exceptional regime captured by special interests, seeking to neutralize or dismantle democratic institutions and the normal play of democracy, and thereby making class power in the US ever more visible. In this regard the war on terrorism and promotion of self-help through 'faith communities' (with the exception of Islamic faith communities) have now become the 'exceptional' flanking mechanisms of an increasingly irrational pursuit of neo-liberalism and neoconservativism in the US. This stands in contrast to the earlier turn in neo-liberal regimes to 'Third Way' rhetoric and policy solutions to provide flanking and supporting mechanisms as they turned from rollback to roll-forward neo-liberalism. In this sense, the ecological dominance of neo-liberalism is crucially mediated through (and made less accountable than normal) through the exceptional character of its primary political protagonist. Indeed, in terms of the approach presented above, it could be argued that the 'war on terrorism' introduces a temporary rise in the primacy of security and the territorial logic of the state at the expense of accumulation – which is reflected in the American economy in problems in securing skilled knowledge workers from abroad and in the intensification of federal government deficits. But this does not mean that the coming end of the Bush regime (due to limited presidential terms and the fallout from Iraq) and success in what is bound to prove a very difficult rollback of its economic and political legacies will end the ecological dominance of neo-liberalism. At most, it will end this particular political mediation of neo-liberalism. More fundamental and more durable is the place of neo-liberal financial capital within the circuit of capital and the impact of shareholder value as the supreme value in corporate governance.

The Ecological Dominance of Financial Capital over Other Fractions of Capital

In my earlier work on the periodization of capitalism, I predicted that the most likely form of accumulation regime in post-Fordist economies would be the globalizing knowledge-based economy. This prediction was based on two sets of argument: First, an investigation of the changing economic imaginaries and political strategies in Fordist regimes following the deepening of the crisis of Fordism in the late 1970s and 1980s; and, second, concern with the structural coherence and reproducibility of knowledge-based economies at the level of urban, regional and national economies. In this sense, my prediction took the viewpoint of productive capital and, notwithstanding my recognition of the importance of the world market, looked at the dynamics of variegated capitalism in terms of the compatibility among different knowledge-based economies specializing in different types of knowledge- or design-intensive products and services. What this approach ignored was the growing disjunction between productive capital and financial capital and the implications of financialization as the ecologically dominant logic of accumulation on the viability of knowledge-based economy strategies. This is reflected in a further set of contradictions expressed in the conflict between the hegemony of the globalizing knowledge-based economy as the material and ideological expression of productive capital and its antagonistic relation to the logic of a finance-led, shareholder-value oriented process of capital accumulation.

In short, my earlier work ignored two related issues: First, the specificity of the contemporary US federal state as an exceptional rather than normal capitalist type of state; and, second, the ecological dominance of financial capital within the overall organization of the capital relation as the ecologically dominant institutional order within world society. The logic of financialization (wherever it occurs, i.e., not just in relation to US financial capital, if, indeed, this can be identified as a distinct fraction of capital outside the global financial system in general) undermines or restricts the operation of economic determination in the first instance (i.e., the primacy of productive capital) within the overall logic of capital accumulation. In contrast to the structured coherence of Fordism and the post-Fordist knowledge-based economy, the post-Fordist neo-liberal financial regime militates against the long-term structured coherence of accumulation regimes and their modes of regulation. In particular, it weakens the spatio-temporal fixes with which regimes based on the primacy of productive capital manage the contradictions between fixity and motion in order to produce zones of relative stability by deferring and displacing their effects. This can be seen in the impact of financialization not only in Atlantic Fordism but also in the export-oriented economies of East Asian and the viability of import-substitution industrialization strategies in Latin America and Africa. The destructive impact of financialization in this regard is reinforced through the neo-liberal approach to accumulation through dispossession (especially the politically-licensed plundering of public assets and the intellectual commons) and the dynamics of uneven development (enabling financial capital to move on when the disastrous effects of financialization weaken those productive capitals that have to be valorized in particular times and places). It is also supported by the growing markets opened for the 'symbionts and parasites' of the ecologically dominant fractions of capital in their heartlands – associated in turn with their own forms of uneven development on regional, national and global scales.

Conclusions

This chapter has emphasized the need to look beyond conventional approaches to the periodization of capitalism and the analysis of neo-liberalism. In particular, it has introduced a new vocabulary and theoretical approach to dealing with issues of economic determination and historical blocs and has highlighted the importance of the notion of ecological dominance to explore economic determination in the last instance and to interpret the impact of neo-liberalism. This approach needs to be supplemented with a new account of the bases of economic, political and ideological class domination, which lie beyond the scope of this chapter – apart from the few comments that I have made on the exceptional nature of the American federal state. In these terms, I have suggested that the logic of rollback neo-liberalism is still ecologically dominant at the level of the world market even though it is in retreat at other levels (with the significant exception of the US) in favour of a roll-forward neo-liberalism flanked and supported by other mechanisms to maintain and reinvigorate the momentum of neo-liberal restructuring in the subset of neo-liberal regimes. Given the nature of ecological dominance, I suspect that it will be far more difficult to 'rollback' neo-liberalism on a world scale and/or to tame it through new forms of roll-forward neo-liberalism on a world scale than has been the case to date in particular national states where mechanisms of political accountability through normal forms of bourgeois politics still operate. Indeed, it should be a major concern that the ecological dominance of neo-liberalism may be ended by the ecological dominance of the natural environment in a period of growing environmental crisis. To use Polanyi's language, it is not only 'society' that is fighting back – 'nature' also appears to be mobilizing against neo-liberalism and the more general logic of capital accumulation. As yet, however, there is no unified struggle against neo-liberalism or the logic of accumulation on a world scale; and there is no common global space for a unified struggle. The contributions in the second part of the collection nonetheless offer some important insights and guidelines on present and future struggles that can create new spaces of resistance and lead on to more unified struggles in the future.

Notes

1. In earlier work focusing on the advanced capitalist economies, I distinguished only three types of neo-liberalism (e.g., Jessop, 2002). Given my current concern with global capitalism, it has been necessary to introduce a fourth type (albeit in third place in the current list).
2. The temporal dimension of flow is captured in the metaphors of 'liquidity' and 'stickiness'.

3. These distinctions are not directly linked to issues of economic class domination. This occurs in and through the struggle for dominance in the wage relation and in the structuring and regularizing modes of growth (including the wage relation). In turn, political class domination refers to the struggle over state formation and restructuring, over state policies, and at a distance from the state (including the forms of representation, the institutional architecture of the state, and forms of state intervention). Finally, ideological class domination involves the struggle over means of mental production, specific ideological forms and specific imaginaries.
4. This argument about ecological dominance applies to other actors in other types of social ecology, such as organizations and networks. These can also be more or less ecologically dominant in their respective social worlds.
5. There is much research to be done on symbionts and parasites in the field of luxury consumption (Department III), the commercialization of political lobbying, and similar forms of parasitism.
6. Centre-periphery relations refer to differentiation in terms of geographical cores and peripheries (e.g., the economic hegemony and domination of US capitalism in Atlantic Fordism and of the industrial and financial heartlands of the quasi-continental US economy in relation to their respective hinterlands); and stratification refers to the hierarchical organization of social relations, with an upper class organized on national, macro-regional (e.g., European or transatlantic), or even transnational lines (e.g., the World Economic Forum).
7. This apt phrase comes from Blühdorn's commentary on Luhmann (2000, p. 351).
8. Luhmann notes that the structural coupling of function systems is especially promoted by organizations whose multi-functionality is the most likely to be disturbed by artificial distinctions among systems (1994; 1997, p. 843; 2000). Simsa reinforces this in noting that organizations are the source of the societally most relevant, most stable, and most far-reaching decisions (2002, p. 162).
9. Luhmann (2002, p. 55), as cited by Wagner (2006, p. 5).

References

Baecker, D. 2001. 'Managing Corporations in Networks', *Thesis Eleven*, 66, 1.
—. 2006. 'Network Society', in Lehmann, N. O., Qvortup, L., Walter, B. K. (eds.), *The Concept of the Network Society: Post-Ontological Reflections.* Copenhagen: Samfundslitteratur.
Baraldi, C., Corsi, G. and Esposito, E. 1998. *GLU. Glossar zu Niklas Luhmann's Theorie sozialer Systeme.* Frankfurt: Suhrkamp.
Bateson, G. 1972. *Steps to an Ecology of Mind: Collected Essays in Anthropology, Psychiatry, Evolution, and Epistemology.* London: Intertexts Books.
Blühdorn, I. 2000. 'An Offer One Might Prefer to Refuse: The Systems Theoretical Legacy of Niklas Luhmann', *European Journal of Social Theory*, 2, 2.
Bonefeld, W. 2000. 'The Spectre of Globalization: On the Form and Content of the World Market', in Bonefeld, W. and Psychopedis, K. (eds.), *The Politics of Change: Globalization, Ideology, and Critique.* Basingstoke: Macmillan.
Bryan, D. and Rafferty, M. 2006. *Capitalism with Derivatives: A Political Economy of Financial Derivatives, Capital and Class.* Basingstoke: Palgrave.
Bryan, D. and Rafferty, M. 2007. 'Financial Derivatives and the Theory of Money', *Economy and Society*, 36, 1.

Bryer, R. A. 2006. 'Accounting and Control of the Labour Process', *Critical Perspectives on Accounting*, 17, 5.

Elchardus, M. 1988. 'The Rediscovery of Chronos: The New Role of Time in Sociological Theory', *International Sociology*, 3, 1.

Fukuyama, F. 1992. *The End of History and the Last Man*. Glencoe: Free Press.

Gramsci, A. 1971. *Selections from the Prison Notebooks*. London: Lawrence & Wishart.

Jessop, R. 2000. 'The Crisis of the National Spatio-temporal Fix and the Ecological Dominance of Globalizing Capitalism', *International Journal of Urban and Regional Studies*, 24, 2.

—. 2001. 'What follows Fordism? On the Periodisation of Capitalism and its Regulation?' in Albritton, R., Itoh, M., Westra, R. and Zuege, A. (eds.), *Phases of Capitalist Development: Booms, Crises, and Globalization*. Basingstoke: Palgrave.

—. 2002. *The Future of the Capitalist State*. Cambridge: Polity.

—. 2003. 'From Thatcherism to New Labour: Neo-liberalism, Workfarism, and Labour Market Regulation', in Overbeek, H. (ed.), *The Political Economy of European Unemployment*. London: Routledge.

Keddy, P. A. 1989. *Competition*. London: Chapman & Hall.

Lange, S. 2003. *Niklas Luhmanns Theorie der Politik. Eine Abklärung der Staatsgesellschaft*. Opladen: Westdeutscher Verlag.

Lohmann, G. 1991. *Indifferenz und Gesellschaft. Eine kritische Ausein-andersetzung mit Marx*. Frankfurt: Suhrkamp.

Luhmann, N. 1988. *Die Wirtschaft der Gesellschaft*. Frankfurt: Suhrkamp.

—. 1996. 'Politics and Economics', *Thesis Eleven*, 53.

Marx, K. 1965. *Capital*, vol I. London: Lawrence & Wishart.

—. 1971. *Theories of Surplus Value III*. London: Lawrence & Wishart.

—. 1973. 'Introduction', in *idem*, *Grundrisse*. Harmondsworth: Penguin.

Marx, K. and Engels, F. 1976. *The German Ideology*, in *idem*, *Marx-Engels Collected Works*, vol. 5. London: Lawrence & Wishart.

Mészáros, I. 1995. *Beyond 'Capital'*. London: Merlin Press.

Morin, E. 1980. *La méthode: volume 2. La vie de la vie*. Paris: Seuil.

Peck, J. and Tickell, A. 2002. 'Neo-liberalizing space', *Antipode*, 34, 3.

Poulantzas, N. 1978. *State, Power, Socialism*. London: Verso.

Simsa, R. 2002. 'Strukturelle Kopplung: die Antwort der Theorie auf der Geschlossenheit sozialer Systeme und ihre Bedeutung für die Politik', in Hellmann, K. U. and Schmalz-Bruns, R. (eds.), *Theorie der Politik. Niklas Luhmanns politische Soziologie*. Frankfurt: The Institute for Science and Technology Studies (IWT).

Stichweh, R. 2000. *Die Weltgesellschaft. Soziologische Analysen*, Frankfurt: Suhrkamp.

Wagner, T. 2006. Funktionale Differenzierung und ein ökonomischer Primat? Paper available at http://www.sozialarbeit.ch/dokumente/oekonomischer_primat.pdf, last accessed 19.12. 2006

Willke, H. 1997. *Die Supervision des Staates*. Frankfurt: Suhrkamp.

Chapter 5

MONETARY POLICY IN THE NEO-LIBERAL TRANSITION: A POLITICAL ECONOMY CRITIQUE OF KEYNESIANISM, MONETARISM AND INFLATION TARGETING[1]

Alfredo Saad-Filho

The transition from the Keynesian 'golden age' to the current 'age of neo-liberalism' was one of the defining events of the international political economy in the post-war era.[2] This chapter examines this transition in terms of changes in the theory and practice of monetary policy across these two periods, and their socio-economic implications. It is argued that monetary policy regimes are irreducibly political. They do not simply offer alternative approaches to macroeconomic management; policy regimes also discipline nation states and social actors in different ways. For example, they constrain the choice of economic policy priorities and the use of the available policy tools, influence inter-capitalist relations within and between countries, and limit the demands of the working class. The macroeconomic policy regime is one of the basic features of the system of accumulation. By the same token, crises of the policy regime can bring to light limitations of the hegemonic processes of economic production and social reproduction.

This chapter shows, first, that the demise of Keynesianism was the outcome of intractable social, economic and political problems in the late 1960s and 1970s, including monetary and exchange rate disturbances, social discord and the weakening US hegemony. The neo-liberal transition was the historically specific (contingent) outcome of the search for solutions to these mounting problems in the accumulation process. The development of a new monetary and exchange rate policy regime was one of the decisive aspects of this transition. These policy changes responded to the problems of economic management in each sub-period, and supported the consolidation of the new system of accumulation.

Second, the monetary and exchange rate policy regime appropriate for the current phase of *mature neo-liberalism* is finally in place: The 'new monetary policy consensus' (NMPC)[3] includes inflation targeting (IT), central bank independence (CBI) and floating exchange rates. The NMPC has become the dominant monetary policy paradigm in the world because it is theoretically robust, can secure the low inflation rates recently achieved in most countries, and supports the reproduction of neo-liberalism.[4]

Third, the chapter offers a political economy critique of the NMPC. It shows that the NMPC systematically exaggerates the costs of inflation and underestimates the costs in output, income, employment, distributional, financial and balance of payments in pursuing permanently low inflation through IT and CBI. It also downplays the social, political and economic consequences of locking in a rigid institutional framework for monetary policy. Finally, the NMPC expresses the hegemony of capital in general in the field of economic policy, through the imperatives of finance.

These claims are developed and explained in seven sections. This introduction is the first. Section two outlines the main features of Keynesianism and the reasons for its decline from the point of view of the typical monetary and exchange rate policy regime in this period – the Bretton Woods System. Section three examines the pursuit 'austerity by consent' in the mid 1970s. Section four reviews the monetarist imposition of austerity in the late 1970s. Section five offers a political economy critique of neo-liberalism, the hegemonic policy paradigm in the contemporary world. Section six critically reviews the NMPC and the last section presents my conclusions.

Keynesianism

Keynesianism was the hegemonic system of accumulation and the most important structure of socio-political domination during the 'golden age' in the centre, and the 'age of developmentalism' in the periphery.[5] It evolved as a pragmatic response to the breakdown of its predecessor – liberalism – in the interwar period.[6]

The Keynesian Compact

Keynesianism had distinguishing features in the fields of economic policy, social relations and international relations. Keynesian economic policies were characterized by fixed exchange rates, accommodating ('easy') monetary policies, expansionary fiscal policies (especially through state-led investment and transfers)[7] and 'financial repression', including regulations to stabilize the financial system, reduce interest rates and direct credit flows to priority sectors.[8] These policies were prominent in most Organization for Economic Cooperation and Development (OECD) countries, especially France, West Germany and Japan, and in such newly industrializing countries as Brazil, India, South Korea, Mexico, South Africa and Turkey. Financial sector regulations varied considerably between countries and over time, ranging from the nationalization of the banking system and its instrumentalization in order to facilitate breakneck growth, as in South Korea, to the predominance of 'market-based' financial systems in the UK and the US. These countries were special cases not only for historical and institutional reasons, but also because of their leading role financing foreign direct investment (FDI) flows.[9] The expansion of regulated credit and stimulating fiscal and monetary policies delivered high levels of investment, employment, output and productivity growth and rising incomes, consumer demand and macroeconomic stability in several countries for an extended period of time.

The second key aspect of Keynesianism was social integration. In the centre,[10] especially the core Western European countries, it included the institutionalization of a social democratic political settlement drawing on the post-war anti-fascist consensus, the expansion of the entitlements of the working class through a welfare state funded by progressive taxation, the institutionalization of the downward rigidity of the nominal wage and workers' right to claim a share of the productivity gains.[11] This type of wage relation is stabilizing when output and productivity are growing rapidly, because it channels social dissent into monetary demands and employment guarantees bounded by the initial income levels and mediated by negotiations between the 'social partners'. Disputes, however heated, normally involve only the allocation of the *additional* resources made available by the expansion of the economy, and do not normally challenge the current (baseline) revenues of the negotiating parties. This model of social inclusion led to significant improvements in the distribution of income and wealth in most countries. It also facilitated the integration of the reformist left into the Keynesian system, contributing to the remarkable political stability in the centre during this period, in spite of the pressures of the Cold War and the retreat of traditional (colonial) forms of imperialism.

Social integration was invariably limited. For example, the radical left was normally excluded from the political settlement, and there were ongoing disputes about citizens' rights, e.g., the extent to which they should include women, disabled people, homosexuals, ethnic minorities, new immigrants and other marginalized groups. The level of the social wage was also contested. Social provision differed significantly between countries and over time, ranging from its near absence in most peripheral countries and the US (especially in the 1950s), to its relatively 'generous' levels in West Germany and Sweden, especially in the later stages of Keynesianism. The third important feature of the Keynesian era was the international hegemony of the US.[12] Hegemony was based on US control of the commanding heights of capital accumulation (including its unmatched levels of output and productivity, the availability of large blocks of capital, greater financial system depth and US control of the development of technology), and its gold reserves and military power. They ensured that the dollar would be the international currency of this period. US hegemony facilitated the expansion of (mainly) US transnational companies around the world, which helped to harmonize economic policies and integrate resource extraction and use internationally. FDI also supported the convergence of cultural and consumption patterns across different countries.[13]

The Bretton Woods System provided a US-dominated institutional framework for the integration of the national Keynesian compacts into the process of international accumulation. It supported the expansion of trade, FDI and international finance, favouring US capital above its competitors. The smooth functioning of the system also required the US to run regular balance of payments deficits in order to irrigate the international economy with dollars. They allowed the US to fund domestic consumption, foreign investment and military engagements more liberally than would have been possible under a stringent balance of payments constraint. Finally, the fixed exchange rate system created incentives for the other countries to mirror US policies in order to achieve similar rates of productivity growth and inflation, which minimized the risk of exchange rate instability. Failure to achieve these outcomes would generate tensions with the parities, which would always be felt more strongly in the other economies than in the US. For example, relatively slow growth and high inflation in the UK created recurrent pressures for the devaluation of sterling, while faster growth and lower inflation in West Germany induced the periodic revaluation of the deutschmark.

The achievement of the Keynesian goals outlined in this section required the constant calibration of the monetary and fiscal policy stance. These were the most important tools available to control the rhythm of the economy and regulate the balance of class forces, in order to make them compatible with the requirements of international accumulation. The inability to do so, for example, because of high inflation or sluggish productivity growth due to the breakdown of industrial relations would tend to reduce FDI inflows and raise local production costs, creating the threat of balance of payments deficits and currency collapse. This threat was a powerful disciplining tool on the economic policymakers and the class relations in most countries.

Limitations and Crisis of Keynesianism

The unravelling of Keynesianism between the late 1960s and the early 1970s was the outcome of limitations in the areas examined above. They included economic management problems, the weakening of US hegemony and widespread labour and social conflicts.

The economic limitations of Keynesianism were largely due to the long expansion ushered by this system of accumulation. High levels of domestic and foreign investment, the growth of output, productivity and trade, and technological advances in the fields of telecommunications, transport and computing power fuelled the development of finance, especially offshore banking and the euro – dollar market. In turn, financial development contributed to the emergence of innovative business practices, among them international loan syndicates, hedging and derivatives trading. It also fostered the accumulation of financial assets bypassing state regulation, and independently of the demands of industrial capital.[14] Most governments and large industrial corporations welcomed these developments, because they offered access to cheaper and relatively unregulated funds. However, in the longer run, financial deepening loosened the relationship between money and commodities, facilitated purely financial (speculative) accumulation, and breached the financial controls that were essential for the implementation of the Keynesian policies.

The second limitation of Keynesianism was due to the erosion of US hegemony. This was partly the outcome of the continuing expansion of the world economy, which reduced the relative prominence of the US in the fields of production and technology. The successes of such countries as France, Italy, Japan and West Germany, and Brazil, Mexico, India, South Korea and Taiwan, created alternative dynamic poles in the world economy – not because of US 'failure' to keep up with the competition, but because of the *success* of the US-led system of international accumulation. At the same time, the USSR and China offered a rival model that was especially appealing to the weaker economies aiming to supplement their political independence with rapid growth and greater 'economic independence'. In several countries, these pressures fostered the demand for state economic intervention as part of a strategy of accelerated growth, and for a new international economic order and international producers' cartels. All of them potentially conflicted with US hegemony. These difficulties were compounded by the increasing instability of the US economy because of its fiscal and balance of payments deficits. These resulted from poorly funded expansionary social programmes at home and spiralling military commitments abroad, especially during the Vietnam War. They fuelled US inflation and flooded the world economy with dollars. Although these outflows supported the development of finance, they also impaired US capacity to guarantee the convertibility of dollars into gold at the official rate of US$35 per ounce. More immediately, US deficits exported inflation to surplus countries, especially West Germany, Japan and Switzerland. The instability of the system of international accumulation and the US defeat in Vietnam created incentives *and* the political space for other countries to search for domestic solutions to their accumulation problems, as had been the case in the 1930s, which could have been disastrous for US hegemony.

The third limitation of Keynesianism concerned the diffusion of social conflicts in the late 1960s. They were due, in part, to the greater bargaining power of the working class in these circumstances of rapid growth and low unemployment,[15] and, in part, to the (closely related) emergence of a radicalized youth around the world. Their demands fuelled anti-systemic revolts that reduced significantly the degree of managerial control of the workplace and capitalist control of social reproduction as a whole, including the material and cultural levels. The erosion of the hegemony of capital in international accumulation, class relations and material and social reproduction turned the crisis of Keynesianism into a crisis of the *capital relation*. This crisis was associated with declining profit rates in most economies, rising corporate debt, falling share prices and investment ratios, the fiscal crisis of the state and widespread social unrest.[16] Keynesianism was increasingly unable to regulate international accumulation and discipline the working class, as was shown by the rising inflation rates in most countries and the international crisis of the dollar.

Austerity by Consent

Capital accumulation was facing two structural problems in the early 1970s: First, the partial disarticulation of the conditions for rapid accumulation, including grave social conflicts, the declining efficacy of the main economic policy tools, falling rates of profit and productivity growth and rising inflation;[17] second, the erosion of the ideological hegemony of capitalism, including the rapid growth of the left and the partial disarticulation of US hegemony.

The strategy initially adopted in the West to tackle these problems was 'austerity by consent'. It included measures to stabilize the international economy and increase policy flexibility in the US and elsewhere, especially the abandonment of the fixed exchange rate system between 1971–3, and initiatives to restore social discipline and the conditions for accumulation in the centre, including negotiated austerity policies to control inflation without costly head-on confrontations with the workers. The anti-inflation strategy generally comprised fiscal and monetary austerity, curbs to domestic credit and income policies negotiated between the state and representatives of capital and the trade unions, aiming to impose wage restraint.[18] These policies achieved only limited success partly because of the adverse international circumstances in that period, and partly because it sparked revolts of the workers against the trade unions and the state, particularly in France, Italy and the UK. These revolts made it difficult for the unions to deliver their commitments to the state and the 'business community', which undermined their legitimacy and political leverage. The ineffectiveness of austerity by consent (see Figures 1–3) and the inability of most states to broker a negotiated settlement to the crisis compelled these states to manage social relations more closely, for example, by manipulating labour regulations, limiting welfare and employment benefits, and by other initiatives to reduce industrial costs and boost 'business confidence'. But these policy changes eroded the legitimacy of the post-war consensus and aided the ideological disintegration of Keynesianism. The economic crisis of Keynesianism triggered a crisis of the Keynesian state.

Figure 1: GDP per capita growth rates (%)

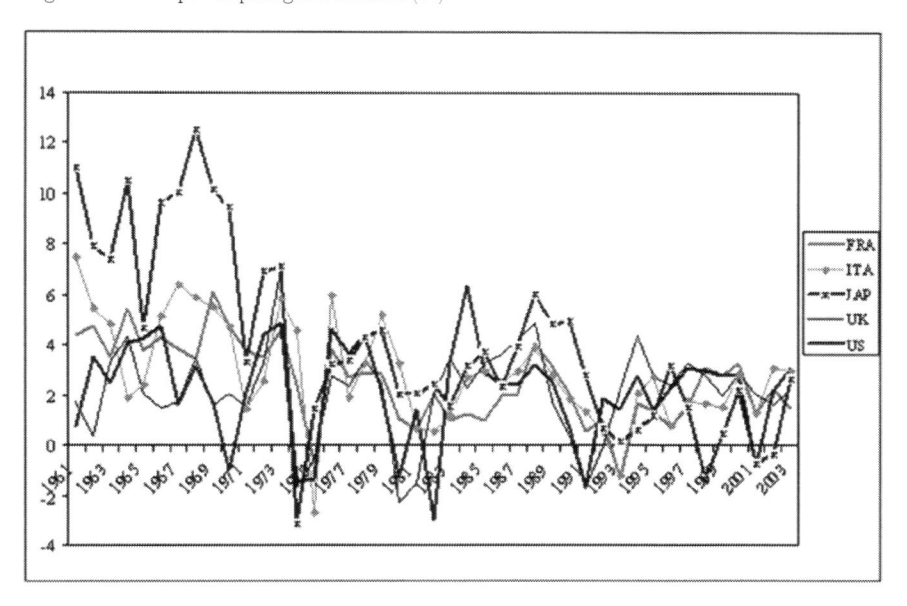

Source: World Development Indicators

Figure 2: Rate of unemployment (% labour force)

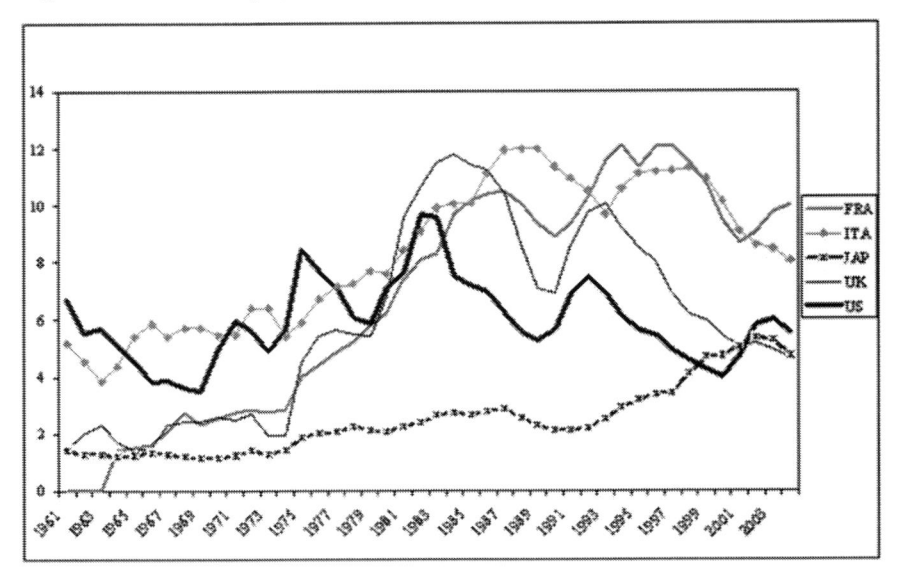

Source: World Development Indicators

Figure 3: Inflation rates (GDP deflator, %)

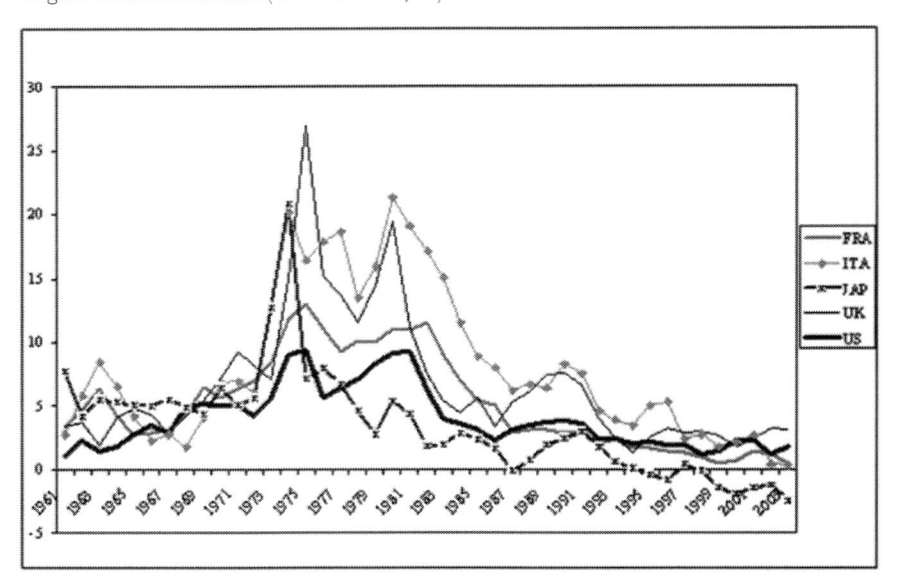

Source: World Development Indicators

The fixed exchange rate system agreed at Bretton Woods was abandoned largely because of such tensions. Relaxing the discipline imposed by the fixed exchange rate system permitted the introduction of more flexible fiscal and monetary policies. These policies were limited by the intensity of the conflicting demands of industrial capital, finance and the working class, the requirements of stable accumulation and the need to accommodate the inflow of dollars — but at least, it was no longer necessary to defend the parity. In this sense, exchange rate fluctuation was not a choice but rather a pragmatic response to political and economic imperatives. The new exchange rate regime also helped to accommodate the US fiscal and balance of payments deficits and safeguard the remaining US gold reserves.

The new exchange rate system offered an alternative means to manage international accumulation. In contrast to the political determination of fixed exchange rates under Keynesianism, the new 'dirty floating' system was based on 'automatic' financial market-led parity adjustments, limited by central bank interventions to avoid large misalignments or severe instability. Rather than presenting the threat of sporadic but potentially catastrophic changes to the parities, floating exchange rates discipline capital accumulation and domestic social relations through the *continuous* threat of instability. The new disciplining mechanism removed the insulation of accumulation from speculative finance that underpinned Keynesian economic management. It also institutionalized the role of financial markets (the main agents of currency speculation) in economic policymaking: floating exchange rates embedded financial market intervention into the fabric of the international monetary system. Reciprocally, domestic accumulation had to be validated continually by the financial markets via their assessment of the 'credibility' of each country's economic policies.

Exchange rate floating increased significantly the scope for the international financial system and its resources to expand. Abolition of fixed parities reduced the reserve discipline on the private financial institutions and the central banks and curtailed their ability to align the supply of credit money with demand. At the same time, it created incentives for hedging and financial speculation by international firms, banks and states, precisely when technological progress had expanded the room for financial sector autonomy relative to real accumulation. Given growing fiscal deficits in most countries and the recycling of petrodollars after the first oil shock, an enormous margin existed for innovative financial instruments to fuel the growth of finance.[19]

The strategy of austerity by consent failed to resolve the crisis of Keynesianism because it could not discipline the working class and restore a stable process of accumulation in most countries. Its failure was symptomatic of the exhaustion of Keynesianism. It also indicated that a stable solution to the problems of the international economy must address the crisis of accumulation in the US.

At that stage, this could only be achieved by introducing a new international system of accumulation: a new hegemonic structure of socio-economic integration and social subordination imposing social stability and supporting the resumption of growth worldwide. For the US and the local classes linked to the US ruling class, it should also help to restore US international hegemony.

Austerity Imposed: The Monetarist Experience

The demand to restore the conditions for stable accumulation was justified theoretically by recourse to the Austrian liberalism associated with Hayek and Friedman's monetarist economic theory.[20] Liberalism rejected social democracy and Keynesianism in the name of individual freedom and 'superior rationality' of the market. In turn, monetarism offered a detailed critique of Keynesianism's propensity to generate runaway inflation because of macroeconomic mismanagement and the accommodation of the workers' demands. For the purposes of this chapter, it is important to review the principles of monetarism.

Monetarist theory includes two basic elements:[21] First, a theory of the real side of the economy, explaining the distribution of income and the level of employment. Monetarism claims that there will be full employment if the factors of production (capital and labour) are paid according to their marginal productivity and relative scarcity. This theory rejects the productivity sharing deals, welfare entitlements and income guarantees associated with Keynesianism, because they allegedly generate unemployment and poverty traps. Instead, monetarism suggests that if the labour markets are 'liberalized' the workers will naturally price themselves into jobs. The most important macroeconomic problem for Keynes is removed by a stroke of theory: unemployment becomes either voluntary or the outcome of institutional distortions which should be removed politically. Monetarist theory justifies the shift of government policies away from the offer of income guarantees, and towards the 'flexibilization' of the labour markets. It legitimizes government neglect of unemployment, validates the alignment of the state with the interests of capital as if it represented society as a whole. Further, it also set the stage for a state-led offensive against the organized working class.

The second element of monetarism is the theory of money and inflation. This theory is based on the revival of the pre-Keynesian quantity theory of money (QTM), which states that inflation is a purely monetary phenomenon which occurs when too much money chases after too few goods. Friedman added the claim that the long-run Phillips curve is vertical, or that there is no long-run trade-off between nominal variables, such as inflation, and real variables such as output, output growth and unemployment.[22] In this case, there will be accelerating inflation if (Keynesian) governments attempt to increase artificially the level of activity in order to keep unemployment below the so-called 'natural rate of unemployment'.

Monetarism offers a straightforward cure for inflation: governments simply have to limit the growth of the money supply to a rate compatible with long-run price stability (money supply targeting). Policy rules such as money supply targeting are useful because they 'depoliticize' economic management. Monetarists claim that policymakers have an incentive to misuse the short-term power of monetary policy to inflate the economy for crass electoral reasons, even though this is destabilizing (inflation bias due to the political business cycle).[23] The monetarist emphasis on policy rules suggests that political will should be *sufficient* to achieve socially desirable outcomes, and that objections to these rules-based policies are invariably due to sectional interests.

Monetarism also advocates floating exchange rates and the liberalization of the capital account of the balance of payments. The monetarist financial, monetary and exchange rate policies *transfer* the imposition of economic discipline from the state to the financial system. The abolition of Keynesian macroeconomic fine-tuning should expand the scope for automatic (overtly non-political) market processes, and reduce the ability of the working class to deflect the costs of adjustment. In sum, under Keynesianism monetary policy supported the subordination of the working class *indirectly*, through rapid capital accumulation and income growth. In contrast, for the monetarists monetary policy should discipline the workers *directly*. Restrictions on the supply of money should limit the level of activity and the level of employment which, in turn, should curb the workers' ability to pursue 'unreasonable' claims for higher wages and better working conditions.[24] Finally, capital ('the market') was expected to resolve the problems of accumulation and growth spontaneously.

Monetarism was imposed in four stages. The first experience followed the 1973 coup in Chile. The Pinochet administration showed that it is possible to impose harsh economic policy changes, at a great cost to the majority, if these policies are backed up by sufficient force. The second experience was the New York City financial crisis in 1974–5. This crisis showed that budgetary imbalances can trigger a catastrophic withdrawal of 'investors' confidence', which can justify monetarist policy reforms including regressive changes in the tax and welfare systems. The third experience followed the UK balance of payments crisis in 1976. Its resolution showed that balance of payments problems could justify monetarist policy changes even in large economies. Finally, the most important experience by far was the US monetary policy change in 1979, through the Volcker shock. This policy shift marked the end of the Keynesian era.[25] The Volcker shock included elements from all the previous monetarist experiences: it was imposed without negotiations or social agreement, and it was justified by the domestic need to curb inflation and improve investors' confidence, and the external imperative of safeguarding the currency. Monetarism routinized the use of financial market imperatives, especially inflation control, in macroeconomic management, and it supported the continuing development of the (US-dominated) international financial system. The Keynesian emphasis on the accumulation of industrial capital, social integration and full employment was abandoned.[26]

Despite its ability to dismantle Keynesianism, defeat the working class in several countries and impose social discipline – monetarism was limited. Gross domestic product (GDP) growth in the centre did not recover between the mid 1970s and the mid 1980s, while unemployment increased relentlessly. Moreover, the monetarist experiences in West Germany, Switzerland, the UK and the US did not vindicate the claims that money supply targeting was either feasible or conducive to rapid inflation stabilization (see Figures 1–3).[27] In addition to these practical difficulties, monetarist theory was damaged by the criticisms inflicted by the new classical, Keynesian and radical political economists.[28] In sum, although monetarism was part of a successful project of social domination, it did *not* offer a viable system of accumulation.

The Political Economy of Neo-liberalism

Neo-liberalism offered a stable solution to the problems of capitalist reproduction in the centre and the periphery after the exhaustion of Keynesianism. Neo-liberalism is not simply a set of economic and social policies. It combines an accumulation strategy, a form of regulation of socio-economic reproduction and a mode of exploitation and social domination based on the systematic use of state power to impose, under the ideological veil of non-intervention, a hegemonic project of recomposition of the rule of capital in each area of social life. This project is guided by the imperatives of the international reproduction of capital, represented by the financial markets and the interests of US capital.

Foundations of Neo-liberalism

The rise of neo-liberalism is closely related to the perceived failure of Keynesianism, developmentalism and Soviet-style socialism in the 1980s, the development of economic theory after the exhaustion of monetarism,[29] the rise of conservative political forces in the US and the UK, and the recomposition of class relations in these countries. These socio-economic and political shifts spread to the periphery through persuasion (including the images of success beamed by the media, the slanted development of economic and political theory and the deliberate promotion of serviceable intellectual fashions) and coercion. For example, central governments have routinely used the international financial institutions, the United Nations (UN) system and the General Agreement on Tariffs and Trade/World Trade Organization (GATT/WTO) to inflict neo-liberal policies on the peripheral and 'transition' countries, as a condition for access to funds, wealthy country markets and aid ('conditionality').

Neo-liberalism draws upon the Austrian critique of Keynesianism and socialism, and upon mainstream (neoclassical) economic theory, both in its traditional (monetarist) guise, and in the revamped version supplied by new Keynesianism and new institutionalism.[30]

Neo-liberal economic policies are based on three main planks.[31] First, at the microeconomic level, it assumes that the market is efficient and the state is inefficient. Therefore, relative prices should be determined by resource availability and consumer preferences, and the market should address such economic problems as employment creation, industrial development and international competitiveness. The state should essentially provide legal and economic infrastructure for the development of markets, mediate between social groups in order to expand market relations, and defend the country against foreign aggression.[32] Beneficial economic policies here include deregulation (e.g., privatization and the abolition of state planning), fiscal and monetary policy discipline (tax reforms, expenditure cuts and the shift of government investment towards basic goods and services), financial liberalization (to increase the availability of savings and the rate of return of investment) and labour market 'flexibilization' (supposedly to raise productivity and employment).

Second, at the macroeconomic level, the world economy is marked by capital mobility and the relentless advance of (an ill-defined process of) 'globalization'.[33] Although they offer the possibility of rapid growth through the attraction of foreign capital, this can only occur if domestic policies conform to the short-term interests of the (financial) markets, otherwise foreign and domestic capital will be driven elsewhere. These assumptions justified the transfer of state capacity to allocate resources intertemporally (the balance between investment and consumption), intersectorally (the allocation of investment funds and the composition of output and employment) and internationally (the pattern of international specialization) towards an increasingly integrated and US-led financial sector. These policy reforms support the recomposition of the system of production at a higher level of productivity (at least at firm-level) through the transnationalization of production and finance and the integration of local capitals into international capital circuits (a new mode of competition). This new relationship between domestic capitals, foreign capitals and the state requires the liberalization of foreign trade, domestic finance and the capital account of the balance of payments.

Third, neo-liberalism institutionalizes the pre-eminence of financial market imperatives on the key aspects of macroeconomic policymaking. This is evident in the neo-liberal claims for the efficacy of monetary policy instruments. In particular, interest rate manipulation becomes the most important tool for economic management and the imposition of discipline under neo-liberalism (as is especially obvious under the NMPC, see Section six). Presumably, in a liberalized economy the 'correct' interest rates can deliver balance of payments equilibrium, low inflation, sustainable investment and consumption and high growth rates in the long term.

These claims are not simply due to the overestimation of the potential of monetary policy to regulate economic activity. The rise of liberalized finance and the prominence of monetary policy evince the growing *material* articulation between the processes of economic and social reproduction across the world, and the trend towards the increasing integration between the international production and financial systems. Even when a bewildering array of products is available, often made to order by competing firms, production in its broadest sense – encompassing planning, design, logistics, hiring, training and managing the workforce, manufacturing, marketing, distribution, trading, accounting and the provision of financial services, including such related activities as hedging, foreign exchange and derivatives trading on behalf of productive capital – has become increasingly integrated. Each stage is closely intertwined with the others and with production carried out elsewhere. Even when individual firms are small, downsize or spin-off independent companies, the process of production of the material conditions of social reproduction is increasingly integrated vertically into vast transnational systems of provision, employing large numbers of workers in different countries to produce commodities for sale in 'local' markets.

In this system of accumulation, finance is *not* an independent sector competing against industrial capital. In advanced capitalist economies with developed financial systems, finance is the pool of liquid capital held by the financial *and* industrial sectors and, at a more abstract level, the mode of existence of capital in general.[34] The liberalization of domestic finance and the capital account of the balance of payments promote the integration between industrial and interest-bearing capital and between domestic and international capital. In this sense, the inability of the neo-liberal reforms to support higher levels of investment is irrelevant; so is the heterodox critique that the neo-liberal reforms increase the returns of financial capital at the expense of industry.[35] The primary purpose of the neo-liberal reforms is not to promote high rates of economic growth, reduce inflation (in spite of the rhetoric of the NMPC, see Section six) or increase the portfolio choices of the financial institutions. Their primary aims are to subordinate domestic accumulation to international imperatives, promote firm-level integration between competing capitals, mediated by finance, and expand the scope for financial system intermediation in the financing of the state.

The transfer of the main levers of accumulation to (international) capital, mediated by (US-led) financial institutions, and regulated by (US-controlled) international organizations, especially the International Monetary Fund (IMF) and the Bank for International Settlements (BIS), has established the material basis of neo-liberalism.[36] In this system of accumulation, stable capital flows are essential to close both the balance of payments and finance domestic activity as well as the public sector. In turn, the stability of these flows depends on compliance with neo-liberal prescriptions. Internationalized finance is the main instrument for the imposition of this project of accumulation and social domination, in which production and finance are inseparably linked. Less directly, the prominence of finance subsumes sectoral interests under the interests of capital as a whole. In policy terms, it ensures that accumulation is not regulated by sectoral coalitions, but by the capitalist *class*. It denies antagonistic relations between production and finance under neo-liberalism and does not expect industrial capital to 'rebel' against finance and push to restore Keynesianism. Industrial capital (the 'domestic bourgeoisie' in the traditional development discourse) has a stake in the neo-liberal model and is committed to its reproduction. It is a *part* of finance and benefits from the suppression of working class demands and from the enhanced international connections established under neo-liberalism, including the restoration of US hegemony. Dissenting voices soon realize that the internationalization of the circuits of capital and financial market control of state funding have made investments and the realization of profits dependent on world market conditions and the interests of international capital. This would make any attempt to 'decouple' from the neo-liberal compact very costly indeed.

The neo-liberal restructuring of socio-economic reproduction drastically reduces the scope for debates about economic policy direction. The economic authorities are no longer tasked with stabilizing accumulation and arbitrating among competing fractions of capital (and other sections of society) as occurred under Keynesianism. Their primary job now is to ensure that financial market signals – expressing the interests of capital in general – are read by the state institutions and the individual (domestic and international) capitals with minimal distortion.

Outcomes and Limitations of Neo-liberalism

The neo-liberal transition includes three main elements, restoring capitalist social domination, restructuring production after the collapse of Keynesianism and recomposing US hegemony (through the pivotal position of US financial institutions in global accumulation, the restoration of the role of the dollar and the US-led integration of the international elite). The transition has led to a significant worldwide shift in power relations away from the majority. The political spectrum has shifted rightwards, left parties and mass organizations have imploded, and many trade unions are muzzled or disabled. The working class has been disorganized and disciplined through a wide range of mechanisms of control, including higher unemployment, labour turnover and personal debt, greater international competition and legal changes, including cuts in Keynesian wages, benefits and entitlements systems. Neo-liberalism has facilitated concentration of power and wealth, increased workers' exploitation,[37] and demoralized and suppressed the alternatives.

Having emphasized the strengths of neo-liberalism, we should briefly note five of its limitations. First, neo-liberal policies accept the imperative of 'business confidence' even though confidence is intangible, elusive and self-referential, and it is subject to sudden and arbitrary changes. The neo-liberal approach invariably overestimates the levels of investment that can be generated by adhering to neo-liberal demands. Second, these policies systematically favour finance and large capital at the expense of smaller capitals and the workers. The ensuing transfer of resources to the rich, and the global growth slowdown triggered by the neo-liberal obsession with low inflation (see the case of the NMPC in Section six) have increased unemployment and fostered the stagnation of wages and the concentration of income in most countries.[38] Third, economic 'deregulation' disintegrates the established systems of provision, reduces state policymaking capacity and the degree of coordination of economic activity, creates undesirable employment patterns and precludes the use of industrial policy instruments for the implementation of socially determined priorities. 'Market freedom' increases economic uncertainty, volatility and vulnerability to crisis.[39] Fourth, the neo-liberal reforms introduce mutually reinforcing policies that destroy jobs and traditional industries that are defined – often *ex post* – as being inefficient. The depressive impact of their elimination is rarely compensated by the rapid development of new industries, leading to structural unemployment, greater poverty, marginalization and a more fragile balance of payments. Fifth, the neo-liberal policies are not self-correcting. Failure to achieve their stated aims generally leads to the *extension* of the reforms, with the excuse of ensuring implementation and the promise of 'imminent' success compounding their adverse implications. Finally, neo-liberalism is inimical to economic democracy, and it hollows out political democracy, making neo-liberalism vulnerable to *political* challenges (see Section seven).[40]

Monetary Policy for Mature Neo-liberalism

The NMPC belongs to the set of monetary policies based on nominal anchors. Similar policies include the gold standard, exchange rate targeting, currency boards and money supply targeting, with which the NMPC has much in common. The NMPC evolved gradually over time, drawing on the insights of the monetarist, new classical and new Keynesian schools of thought to become the dominant ('best practice') monetary policy paradigm in several rich and middle-income countries since the early 1990s.[41] Its popularity is based on its theoretical strengths, the alleged successes of the countries implementing inflation targeting (IT) and central bank independence (CBI), and the elimination of several shortcomings of the previous anti-inflation strategies.

The difficulties of trying to stabilize dynamic credit-money economies with bloated financial systems in the absence of exogenous anchors to the value of money cannot be underestimated. Policy management can become especially challenging when society is split by conflicting political and economic demands, as was the case in several countries until the 1980s. However, the period of high inflation associated with the collapse of the post-war boom has ended, and inflation is no longer a serious problem in most countries (see Figure 3).[42] This section reviews the process of inflation stabilization and the role of the NMPC in the consolidation of these achievements.

CBI and IT

The shortcomings of monetarism as well as the heavy criticisms levelled against it have contributed – since the mid 1980s – to a vast mainstream literature on inflation and stabilization. These developments were based on three vectors: First, the convergence between the monetarist, new classical and new Keynesian approaches; second, the formalization of the assumption that government intervention in the economy is either useless or counterproductive; and third, the establishment of a causal relationship between lack of government policy credibility, adverse expectations and inflation. These insights have buttressed the argument that inflation control requires the implementation of 'credible' (neo-liberal) macroeconomic policies (Section five), monetary policy rules (Section four) and the elimination of residual inflationary pressures through the repression of working class demands and the removal of selected features of the welfare state. These policies have been supplemented institutionally by the shift towards CBI and the introduction of nominal anchors, especially exchange rates or inflation targets. These anchors are ostensibly designed to 'discipline the politicians' and remove the inflation bias.

IT is a monetary policy paradigm for *mature neo-liberalism*. In contrast to exchange rate targeting, IT is not an inflation stabilization strategy (it can be introduced only when inflation is already low), and it operates optimally when the financial markets have already been liberalized. Despite these limitations, IT is the policy regime most conducive to the consolidation of low inflation, because there is very limited scope for the deviation of the goals of monetary policy from the preservation of value of money. Moreover, in contrast to exchange rate targeting, IT allows monetary policy to respond flexibly to adverse shocks, reducing its vulnerability to speculation, instability and crisis. Even more significantly, IT locks government policy into the neo-liberal framework institutionally. This makes IT a stable and potentially durable monetary policy regime that is singularly appropriate for those countries completing the transition to neo-liberalism. These features help to explain the adoption of IT in an increasing number of countries.

Supporters of IT claim that this policy regime can 'deliver as much price level stability as a commodity [gold] standard'.[43] To achieve this desirable outcome, the government should signal its 'acknowledgement that low and stable inflation is the overriding goal of monetary policy'[44] by setting a legally binding target rate for inflation, usually defined as a low positive interval, including a small tolerance margin. This should be the only nominal anchor in the economy, as IT cannot be pursued simultaneously with money supply, wages, employment or exchange rate targets (i.e., IT requires a 'dirty' floating exchange rate regime).[45]

The inflation targeting regime (ITR) operates at multiple levels. It institutionalizes 'good' (i.e., mainstream) monetary policies, increases the 'transparency' of central bank policies and provides a trend for the inflation expectations of the private sector, which should reduce uncertainty and facilitate economic planning and coordination. The transition costs to the new policy regime depend on the credibility of the government's commitment to IT and the reputation of the central bank. The higher they are, the faster the expectations will converge to the IT and the lower the output costs of reducing inflation (the 'sacrifice ratio'). Once established, the ITR should bring several benefits, including lower and more stable inflation, higher economic growth rates and a lower sacrifice ratio. These potential benefits suggest that other policy objectives such as employment generation, economic growth and income distribution should be subordinated to the IT.[46]

CBI institutionalizes the primary responsibility of the central bank for achieving the IT, which presumably limits the influence of the politicians over economic policymaking, greatly reducing uncertainty and eliminating time-inconsistency, the political business cycle and the inflation bias. Therefore, CBI should help improve economic performance. CBI can include two types of independence. Political or administrative independence involves the appointment of bank directors for fixed terms (preferably not coinciding with the mandate of the country's president or the legislators in order to ensure policy continuity), and the regular assessment of the bank's performance through the trajectory of inflation and the bank's reports to the government, the parliament and the media. Instrument independence involves the bank's autonomy to conduct monetary policy, essentially calibrating interest rates to fine-tune economic activity and, therefore, the rate of inflation. The institutional arrangements underpinning CBI regimes vary between countries and over time. Differences may include the precise duties of the bank, the policy instruments that it controls, its degree of autonomy, the relationship between the central bank and other government departments, the procedure for appointing bank directors and the limits on government borrowing from the bank. In spite of their practical significance these details will be ignored in what follows, in order to permit a general assessment of the NMPC.

Performance of IT and CBI Regimes

There is a vast literature assessing the performance of IT and CBI. These studies are substantively similar; this section considers only the former in detail for reasons of space. Several studies have identified gains stemming from IT in such areas as lower inflation rates, volatility and inertia, improved expectations, faster absorption of adverse shocks, lower sacrifice ratio, output stabilization and the convergence of poorly performing countries towards well performing country standards.[47] Similar gains are attributed to CBI.[48] However, other studies claim that there is no evidence that IT and CBI improve economic performance.[49]

These conflicting views are partly due to variation in approaches and econometric methodologies – which is common in other areas of macroeconomics. However, there may be five additional reasons for these discrepant views of IT and CBI. First, it is difficult to classify policy regimes rigorously. Countries can be grouped differently according to whether they follow 'explicit' or 'implicit' IT policies, and the extent to which their central banks have administrative and instrument independence.[50] If one also controls for the structural differences among the relevant economies, available samples become insignificantly small, making meaningful comparisons impossible.

Second, IT and CBI experiences are relatively new. For example, Stone and Bhundia (2004) list 20 'full-fledged' IT countries, only five of which have been targeting inflation for more than ten years.[51] Another five have been targeting for more than five years,[52] and ten for a shorter period.[53] It is impossible to draw any conclusions based on these short and disparate sample periods. Third, even its supporters admit that IT is not an inflation stabilization strategy (see above). Consequently, although high inflation countries may be more inclined to adopt IT, they can do so only *after* a successful disinflation programme that is unrelated to IT. On adoption, the ITR will almost invariably inherit declining inflation rates, growing monetary policy credibility and, quite possibly (if their economies have been in the doldrums for long periods), healthy growth rates. These favourable developments are *conditions* for IT rather than outcomes of this policy regime, and they should be factored in when assessing the performance of ITR. Fourth, the last 15 years have been relatively tranquil by post-Bretton Woods standards. Although growth rates have tended to deteriorate, performance in terms of inflation, output volatility and interest rates has improved in most OECD countries. These improvements are obvious both in IT and non-IT countries, which may indicate that they are not due to IT.[54] Fifth, even when the performance of IT countries improves *more* than that of non-IT countries, it cannot be assumed that the difference was *due* to IT. For example, Ball and Sheridan (2003) find evidence that the countries showing the greatest performance improvements recently were those with the worst performance in the previous period, and these tend to be IT countries. However, these improvements were due to their *regression towards the mean*, which helps to explain why performance also improved in the non-IT countries. Therefore, the apparent success of IT countries is merely due to their having 'high initial inflation and large decreases, but the decrease for a given initial level looks similar for targeters and non-targeters' (p. 16). Controlling for regression towards the mean, Ball and Sheridan find no evidence that IT improves any aspect of economic performance.[55]

In conclusion, IT and CBI seem to have little influence on economic performance. So why does mainstream discourse place so much emphasis on IT and CBI and why do IMF publications present such a favourable assessment of IT and CBI?[56] Three contributing factors can be readily identified. First, mainstream theory is structurally predisposed to see value in IT and CBI, since they share methodological foundations (real-monetary dichotomy, quantitativism, abhorrence of state intervention and so on). Second, IT and CBI are a *fashionable* part of the 'common sense' of our age, and these policy recommendations tend to creep into even heterodox discourse. Third, IT and CBI promote the interests of domestic and international finance, ensuring that they will find support among a very powerful constituency (see next page).

Costs of the NMPC

This section examines four costs of the NMPC. They are intrinsic to this inflation strategy, in the sense that they derive from the choice of economic policy instruments for inflation control and the institutional structure associated with IT and CBI.

The cost of high interest rates: Modern mainstream economic theory suggests that the manipulation of interest rates is the most efficient tool to secure low inflation in the long term. This implies that real interest rates tend to be higher under IT and CBI than under an alternative regime in which other instruments play more significant role in inflation control. There is no question that high interest rates can reduce demand and inflation. They increase the costs of production, investment and consumption and trigger public expenditure cuts because they raise the domestic public debt service. Higher costs and depressed demand may force highly leveraged or financially weaker firms into bankruptcy – regardless of their economic prospects, technical efficiency, employment potential or strategic importance. The imperatives of survival can compel the remaining firms to attack the welfare of their workforce which, among other destructive outcomes, could fatally wound the Keynesian settlement. This strategy has been used in countless transitions to neo-liberalism. Higher interest rates offer profitable opportunities for financial institutions combined with higher risks. They include not only cost and demand pressures also experienced by industrial capital, but specific problems of liability mismatches, the emergence of new financial assets and investment strategies and, generally, the demands of a more volatile economic environment. These are only some of the ways in which high interest rates discipline industrial capital and finance and impose regressive changes in the structure of the economy and in the distribution of income (Figure 4 indicates that there is a positive relationship between high interest rates and high Gini coefficients).[57] In extreme cases, rigid rates of inflation (because of cost or balance of payments pressures or deep social divisions) or excessively ambitious IT can lead to very high real interest rates, which may foster output volatility and even lock the economy into a stabilization trap: a low-level equilibrium with low growth, high unemployment and intractable problems of poverty and inequality.[58]

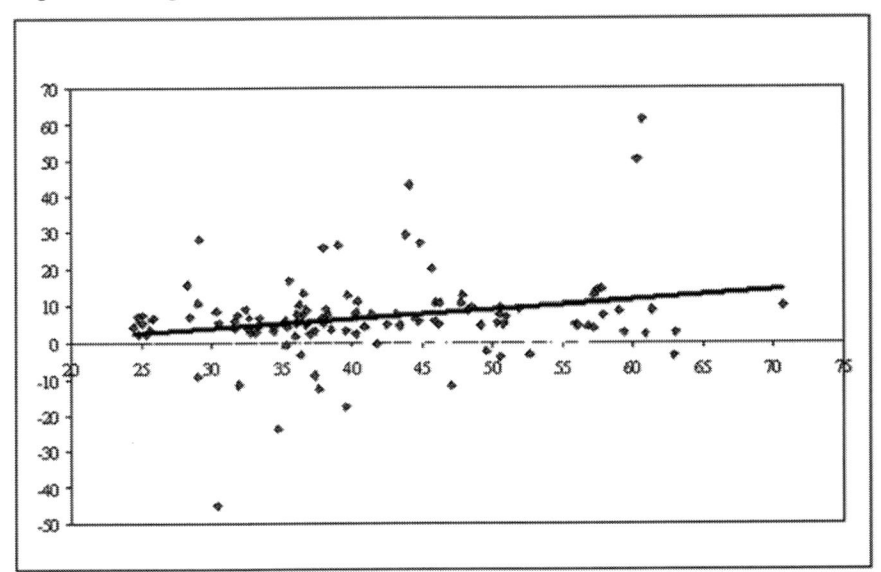

Figure 4: Average Real Interest Rate and Gini Coefficient, 1961–2001

Vertical axis: real interest rates (annual average for 112 countries).
Horizontal axis: Gini coefficient (latest year).
Source: World Development Indicators.

The Cost of Balance of Payments Instability

The interest rates required to achieve the IT may conflict with those needed to ensure balance of payments sustainability. If the former is higher there may be destabilizing inflows of foreign capital which, if they are sterilized, inflate the domestic public debt and may trigger unsustainable consumption or financial bubbles. Alternatively, if the latter is higher, the economy could face destructive capital outflows.[59] Finally, IT is inappropriate if the private sector has large liabilities denominated in foreign currency (liability dollarization). Currency depreciations could be extraordinarily costly if the financial institutions and their customers are saddled with unhedged currency mismatches, creating demands for the central bank to maintain exchange rate stability even where incompatible with the ITR.[60]

The Cost of Financial Instability

Although the central bank is primarily responsible for achieving IT, it must continue to be the bank of banks and the institution responsible for preserving the stability of the domestic financial system.[61] These mandates may occasionally become mutually incompatible, especially if the asset and product markets give contradictory signals about inflation, if asset prices are very volatile, or if asset values rise rapidly as a proportion of GDP. For example, if price inflation threatens to escalate, the central bank may be compelled to raise interest rates, which could undermine financial system stability and trigger a costly crisis. Alternatively, if deflation looms, the central bank may be forced to lower interest rates, although this may fuel a destabilizing bout of asset price inflation and a debt and consumption bubble based on loans secured on those rising asset prices.[62] The close relationship between price inflation, personal and company debt, financial system stability and asset price inflation – especially when interest rate manipulation becomes the most important instrument of economic policy – and the potentially large cost of financial crises indicate that the central bank ought to monitor asset prices and levels of debt as part of its duty to maintain economic stability. In other words, the excessive focus of the NMPC on inflation control tends to distract attention from the financial sector as a major source of *instability*. This is misguided, because the output and employment costs of financial crises can easily exceed the costs of moderate inflation. In this sense, the NMPC offers poor guidance for monetary policy.

CBI is Incompatible with Economic Democracy

CBI is undemocratic because the insulation of monetary policy from public debate *reduces* central bank accountability and *curtails* the legitimacy of monetary policy.[63] In this policy regime the central bank is free to consult only the financial institutions when determining the interest rates, among other policy adjustments. In contrast, in previous monetary policy regimes claims for higher interest rates would have to be argued politically at several levels of government. In this process, counter-claims expressing the interests of other social groups could, in principle be heard, offering the opportunity to reach a more balanced decision. More generally, anti-inflation policies ought to be selected through an assessment of the socio-economic costs of inflation, their distributive implications and the distribution of the gains of stabilization.

The improved indicators of credibility that accompany CBI and IT express the appreciation of a relatively narrow circle of powerful individuals for these quintessentially neo-liberal policies. By the same token, 'improved expectations' reflect the closer relation between the central bank and the financial markets under this policy regime, the financial operators' appreciation of the central bank's performance, and their confidence that monetary policy will continue to be determined by their narrow interests. The 'credibility' of CBI and IT indicates the *takeover* of monetary policy by finance in mature neo-liberalism.

The institutional rigidities imposed by both CBI and IT are part of an attempt to impose a specific form of monetary policy discipline upon the state, industrial capital, financial institutions and the working class. This is not only regressive, it is also misguided. First, it presumes that the independent central bank can deliver the IT if it *really* wants to. This simply revamps the discredited monetarist claim that money supply targeting is feasible and sufficient to control the rate of inflation. Second, it ignores the real dilemmas involved in central bank policy, especially the potential conflicts between monetary, financial and balance of payments stability. Third, if inflation is complex and contingent, it is important to preserve monetary policy flexibility. Institutional rigidity is hardly the most efficient way to tackle changing economic problems.

CBI and IT lock into place the mainstream theory of inflation and the anti-inflation policies associated with the reproduction of neo-liberalism, and serving primarily the interests of finance. These rigidities are bound to create unnecessary costs and political difficulties when the causes of inflation change or when shifts in the correlation of social forces permits the implementation of less regressive policies.

Finally, the insulation of monetary policy from public scrutiny and political control can thwart policy coordination essential for the success of *any* significant government initiative. It is much harder to deliver the outcomes chosen by the electorate if the government can count on only one set of (fiscal policy) instruments, while monetary and exchange rate policy may be pursuing entirely different targets that may even compromise the achievement of other socially desirable objectives.

Conclusion

Monetary policy is political. It regulates and disciplines the process of accumulation in each country and internationally, and helps to perpetuate the inequalities underpinning the production of the material conditions of social reproduction.

In the Keynesian era, monetary policy contributed to social stability through the maximization of the rate of accumulation, subject to the preservation of macroeconomic stability. In the centre, rapid growth of output and income helped to contain the lure of communism and supported the achievement of political stability within a social democratic framework. In the periphery, rapid accumulation was usually accompanied by harsher political regimes. The Bretton Woods System provided the framework for the integration of domestic accumulation within a process of international accumulation under the hegemony of the US.

The Keynesian compact was unravelled between the late 1960s and the early 1970s, and this chapter reviewed the protracted search for an alternative monetary policy regime. The failure of 'austerity by consent' led to the introduction of monetarist policies in several countries. Monetarism validated the abandonment of government commitments to full employment and social integration, and rationalized the shift of monetary policy away from output growth and towards inflation control. Monetarism also helped to institutionalize the floating exchange rate regime, in which the financial markets are embedded into the fabric of macroeconomic policy formulation and implementation.

Monetarism contributed to the elimination of high inflation; it also helped to restore US hegemony and discipline a restless working class in several countries. However, monetarism was theoretically flawed, money supply targeting was generally ineffective and monetarist policies did not facilitate the resumption of rapid growth. The subsequent transition to neo-liberalism was due to the growing pressure of capitalist interests for the imposition of social discipline and the restoration of the conditions of accumulation through the prominence of finance. These trends culminated in the NMPC – the monetary policy framework for mature neo-liberalism.

IT and CBI are primarily political rather than 'technical' choices. They support the processes of socio-economic reorganization engineered by the neo-liberal transition, including the takeover of the state's legitimacy, resources and policymaking capacity by finance, and its deployment to strengthen minority power and promote the interests of capital in general dressed up as the general good. These objectives are thinly disguised by the veil of 'technical objectivity', 'rules' and 'policy neutrality' supplied by mainstream economics. The NMPC excludes inconvenient political dilemmas from public scrutiny, entrenches the current balance of social forces into the institutional fabric of the economy, and creates rigidities preventing the consideration of alternative economic policy objectives. These policy changes are normally introduced in response to domestic political imperatives, and they are validated by the financial markets, the international financial organizations and the US Treasury Department. These institutions help to monitor the outcomes of their preferred monetary policy framework, and they can supply expertise and resources to assist the implementation of the NMPC. Finally, mainstream economics provide academic credibility for this emerging consensus by lending theoretical density and depth to the NMPC.

The NMPC can deliver low inflation for long periods, because demand control through interest rate manipulation can reduce inflation regardless of its causes. Its most important vulnerabilities are not due to its theoretical weaknesses or the failure of CBI and IT to reduce inflation. The NMPC's most important vulnerability is its *lack of political legitimacy*. Its policies are blunt, inefficient and costly. They grind down inflation only through high unemployment and reduced growth potential; and they increase vulnerability to financial and balance of payments instability. NMPC policies are also regressive. They facilitate the transfer of income and political power to the minority and lock rich and poor countries into economic development strategies inimical to democratic outcomes. NMPC's lack of legitimacy and the neo-liberal system of accumulation render both vulnerable to political challenges. Their economic resilience should not detract from neo-liberalism's political fragilities and its monetary policy offspring – the NMPC.

Notes

1. I am grateful to Al Campbell and Lecio Morais for their generous comments to a previous version of this paper. The usual disclaimers apply.
2. In this chapter, Keynesianism, monetarism and neo-liberalism are both economic theories and economic policy paradigms. Keynesianism was typical of the period between the mid 1930s and 1973 and, more specifically, of the post-war 'golden age'. Neo-liberalism is typical of the period after 1979 (all dates are approximate). For an overview of Keynesian policies and experiences, see Clarke (1988) and Marglin and Schor (1990). Neo-liberalism is critically scrutinized by the contributions in Saad-Filho and Johnston (2005).
3. This term is suggested by Arestis and Sawyer (2005).
4. For a clear statement, see Bordo et al. (2003, p. 1).
5. See Jomo (2005).
6. See Arrighi (1994) and Hobsbawm (1994, chs. 3–4, 8–9).
7. One of the most important Keynesian innovations in the field of economic policy was the use of the fiscal budget not only to finance the state, but also to fine-tune aggregate demand.
8. See Fry (1995), Grabel (2003) and World Bank (1989).
9. Different types of financial system are reviewed by Zysman (1983); see also Aybar and Lapavitsas (2001).
10. Experiences in the periphery were very diverse, and they cannot be reviewed in this chapter.
11. See Aglietta (1979) and Panitch (1976).
12. See Panitch and Gindin (2004; 2005).
13. See, for example, Ietto-Gillies (2004).
14. See Panitch and Gindin (2005).
15. For a prescient study of this contradiction of Keynesianism, see Kalecki (1943).
16. See Duménil and Lévy (2004; 2005).
17. See, for example, Brenner (2002).
18. See, for example, Panitch (1976).
19. For a detailed study of finance under neo-liberalism, see Duménil and Lévy (2004, esp. chs. 13, 23).
20. See Munck (2005).
21. See Laidler (1993) and Screpanti and Zamagni (1993, ch. 9).

22. '[I]f one believes that, in the long-run, there is no trade-off between inflation and output then there is no point in using monetary policy to target output ... [You only have to adhere to] the view that printing money cannot raise long-run productivity growth, in order to believe that inflation rather than output is the only sensible objective of monetary policy in the long-run' (Mervyn King, current Governor of the Bank of England, cited in Arestis and Sawyer, 2005).
23. See Gärtner (2000, p. 529).
24. See Panitch and Gindin (2005, pp. 60–4).
25. M.J. Horgan, vice president of Citibank, claimed that 'the world had changed' since the Fed's policy shift, while the future chairman of the US Federal Reserve System, Alan Greenspan, remarked that Volcker's policy shift was 'the most important monetary policy change since World War II' (Business Week, 5 November 1979, p. 91 and 22 October 1979, p. 67).
26. See Campbell (2005) and Duménil and Lévy (2005).
27. See Arestis and Sawyer (1998).
28. See Levacic and Rebmann (1982) and Sawyer (1989).
29. See Screpanti and Zamagni (1993, ch. 9).
30. See Fine, Lapavitsas and Pincus (2001).
31. See Saad-Filho (2005).
32. Michel Camdessus (1996), managing director of the IMF, claimed that '[a] key step [to control inflation] ... is to establish a positive perception of the government's role in the economy. Governments can do this by concentrating on doing a few things well: ensuring law and order, providing reliable public services, and establishing a simple, transparent regulatory system that is equitably enforced'.
33. For a critique of mainstream theories of globalization, see Kiely (2005), Radice (2005) and Saad-Filho (2003, introduction).
34. For a Marxian analysis of the relationship between production and finance, see Itoh and Lapavitsas (1999) and Fine and Saad-Filho (2004, ch.12).
35. The inability of financial and capital account liberalization to increase levels of investment was demonstrated by Feldstein and Horioka (1980) and Helleiner (1998). For a heterodox critique of the prominence of finance, see Chang and Grabel (2004, ch. 9).
36. See Rude (2005).
37. See Duménil and Lévy (2004).
38. See Milanovic (2002).
39. Volatile capital flows have triggered severe financial crises in several countries recently, e.g., Mexico (1994), East Asia (1996–7), Russia (1998), Brazil (1999) and Turkey and Argentina (2001). For a review, see Palma (2003) and Jomo (2001).
40. See Wood (1995).
41. An incomplete list includes Australia, Brazil, Canada, Chile, Colombia, Czech Republic, Hungary, Iceland, Israel, Mexico, New Zealand, Norway, Poland, South Africa, South Korea, Sweden, Thailand and the UK. Other countries following similar strategies include Argentina, the eurozone, Japan, Singapore, Switzerland and the US.
42. '[C]entral banks appear to have learned how to maintain inflation at a low level. For many central banks, this new era has been characterized by central banks adopting implicit or explicit inflation targets' (Bordo et al., 2003, p. 1).
43. Bordo et al. (2003, p. 1).
44. Bernanke and Mishkin (1997, p. 97).

45. See Agénor (2002).
46. See Carare et al. (2002, p. 5).
47. See, for example, Bernanke et al. (1999), Debelle et al. (1998), Landerretche et al. (2001), Mishkin (1999), Mishkin and Schmidt-Hebbel (2002) and Svensson (1997a; 1997b).
48. See, for example, Alesina (1988; 1989), Alesina and Summers (1993), Cukierman (1992) and Grilli et al. (1991).
49. See, for example, Agénor (2001, pp. 43–4), Cecchetti and Ehrmann (1999), Chang and Grabel (2004, pp. 183–4), Debelle et al. (1998) and Neumann and von Hagen (2002).
50. See, for example, Carare and Stone (2003), Eichengreen (2002) and Stone and Bhundia (2004).
51. Australia, Canada, New Zealand, Sweden and the UK.
52. Brazil, Chile, Czech Republic, Israel and Poland.
53. Colombia, Hungary, Iceland, Norway, Mexico, Peru, Philippines, South Africa, South Korea and Thailand.
54. See Arestis and Sawyer (2005).
55. 'There is no evidence whatsoever that inflation targeting reduces inflation variability... Our robust finding is that inflation targeting has no beneficial effects ... [T]here is no evidence that targeting affects inflation behavior' (Ball and Sheridan, 2003, pp. 11–2).
56. See, for example, Camdessus (1996) and IMF (2002).
57. For a detailed study of the distributional impact of high interest rates in the US and the UK, see Argitis and Pitelis (2001).
58. See McKinley (2003).
59. See Arestis and Glickman (2002), Jomo (2001), Palma (1998) and Weller (2001).
60. See Eichengreen (2002, pp. 38–41).
61. See Lapavitsas (1997).
62. See Arestis and Sawyer (1997; 2005) and Toporowski (2000). For estimates of the cost of financial crises, see World Bank (1989, ch. 5).
63. See Epstein and Yeldan (2004) and Forder (2003).

References

Agénor, P. R. 2002. Monetary Policy under Flexible Exchange Rates: An Introduction to Inflation Targeting, in Layza, N. and Soto, R. (eds.), *Inflation Targeting: Design, Performance, Challenges*. Santiago, Chile: Central Bank of Chile. http://www1.worldbank.org/wbiep/macro-program/agenor/pdfs/cmi_target_wp

Aglietta, M. 1979. *A Theory of Capitalist Regulation*. London: Verso.

Alesina, A. 1988. 'Macroeconomics and Politics', in Fischer, S (ed.), *NBER Macroeconomics Annual*. Cambridge, Mass: MIT Press.

—. 1989. 'Politics and Business Cycles in Industrial Democracies', *Economic Policy*, 8.

Alesina, A. and Summers, L. 1993. 'Central Bank Independence and Macroeconomic Performance: Some Comparative Evidence', *Journal of Money, Credit, and Banking*, 25, 2.

Arestis, P. and Glickman, M. 2002. 'Financial Crisis in Southeast Asia: Dispelling Illusion the Minskyan Way', *Cambridge Journal of Economics*, 26.

Arestis, P. and Sawyer, M. 1997. 'The Problematic Nature of Independent Central Banks', in Cohen, A. J., Hagemann, H., and Smithin, J. (eds.), *Money, Financial Institutions and Macroeconomics*. Dordrecht: Kluwer Academic.
—. 1998. 'New Labour, New Monetarism', *Soundings*, 9.
—. 2005. 'Inflation Targeting: A Critical Appraisal', Available at http://www.levy.org/pubs/wp/388.pdf, last accessed 27 March 2007.
Argitis, G. and Pitelis, C. 2001. 'Monetary Policy and the Distribution of Income: Evidence for the United States and the United Kingdom', *Journal of Post Keynesian Economics*, 23, 4.
Arrighi, G. 1994. *The Long Twentieth Century: Money, Power, and the Origins of Our Times*. London: Verso.
Aybar, S. and Lapavitsas, C. 2001. 'Financial System Design and the Post-Washington Consensus', in Fine, B. Lapavitsas, C. and Pincus, J. (eds.), *Development Policy in the Twenty-first Century: Beyond the Post-Washington Consensus*. London: Routledge.
Ball, L. and Sheridan, N. 2003. *Does Inflation Targeting Matter?* IMF Working Paper No. 03/129.
Bernanke, B. S., and Mishkin, F. 1997. 'Inflation Targeting: A New Framework for Monetary Policy?' *Journal of Economic Perspectives*, 11, 2.
Bernanke, B. S., Laubach, T., Mishkin, F and Posen, A. S. 1999. *Inflation Targeting: Lessons from the International Experience*. Princeton: Princeton University Press.
Bordo, M. D., Dittmar, R. T and Gavin, W. T. 2003. *Gold, Fiat Money, and Price Stability*. NBER Working Paper No. 10171.
Brenner, R. 2002. *The Boom and the Bubble: The US in the World Economy*. London: Verso.
Camdessus, M. 1996. *Is the New Bretton Woods Conceivable?*, Address by the Managing Director of the International Monetary Fund, Société d'Economie Politique, Paris, January 19, http://www.imf.org/external/np/sec/mds/1996/mds9601.htm.
Campbell, A. 2005. 'The Birth of Neoliberalism in the United States: A Reorganisation of Capitalism', in Saad-Filho, A. and Johnston, D. (eds.), *Neoliberalism: A Critical Reader*. London: Pluto Press.
Carare, A. and Stone, M. R. 2003. *Inflation Targeting Regimes*. IMF Working Paper No. 03/9.
Carare, A., Shaechter, A., Stone, M. and Zelmer, M. 2002. *Establishing Initial Conditions in Support of Inflation Targeting*. IMF Working Paper No. 02/102.
Cecchetti, S. G. and Ehrmann, M. 1999. 'Does Inflation Targeting Increase Output Volatility? An International Comparison of Policymakers' Preferences and Outcomes'. NBER Working Paper No. 7426.
Chang, H.-J. and Grabel, I. 2004. Reclaiming Development: An Alternative Economic Policy Manual. London: Zed Books.
Clarke, S. 1988. *Keynesianism, Monetarism, and the Crisis of the State*. Aldershot: Edward Elgar.
Cukierman, A. 1982. *Central Bank Strategy, Credibility, and Independence: Theory and Evidence*. Cambridge, Mass.: MIT Press.
Debelle, G., Masson, P., Savastano, M. and Sharma, S. 1998. *Inflation Targeting as a Framework for Monetary Policy*. IMF website.
Duménil, G. and Lévy, D. 2004. *Capital Resurgent: Roots of the Neoliberal Revolution*. Cambridge, Mass.: Harvard University Press.
—. 2005. 'The Neoliberal Counter-Revolution', in Saad-Filho, A. and Johnston, D. (eds.), *Neoliberalism: A Critical Reader*. London: Pluto Press.
Eichengreen, B. 2002. *Can Emerging Markets Float? Should They Inflation Target?* Banco Central do Brasil, Working Paper Series No. 36.

Epstein, G. and Yeldan, E. 2004. 'Alternatives to Inflation Targeting Monetary Policy for Stable and Egalitarian Growth in Developing Countries: A Multi-Country Research Project', Research proposal, Amherst, MA: Political Economy Research Institute.

Feldstein, M. and Horioka, C. 1980. 'Domestic Saving and International Capital Flows', *Economic Journal*, 90.

Fine, B. and Saad-Filho, A. 2004. *Marx's Capital*, 4th edition. London: Pluto Press.

Fine, B., Lapavitsas, C. and Pincus, J. (eds.), 2001. *Development Policy in the Twenty-first Century: Beyond the Post-Washington Consensus*. London: Routledge.

Forder, J. 2003. 'Central Bank Independence: Economic Theory, Evidence and Political Legitimacy', *International Papers in Political Economy*, 10, 2.

Fry, M. J. 1995. *Money, Interest, and Banking in Economic Development*, 2nd edition. Baltimore: The Johns Hopkins University Press.

Gärtner, M. 2000. 'Political Macroeconomics: A Survey of Recent Developments', *Journal of Economic Surveys*, 14, 5.

Grabel, I. 2003. 'International Private Capital Flows and Developing Countries', in Chang, H.-J. (ed.), *Rethinking Development Economics*, London: Anthem Press.

Grilli, V, Masciandaro, D. and Tabellini, G. 1991. 'Political and Monetary Institutions and Public Finance Policies in the Industrial Countries', *Economic Policy*, 13.

Helleiner, G. K. 1998. 'Capital Account Regimes and the Developing Countries: Issues and Approaches', in Helleiner, G, K. (ed.), *Capital Account Regimes and the Developing Countries*. London: Macmillan.

Hobsbawm, E. J. 1994. *Age of Extremes: The Short Twentieth Century, 1914-1991*. London: Michael Joseph.

Ietto-Gillies, G. 2004. *Theories of International Production*. London: Routledge.

International Monetary Fund. 2002. 'IMF Panel of Experts on Safeguards Assessments Review of Experience and Next Steps', IMF website.

Itoh, M. and Lapavitsas, C. 1999. *Political Economy of Money and Finance*. London: Macmillan.

Jomo K. S. 2001. 'Growth After the Asian Crisis: What Remains of the East Asian Model?' G24 Discussion Paper Series: G24 website.

—. (ed.), 2005. *Pioneers of Development Economics*, 2 vols. Amsterdam: Sephis.

Kalecki, M. 1943. 'Political Aspects of Full Employment', *Political Quarterly* 14, amended version reprinted in *Selected Essays on the Dynamics of the Capitalist Economy*, Cambridge: Cambridge University Press.

Kiely, R. 2005. *The Clash of Globalisations: Neo-Liberalism, the Third Way, and Anti-Globalisation*. Leiden: Brill.

Laidler, D. 1993. *The Golden Age of the Quantity Theory*, Brighton: Harvester Wheatsheaf.

Landerretche, O., Corbo, V. and Schmidt-Hebbel, K. 2001. *Does Inflation Targeting Make a Difference?* Central Bank of Chile, Working Papers No. 106.

Lapavitsas, C. 1997. 'The Political Economy of Central Banks: Agents of Stability or Sources of Instability?' *International Papers in Political Economy*, 4, 3.

Levacic, R. and Rebmann, A. 1982. *Macroeconomics: An Introduction to Keynesian-Neoclassical Controversies*. London: Macmillan.

Marglin, S. and Schor, J. 1990. *The Golden Age of Capitalism: Reinterpreting the Postwar Experience*. Oxford: Clarendon Press.

McKinley, T. 2003. 'The Macroeconomics of Poverty Reduction: Initial Findings of the UNDP Asia-Pacific Regional Programme', New York: UNDP.

Milanovic, B. 2002. 'True World Income Distribution, 1988 and 1993: First Calculation Based on Household Surveys Alone', *Economic Journal*, 112.

Mishkin, F. S. 1999. 'Inflation Experiences with Different Monetary Policy Regimes', *Journal of Monetary Economics*, 43.
Mishkin, F. S. and Schmidt-Hebbel, K. 2002. 'A Decade of Inflation Targeting in the World: What do We Know and What do We Need to Know?' in Loayza, N. and Soto, R. (eds.), *Inflation Targeting: Design, Performance, Challenges*. Santiago: Central Bank of Chile.
Munck, R. 2005. 'Neoliberalism and Politics, and the Politics of Neoliberalism', in Saad-Filho, A. and Johnston, D. (eds.), *Neoliberalism: A Critical Reader*, London: Pluto Press.
Neumann, M. J. M. and von Hagen, J. 2002. 'Does Inflation Targeting Matter?' *Federal Reserve Bank of St Louis Review*, 84.
Palma, G. 1998. 'Three and a Half Cycles of 'Mania, Panic and [Asymmetric] Crash': East Asia and Latin America Compared', *Cambridge Journal of Economics*, 22, 6.
—. 2003. 'The Latin American Economies During the Second Half of the Twentieth Century – From the Age of "ISI" to the Age of "The End of History"', in Chang, H.-J. (ed.), *Rethinking Development Economics*, London: Anthem Press.
Panitch, L. 1976. *Social Democracy and Industrial Militancy: The Labour Party, the Trade Unions and Incomes Policy, 1945–1974*. Cambridge: Cambridge University Press.
Panitch, L. and Gindin, S. 2004. 'Global Capitalism and American Empire' in Panitch, L. and Leys, C. (eds.), *Socialist Register: The Empire Reloaded*. London: Merlin Press.
—. 2005. 'Finance and American Empire' in Panitch, L. and Leys, C. (eds.), *Socialist Register: The Empire Reloaded*. London: Merlin Press.
Radice, H. 2005. 'Neoliberal Globalisation: Imperialism without Empires?' in Saad-Filho, A. and Johnston, D. (eds.), *Neoliberalism: A Critical Reader*. London: Pluto Press.
Rude, C. 2005. 'The Role of Financial Discipline in Imperial Strategy', in Panitch, L. and Leys, C. (eds.), *Socialist Register: The Empire Reloaded*. London: Merlin Press.
Saad-Filho, A. 2005. 'From Washington to Post-Washington Consensus: Neoliberal Agendas for Economic Development', in Saad-Filho, A. and Johnston, D. (eds.), *Neoliberalism: A Critical Reader*. London: Pluto Press.
—. (ed.), 2003. *Anti-Capitalism: A Marxist Introduction*. London: Pluto Press.
Saad-Filho, A. and Johnston, D. (eds.), 2005. *Neoliberalism: A Critical Reader*. London: Pluto Press.
Sawyer, M. 1989. *The Challenge of Radical Political Economy*. London: Edward Elgar.
Screpanti, E. and Zamagni, S. 1993. *An Outline of the History of Economic Thought*. Oxford: Oxford University Press.
Stone, M. R. and Bhundia, A. J. 2004. *A New Taxonomy of Monetary Regimes*. IMF Working Paper No. 04/191.
Svensson, L. E. O. 1997a. 'Optimal Inflation Targets, "Conservative" Central Banks, and Linear Inflation Contracts', *American Economic Review*, 87, 1.
—. 1997b. 'Inflation Forecast Targeting: Implementing and Monitoring Inflation Targets', *European Economic Review*, 41.
Toporowski, J. 2000. *The End of Finance: Capital Market Inflation, Financial Derivatives and Pension Fund Capitalism*. London: Routledge.
Weller, C. E. 2001. 'Financial Crises after Financial Liberalisation: Exceptional Circumstances or Structural Weakness?' *Journal of Development Studies*, 38, 1.
Wood, E. M. 1995. *Democracy against Capitalism: Renewing Historical Materialism*. Cambridge: Cambridge University Press.
World Bank. 1989. *World Development Report*. London: Oxford University Press.
Zysman, J. 1983. *Governments, Markets and Growth: Financial Systems and the Politics of Industrial Change*. Oxford: Martin Robertson.

Part II: Political Economy of a Progressive Global Future

INTRODUCTION

In Chapter Six – 'Volatile, Uneven and Combined Capitalism' – Patrick Bond seeks explanations for the last three decades of volatile global capitalism that could inform and guide strategic resistance. In Bond's view, the long economic slowdown since the 1970s has been accompanied by amplified uneven development, which can be directly traced to crisis displacement (not resolution) strategies imposed from Northern power centres. Some of the unevenness is a function of worsening financial volatility; some reflects the resurgent imperial project in the sphere of economic policy since the early 1980s, often termed neo-liberalism. The commodification of life and nature, and the degeneration of eco-social processes have resulted in increasingly common ideological splits, with five core responses discernible: (i) neoconservatism, (ii) neo-liberalism, (iii) a 'Post-Washington' reform agenda, (iv) Third World nationalism, and (v) global justice. These five ideologies approach capitalist crisis and uneven development from differing analytical perspectives and also draw divergent strategic and tactical lessons. Occasionally alliances within and between the five main camps are important. However, for Bond, the crucial challenge to the conflation of crisis and unevenness will be a 'decommodification' programme launched from overlapping, interlocking struggles that are already underway, aiming at the 'deglobalization of capital' via increasing internationalist solidarity.

David Kotz in Chapter Seven – 'The Erosion of Non-Capitalist Institutions and the Reproduction of Capitalism' – follows up Marx's observation that the process of capital accumulation tends to extirpate pre-capitalist social relations the world over. The vigorous accumulation process to which capitalism gives rise, Kotz argues in his chapter, certainly supports Marx's predictions. Thus, feudal and semi-feudal relations throughout the world have, over time, dissolved under the pressure of capitalist penetration; and, although not entirely eliminated, relations of independent commodity production have not only been gradually reduced but also increasingly marginalized. But capitalism has not eliminated all pre-existing non-capitalist institutions but has reshaped some of them to suit its needs because a social system made up entirely of institutions that operate on capitalist principles and embody capitalist relations would not be viable. Three major institutions that have hitherto been regarded as essential to capitalist reproduction precisely because of their *internally* non-capitalist form are states, families and schools. Thus Kotz shows that, in recent times, as capitalist relations have increasingly penetrated states, families, and schools, this has undermined their capacity to contribute effectively to the reproduction of capitalism. He suggests that understanding this process and its consequences may help opposition movements to chart a course aimed at superseding capitalism.

In Chapter Eight – 'The Transformative Moment' – Julie Matthaei and Barbara Brandt argue that a set of transformative processes and movements have arisen in advanced capitalism in reaction to the intense contradictions created by its hierarchical dualism. Hierarchical dualism, which lies at the foundation of capitalism, is a set of social structures and processes that polarize and hierarchize people, personality traits, works and realms of social life. Key hierarchical dualisms include man over and above nature; man over women, whites over people of colour, bosses over workers, rich over poor, mind over body, rationality over emotionality, and monetary over non-monetary. All of these dualisms are overlain by a set of overarching, power/value dualisms: dominator over dominated, strong over weak, good over bad, right over wrong. Finally, capitalist hierarchical dualism finds its unifying structure in class phenomena: the association of power with money; the ranking and judging of people, activities and things according to their monetary value; and the competition among people to move up the class hierarchy. For a person, more money – or the consumer goods it buys – is better, less is worse; the same holds for relations among peoples. What increasingly emerges with capitalist development is a set of money-based values that colonize all arenas of life and push aside other value systems, religious and otherwise.

However powerful and ubiquitous capitalist hierarchical dualism may seem, it is fraught, Matthaei and Brandt maintain, with contradictions that are spawning an ever growing array of people and movements for progressive economic transformation. The injustices of hierarchy have led to movements for equal opportunity based on gender and race, as well as movements to value the devalued, be it women's unpaid work, or what are now labelled 'social capital' and 'natural capital'. Hierarchy is also resulting in equalizing movements, from union and living wage organizing to share the wealth, fair trade and reparations movements. Dualistic polarization is also replete with contradictions. The life imbalances resulting from gender polarization are generating personal and political efforts to integrate paid work with family and parenting, by organizing for shorter work-time, downshifting, and the simplification of consumption; all of these challenge money-based values and institutions. Meanwhile, the increasingly undeniable problems resulting from the absence of caring and other values in economic life have birthed a vibrant and multifaceted set of movements for 'social responsibility'.

The authors conclude that these many transformational processes and movements are beginning to cohere around a shared set of transformational values, and around the urgent necessity of living one's life and of building economic and social institutions around these transformational values. Exemplified by the World Social Forum, and the associated anti-globalization demonstrations, these processes and movements could overturn hierarchical dualism and create economic practices and institutions that are more equal, just, free, fulfilling, balanced and sustainable.

Kees van der Pijl, in 'Frontiers of Cadre Radicalization in Contemporary Capitalism', explores the class structure of a transformation from neo-liberal capitalism toward a mode of survival that has a more pronounced element of authority and collective responsibility, possibly also more democracy. He begins Chapter Nine by outlining how, historically, the socialist movement could never include the technical/managerial cadre of modern capitalist society on its own credentials. Although the political cadre of the socialist and communist parties shared essentially the same class, background and perspective, revolutionary transformations did not settle (either in advance or as in the Soviet experience) the matter of how 'bourgeois specialists' were to be integrated into a changed politico-economic order. Van Pijl then discusses how neo-liberal capitalism in the last decades of the twentieth century has involved a struggle within the managerial/technical cadre that resulted in the defeat of a social-democratic tendency by a radicalized neo-liberal strand that drew its inspiration from neoclassical economics, monetarism, supply side theory, etc. With the end of the stock market boom and the dissipation of the glamour of the neo-liberal episode, this radicalized cadre is clearly heading for a difficult denouement. The concluding section investigates how far this experience has created the possibility for a new 'managerial revolution' in which there is a convergence among cadres associated with certain non-governmental organization (NGO)-related social concerns (but also the corporate social responsibility department in corporations and consultancies) around a reform drive that allies it with the alternative globalization movement.

Richard Westra, in the final chapter of this collection, '*Green* Marxism and the Institutional Structure of a Global Socialist Future', breaks new ground in the political economy of social change by facilitating an interface between two areas of research that hitherto have largely developed in isolation from each other. These are the study of the economic viability of forms of human society (including capitalism and varieties of socialism) and the institutional configuring of an eco-sustainable future. Westra first draws out the key insights of Marx's work on economic viability and then juxtaposes these to arguments drawn from Marxian economics for the essential eco-destructiveness of capitalism to provide a *metric* for assessing economic viability and eco-sanctity of alternative forms of human society. Secondly, the chapter proceeds to briefly assess the potential inherent in the trajectory of globalization to realize an economically viable and eco-sustainable future. Thirdly, Westra applies his metric for economic viability and eco-sustainability in a summary fashion to new ideas of socialism and the benchmark 'small is beautiful' version of *green* theory. Finally, the chapter tabulates the signal lessons from that analysis to suggest an institutional framework for a future global socialist society that is economically viable, eco-sustainable, and which realizes the overall aim of socialism to offer human socio-material betterment. The socialist model advanced in this final chapter holds to Marx's dictum that the new socialist society be institutionally configured out of the current really existing global economy.

Chapter 6

VOLATILE, UNEVEN AND COMBINED CAPITALISM

Patrick Bond

Introduction

This chapter seeks explanations for the last period (roughly three decades) of volatile global capitalism in order to advance strategic resistance. The merits of 'classical political economic theory' include the identification of crisis tendencies at the core of capital's laws of motion, tendencies which are met by countervailing management techniques. Crisis *displacement* techniques became much more sophisticated since the 1930s freeze of financial markets, crash of trade, Great Depression and inter-imperial turn to armed aggression. The chapter documents the global economy's vast credit expansion and the use of geographical power to move devaluation to Third World and emerging market sites, as well as vulnerable markets in the North that have suffered substantial 'corrections' in past years. Extra-market coercion including gendered and environmental super-exploitation has intensified in the process. The result is an 'uneven and combined' capitalism that concentrates wealth and poverty in more intense ways, geographically, and brings capitalist markets and the non-market spheres of society and nature together in ways adverse to the latter.

As for resistance, popular movements across the world are divided on strategies and tactics. While there are some crucial sites of national state control by anti-capitalist forces in Latin America, we can consider the options faced by the popular movements in terms of three alternative orientations: (i) 'autonomism', (ii) 'global governance'; and (iii) 'decommodification' of life/nature alongside the 'deglobalization' of capital. In advocating the latter course, I argue that the leading movements need to continue linking across borders in an internationalist manner, so as to reverse the social, political, military and environmental manifestations of volatile, uneven and combined capitalism. To do so in the future will probably require a shift from sectoral-level battles against the commodity form and global capitalist institutions, towards more coherent explanation and revived *national*-driven but internationally-linked sets of alternative development programmes.

Still by way of introduction, we might consider three central components to this political economic argument about global capitalism's problems. First, the durable late twentieth century condition of 'overaccumulation', as witnessed in declining increases in per capita gross domestic product (GDP) growth and falling corporate profit rates, was displaced and mitigated – 'shifted and stalled' geographically and temporally – at the cost of much more severe tensions and potential market volatility in months and years ahead. Second, the temporary dampening of crisis conditions through increased credit and financial market activity has resulted in fictitious capital expansion – especially in real estate but other speculative markets as well – far beyond the ability of production to meet the paper values. Third, geographical shifts in production and finance continue to generate economic volatility and regional geopolitical tensions, contributing to unevenness in currencies and markets as well as pressure to 'combine' capitalist and non-capitalist spheres of society and nature in search of restored profitability. With durable overaccumulation, financialization and globalization comes not only pressures for war, but also threats of catastrophic climate change and new pandemics (including acquired immune deficiency syndrome (AIDS), severe acute respiratory syndrome (SARS), drug-resistant malaria and avian flu).

The context in the most recent period, since the global justice movement reached the international stage at Seattle in late 1999, includes some incongruent experiences, especially in the US, Euro Area and Japan (Bank for International Settlements 2006, pp. 12–32):

- A recovery in trade, foreign investment flows (especially mergers and acquisitions) and stock market values after early 2000 downturns.
- Rising US and Japanese fiscal deficits.
- An unprecedented US trade deficit (especially due to increased Chinese imports), while nearly all emerging market economies – aside from Turkey, Mexico, South Africa, the Czech Republic and Poland – ran large current account surpluses.
- An upturn in raw material prices from early 2002 (especially in energy and minerals/metals).
- An uptick in corporate profits as a share of GDP accompanied by sluggish private fixed investments.
- Real interest rates below 1 per cent since 2001 in spite of 17 small rate increases by the US Federal Reserve since 2004.
- A fast-rising household debt/asset ratio in the US.

- Uncertainty in global property markets after apparent mortgage-driven peaks in 2005.
- An 18 per cent fall in the value of the dollar from its early 2002 high until year-end 2006; and
- The ongoing role of emerging Asian economies as the engine of world growth, accounting for half of global GDP since 2000.

Can incongruities within these macro-data be reconciled with Marxist political-economic analysis? In contrast, recent orthodox analysis of capitalist disequilibria, especially US trade/budget deficits, often relies upon four key variables: (i) low US national savings rates (below 14 per cent during the early 2000s); (ii) the positive implications of the 'new economy' for US investments (which have been stable at just lower than 20 per cent of GDP during the 1990s–2000s, roughly equal to Europe and Latin America but lower than Japan's 25 per cent and other East Asian countries' 33 per cent); (iii) the argument that a 'global savings glut' (roughly 2 per cent higher than 1990s levels) permits relatively low interest rates in the US in addition to capital inflows; and (iv) a 'Sino-American codependency' situation due to risk avoidance by Asian investors in the wake of the 1997–8 crisis (Bank for International Settlements, 2006, p. 24). For Barry Eichengreen (2006, p. 14), 'the four sets of factors supporting the global imbalance and the US deficit will not last forever. There will have to be adjustment, the question being whether it will come sooner or later and whether it will be orderly or disorderly'.

Moving from US crisis conditions, there have been other 'very long bouts of stagnant or even negative growth', the World Bank (WB) (2006, p. 56) notes: 'The past 25 years have had numerous setbacks afflicting growth in the developing countries'. It offers an explanation for 'Sub-Saharan Africa, the Middle East and North Africa, Latin America, and Europe and Central Asia. They each had specific reasons for these periods of depressed growth ranging from Latin America's debt crisis in the 1980s, the Middle East and North Africa's (and, to a lesser extent, Africa's) energy decline, and Europe and Central Asia's emergence from its transition toward market-based economies'. But in each case, the WB (2006, p. 55) claims, progress can be recorded:

- Improved macroeconomic conditions (such as less inflation and inflationary expectations).
- More sustainable debt levels (at least for developing countries on an average).
- More diversified economies with less reliance on volatile commodities.
- A much greater role for services (which tend to be less volatile).

- Much improved production management with lower inventories (which tended to be a major factor in past business cycles), and
- Better macroeconomic management, particularly monetary policy.

These claims – which has downside the Bank would not logically factor in – lead many elites to smugness. Some, like *The New York Times* economics correspondent Daniel Altman (2006), profess not to worry (unless an exogenous shock emerges), because 'the dollar's decline could continue in an orderly and relatively benign fashion. The economy could see what, under the circumstances, would be the best of all possible worlds: a lower dollar helping to support American exports, while foreign money continues to rush into the country'. For *The Economist* (2006), 'The world economy could well benefit from a gradual slide in the greenback. It would help to reduce global current-account imbalances and, by shifting production into America's tradable sector, would cushion the United States' economy as its housing bubble bursts'. The WB (2006, Chapter 1, p. 24) agrees that 'a soft landing remains likely... even though it may take several years beyond our medium-term projection period (2006–08) before the US current account deficit reaches sustainable levels'.

Others do worry, however, because broader systemic power shifts in the wake of financial and trade adjustments are likely. According to Menzie Chinn, writing for the Council on Foreign Relations:

> A cautionary note regarding America's current path is provided by Britain's loss of military and political primacy in the twentieth century; that development followed a shift from creditor to debtor status. Similarly, a prolonged decline in the dollar's value and increasing indebtedness will erode America's dominance in political and security spheres. These trends threaten the dollar's role as *the* global currency that facilitates international trade and finance, something the United States has gained immeasurably from over the years. A weaker dollar also reduces American leverage in international financial institutions such as the World Bank and International Monetary Fund. Finally, a diminished US currency means that each dollar's worth of military and development assistance has less impact at precisely the time when the nation faces the greatest challenges. Those threats we ignore at our own peril.

Such threats can only be made substantive, however, if popular international resistance to US-centred neo-liberalism picks up much more rapidly and decisively, corresponding with the US military's inclement defeat in Iraq and Afghanistan, the US neoconservative movement's overextension, the Latin American right-wing's loss of national power, the World Trade Organization's

(WTO) recent slide into irrelevance, and the International Monetary Fund's (IMF) troubles as one of the key global financial coordinators.

In a simplistic way, the WB's *Global Economic Prospects* for 2007 specified three upsides of 'the next wave of globalization':

> First is the growing economic weight of developing countries in the international economy, notably the emergence of new trading powerhouses such as China, India, and Brazil. Second is the potential for increased productivity that is offered by global production chains, particularly in services, arguably the most dynamic sector of trade today. Third is the accelerated diffusion of technology, made possible through falling communications costs and improved access to telecommunications and the Internet, as well as through innovative forms of business organization, often linked to foreign investment (WB, 2006, p. vii).

On the downside, the WB (2006, p.vii) continues that 'growing inequality, pressures in labor markets and threats to the global commons' which are not only 'evident in the current globalization' but 'are likely to become more acute. If these forces are left unchecked, they could slow or even derail globalization'. The Bank notes that threats from 'environmental damage, social unrest, or new increases in protectionist sentiment are potentially serious', in part because 'returns to skilled labor will continue to increase more quickly than those to unskilled labor, extending today's natural wage-widening tendencies evident in many, if not most, countries' (WB, 2006, p. vii, p. xxi). If so, making good on such threats to elite coalitions of neo-liberals and neoconservatives at the helm of the global institutions and nearly all national states will require much stronger approaches than an offer from ameliorative and thus far ineffectual centre-left 'Post-Washington Consensus' advocates as well as most Latin American governments. A more sustained, radical decommodification and deglobalization of capital is required.

Stagnation, Volatility and Uneven Development

Post-Keynesian economist David Felix (2003, p. 2) has succinctly addressed the overall economic policy problem, namely the US and global ruling elites' adoption – since the early 1980s – of a specific style of capitalism known as:

> ...neoliberalism, with financial market liberalization and heavy reliance on freely mobile international capital as its leading components. However, their adoption by the industrialized countries has been associated with

exchange rate misalignments, excessive debt leveraging, asset price bubbles, slower and more unstable output and employment growth, and increased income concentration; and additionally in the developing countries by more frequent financial crises, exacerbated by over-indebtedness that forces many of them to adopt pro-cyclical macroeconomic policies that deepen their output and employment losses.

Marxist political economists, in contrast, continue debating whether global capitalism and the imperial order are strong or weak. Judging by recent *Socialist Register* volumes, for example, divergent views continue over the nature of finance within the context of a slower-growing contemporary capitalism and more aggressive geopolitical and military imperialism. Harking back to an earlier debate between Rudolf Hilferding (1910) and Heinrich Grossmann (1929), some emphasize the power and coherence of finance within a restructuring, hegemonic capitalist economy; some the vulnerability and system-threatening contradictions associated with durable capitalist crisis, especially financial system fragility.

In the first category, Leo Panitch and Sam Gindin (2004, pp. 73–5) insist, 'Clinging to the notion of that the crisis of the 1970s remains with us today flies in the face of the changes that have occurred since the early 1980s'. Both Panitch and Gindin remind us correctly, that the 'opposition to [capitalism] is unable after three decades to mount any effective challenge', and hence their message is to redouble efforts to challenge 'neo-liberal and imperial legitimacy', rather than to expect or hope for 'any sudden collapse'. In the same spirit, Chris Rude (2004) provides a convincing statement of the way incidents like the 1997–8 Asian and Long Term Capital Management (LTCM) liquidity crises actually strengthened the system: 'Financial instability and the economic hardship that it creates play an essential role in reproducing capitalist and imperial social relations. The financial instability is functional. It disciplines world capitalism'. There is probably no more striking evidence of this than the 'Volcker shock' rise in the US interest rate in 1979, imposed by Federal Reserve chair Paul Volcker to halt inflation and in the process discipline labour, subsequently drawing the Third World inexorably into debt crisis, austerity, decline and conflict.

What, therefore, is the source, not only of recent economic volatility, but of the long slowdown in capitalist growth? The world's per capita annual GDP increase fell from 3.6 per cent during the 1960s, to 2.1 per cent during the 1970s, to 1.3 per cent during the 1980s to 1.1 per cent during the 1990s followed by a rise to 2.5 per cent for the first half of the 2000s (WB, 2005b, p. 297). GDP measures are notorious overestimates, especially since environmental degradation became more extreme from the mid 1970s, the point at which a typical 'genuine progress indicator' went into deficit.[1] We must also acknowledge the extremely uneven character of accumulation across the world, with some regions – especially Eastern Europe – having dropped vast proportions of their output during 1980s–1990s downturns.

In contrast to Panitch, Gindin and Rude, there have been several powerful statements about the 'crisis' faced by global – and especially the US – capital in restructuring production systems, social relations and geopolitics for the long haul of accumulation under the thumb of Washington's empire (Brenner, 2003; Harvey, 2003; Pollin, 2003; Wood, 2003). It would be tempting to draw upon sources like Volcker himself, who in 2004 publicly warned of a '75 percent chance of a financial crisis hitting the US in the next five years, if it does not change its policies'. As he told the *Financial Times*, 'I think the problem now is that there isn't a sense of crisis. Sure, you can talk about the budget deficit in America if you think it is a problem – and I think it is a big problem – but there is no sense of crisis, so no one wants to listen' (Tett, 2004).

From the standpoint of Marxian political economy, similar sentiments are regularly aired, based not only upon distorted US financial and trade accounts, but also underlying features of production, ecological destruction and social degradation. Yet amongst crisis theorists, disputes remain over the relative importance of:

- Class struggle (especially emanating from late 1960s Europe).
- International political conflict.
- Energy and other resource constraints (especially oil shortages), and
- The tendency to 'overaccumulation' (production of excess goods, beyond the capacity of the market to absorb).

For David Harvey (2003a), also writing in the *Socialist Register*, 'Global capitalism has experienced a chronic and enduring problem of overaccumulation since the 1970s'. Robert Brenner (2004) finds evidence of this problem insofar as 'costs grow as fast or faster in non-manufacturing than in manufacturing, but the rate of profit falls in the latter rather than the former, because the price increase is much slower in manufacturing than non-manufacturing. In other words, due to international overcapacity, manufacturers cannot raise prices sufficiently to cover costs'.

Whether this is a sufficient basis of proof has been disputed, for example by Giovanni Arrighi (2003) who observes 'a comparatively low, and declining, level of over-capacity', drawing upon official statistics. Such data are not terribly useful for measuring overaccumulation, however, because year-on-year capacity measurement does not take into account either the manner in which firms add or subtract capacity (e.g. *temporarily* mothballing factories and equipment) or the ways that overaccumulation problems are shifted/stalled into other sectors of the economy.[2] At the height of the West's devalorization stage of overaccumulation, during the 1980s, other political economists – Simon Clarke (1988, pp. 279–360), Harvey (1989, pp. 180–97) and Ernest Mandel (1989, pp. 30–58) – showed how deindustrialization and intensified uneven development were correlated to overaccumulation. Subsequently, evidence of the ongoing displacement of capitalist crisis to the Third World and via other sectors was documented by Harry Shutt (1999, pp. 34–45) and Robert Biel (2000, pp. 131–89).

Related debates unfold over what I take to be largely a *symptom* of capitalist crisis: declines in the corporate rate of profit during the 1970s–1990s. At first glance, the after-tax US corporate profit rate appeared to recover from 1984, nearly reaching 1960s–1970s highs (although it must be said that tax rates were much lower in the recent period). On other hand, interest payments remained at record high levels throughout the 1980s–1990s. By subtracting real (inflation-adjusted) interest expenses we have a better sense of net revenue available to the firm for future investment and accumulation, which remained far lower than earlier periods (Duménil and Lévy, 2003). Furthermore, we can trace, with the help of Gérard Duménil and Dominique Lévy (2003), the ways that US corporations responded to declining manufacturing-sector accumulation. Manufacturing revenues were responsible for roughly half of total (before-tax) corporate profits during the quarter-century post-war 'golden age', but fell to below 20 per cent by the early 2000s. In contrast, profits were soon much stronger in the financial sector (rising from the 10–20 per cent range during the 1950s–1960s to above 30 per cent by 2000) and in corporations' global operations (rising from 4–8 per cent to above 20 per cent by 2000).

We also know that since the Volcker shock changed the interest/profit calculus, there have been far more revenues accruing to capital based in finance than in the non-financial sector, to the extent that financiers doubled their asset base in relation to non-financial peers during the 1980s–1990s. Moreover, as Gerald Epstein and Dorothy Power (2002) document that rentier income doubled as a share of GDP from around 15 per cent during the 1960s to above 30 per cent for most of the 1980s–1990s. Many such trends continued into the 2000s, with low investment rates, high debt loads and bankruptcy threats to what were once some of the US' most powerful auto companies. Hence, restored profits for capital in general disguised the difficulty of extraction of surplus value, leaving most accumulation hollow, based increasingly upon financial and commercial activity rather than production. Although productivity increased and wage levels fell, we will see that the search for relative and absolute surplus value was augmented by profitability found outside the production process.

Indeed the primary problem for those wanting to measure and document the dynamics of capital accumulation in recent years has been the mix of extreme asset-price volatility and 'crisis displacement' that together make the tracking of valorization and devalorization terribly difficult. Volatility associated with ongoing financial processes and minimalist intrastate regulation is addressed later, but Harvey's (1999) analyses of spatio-temporal 'fixes' (not resolutions), and of systems of 'accumulation by dispossession' (Harvey, 2003a; 2003b), are also appealing as theoretical tools. They help explain why capitalist crisis do not automatically generate the sorts of payments-system breakdowns and mass core-capitalist unemployment problems witnessed on the main previous conjuncture of overaccumulation – the Great Depression.

Accumulation by Dispossession and 'Combined' Development

To be sure, the destruction associated with capitalist crisis tendencies – about which more information is offered in the next section – is accompanied by degradation in the form of spatio-temporal fixes and accumulation by dispossession. Investigating these problems, perhaps the most important intellectual challenges are, as Rosa Luxemburg (1968, pp. 452–3) wrote in her book, *The Accumulation of Capital*:

> [H]ow the right of ownership changes in the course of accumulation into appropriation of other people's property, how commodity exchange turns into exploitation and equality becomes class rule. The other aspect of the accumulation of capital concerns the relations between capitalism and the non-capitalist modes of production which start making their appearance on the international stage. Its predominant methods are colonial policy, an international loan system – a policy of spheres of interest – and war. Force, fraud, oppression, looting are openly displayed without any attempt at concealment, and it requires an effort to discover within this tangle of political violence and contests of power the stern laws of the economic process.

Are these early twentieth century problems still 'predominant' in the early twenty-first century? For Luxemburg (1968, p. 347), a principle concern was 'the deep and fundamental antagonism between the capacity to consume and the capacity to produce in a capitalist society, a conflict resulting from the very accumulation of capital which periodically bursts out in crises and spurs capital on to a continual extension of the market'. Simply put, 'Capital cannot accumulate without the aid of non-capitalist organizations, nor ...can it tolerate their continued existence side by side with itself. Only the continuous and progressive disintegration of non-capitalist organizations makes accumulation of capital possible'. The crisis tendencies, in turn, generate a renewed reliance upon 'primitive accumulation' which remains one of capitalism's persistent and permanent tactics (Perelman, 2000).

Following from these insights Harvey (2003a) has shown that an extreme form of accumulation by dispossession characterizes market penetration of non-capitalist spheres of life and nature, including:

> [C]ommodification and privatization of land and the forceful expulsion of peasant populations; conversion of various forms of property rights (common, collective, state, etc.) into exclusive private property rights; suppression of rights to the commons; commodification of labor power and the suppression of alternative (indigenous) forms of production and consumption; colonial, neocolonial and imperial processes of appropriation of assets (including natural resources)... and ultimately the credit system as radical means of primitive accumulation.

That these systems of dispossession today more explicitly integrate the sphere of reproduction – where much primitive accumulation occurs through unequal gender power relations – reflects a 'reprivatization' of life, as Isabella Bakker and Stephen Gill (2003) remarked. To illustrate the degradation faced by Africans, the denial of access to food, medicines, energy and even water is the most extreme result; people who are surplus to capitalism's labour requirements find that they must fend for themselves or die. The scrapping of safety nets in structural adjustment programmes worsens the vulnerability of women, children, the elderly and the disabled people. They are expected to survive with less social subsidy and greater pressure on the fabric of the family during economic crisis, which makes women more vulnerable to sexual pressures and, therefore, human immunodeficiency virus (HIV)/AIDS (Elson, 1991; Longwe, 1991). According to Dzodzi Tsikata and Joanna Kerr (2002), 'Mainstream economic policymaking fails to recognize the contributions of women's unpaid labor – in the home, in the fields, or in the informal market where the majority of working people in African societies function. It has been argued that these biases have affected the perception of economic activities and have affected economic policies in ways that perpetuate women's subordination'.

Even in relatively wealthy South Africa an early death for millions was the outcome of state and employer AIDS policy, with cost-benefit analyses demonstrating conclusively that keeping most of the country's 6.5 million HIV-positive people alive through patented medicines cost more than these people were 'worth'. In the case of the vast Johannesburg/London conglomerate Anglo-American Corporation, the cut-off for saving workers in 2001 was 12 per cent – the lowest-paid 88 per cent of employees were more cheaply dismissed once unable to work, with replacements found amongst

South Africa's 42 per cent unemployed reserve army of labour (Bond, 2005, Afterword). This is merely one aspect of what is now regularly termed labour's 'precarity' – albeit a life-and-death matter even if merely a cost-benefit calculation for the employer.

The imposition of neo-liberal policies in this spirit has amplified uneven and combined development across the world. In macroeconomic terms, the 'Washington Consensus' entails trade and financial liberalization, currency devaluation, lower corporate taxation, export-oriented industrial policy, austere fiscal policy aimed especially at cutting social spending and monetarism in central banking (with high real interest rates). In microdevelopmental terms, neo-liberalism implies not only three standard microeconomic strategies – (i) deregulation of business, (ii) flexibilized labour markets; and (iii) privatization (or corporatization and commercialization) of state-owned enterprises – but also the elimination of subsidies, the promotion of cost-recovery and user fees, the disconnection of basic state services to those who do not pay, means-testing for social programmes, and reliance upon market signals as the basis for local development strategies. As Gill has shown, enforcement is crucial, through both a 'disciplinary neo-liberalism' entailing constant surveillance, and a 'new constitutionalism' that locks in these policies over time. Of course, in terms of empirical data, these are notoriously difficult areas of political economy and political ecology to measure and to correlate with accumulation, but the connections should be obvious.

One additional feature of the degradation of 'non-capitalist' spheres of life must be flagged, namely the extent to which the ecological basis of life is becoming 'vulnerable'. For James O'Connor (1988), the standard responses to capitalism's 'primary contradiction' (crisis tendencies especially in the form of falling profits) have severe environmental implications, associated with a 'second contradiction'– 'when individual capitals attempt to defend or restore profits by cutting or externalizing costs, the unintended effect is to reduce the "productivity" of the conditions of production and hence to raise average costs'.

This problem emerges in part because when accumulation by dispossession as a capitalist strategy is applied to natural resources, ironically as an alleged 'market solution' to 'market problems' (such as pollution and global warming externalities), new crises invariably ensue. Elmar Altvater (2003) finds these strategies of ecological commodification 'highly doubtful because of the "limits to growth", the exhaustion of resources and sinks and because of military conflicts on resources ("new wars on resources") in Africa and Latin America and in the Middle East. Several wars have been waged on the domination over oil-territories and influences on the oil-price'. Water wars are said to be emerging as the twenty-first century equivalent of petro-related conflicts of the twentieth century. How serious have these socio-political-ecological problems become? For John Bellamy Foster (1998), 'the destruction of the planet in the sense of making it unusable for human purposes has grown to such an extent that it now threatens the continuation of much of nature, as well as the survival and development of society itself' (see Harvey, 1998 for a rebuttal).

There are many ways in which this threat plays out, but consider a few that relate to the super-exploitation of the Third World. According to Joan Martinez-Alier (2003), 'Ecologically unequal exchange is one of the reasons for the claim of the Ecological Debt. The second reason for this claim is the disproportionate use of Environmental Space by the rich countries'. In the first category, Martinez-Alier lists:

- Unpaid costs of reproduction or maintenance or sustainable management of the renewable resources that have been exported.
- Actualized costs of the future lack of availability of destroyed natural resources.
- Compensation for, or the costs of reparation (unpaid) of the local damages produced by exports (for example, the sulphur dioxide of copper smelters, the mine tailings, the harms to health from flower exports, the pollution of water by mining), or the actualized value of irreversible damage.
- (Unpaid) amount corresponding to the commercial use of information and knowledge on genetic resources, when they have been appropriated gratis ('biopiracy'). For agricultural genetic resources, the basis for such a claim already exists under the Food and Agricultural Organization's (FAO) Farmers' Rights.

In the second, he cites 'lack of payment for environmental services or for the disproportionate use of Environmental Space':

- (Unpaid) reparation costs or compensation for the impacts caused by imports of solid or liquid toxic waste.
- (Unpaid) costs of free disposal of gas residues (carbon dioxide (CO_2), chloroflurocarbon (CFCs), etc), assuming equal rights to sinks and reservoirs.

The sums involved are potentially vast. Biopiracy of wild seeds may be worth $66 billion each year to the US alone (Tandon, 2000). Other recent biopiracy cases include a diabetes drug produced by a Kenyan microbe; a Libyan/Ethiopian treatment for diabetes; antibiotics from a Gambian termite hill; an antifungal from a Namibian giraffe; an infection-fighting amoeba from Mauritius; a Congo (Brazzaville) treatment for impotence; vaccines from Egyptian microbes; multipurpose medicinal plants from the Horn of Africa; the South African and Namibian indigenous appetite suppressant *Hoodia*; and many others (McGown, 2006).

In the case of CO_2 emissions, according to Martinez-Alier (2003):

> Jyoti Parikh (1995) (a member of the UN International Panel on Climate Change) [argues that] if we take the present human-made emissions of carbon, the average is about one tonne per person per year... Let us take an average of $25: then a total annual subsidy of $75 billion is forthcoming from South to North.

Depletion of minerals and other non-renewable resources (including fisheries), dumping of toxics, biopiracy and excess use of the planet's CO_2 absorption capacity are merely some of the many ways that the South is being exploited by the North on the ecological front. The amounts involved would easily cover debt repayments.

To maintain 'combined' development between capitalism and non-capitalist spheres of life requires a strong coalition based upon several constituencies: neoconservative politics/culture and petro-military-industrial accumulation, plus the more general interests of financial/commercial capital termed the 'Washington Consensus' (Panitch and Gindin, 2003). Before turning to the political and strategic implications, especially in relation to sites of intense contradiction and politicization that follow from commodification and globalization, we should first review further recent evidence regarding destruction associated with one of the most contradictory facets of crisis displacement, namely financial instability.

Destruction through Financial Volatility

We begin this survey of how financial volatility has contributed to uneven development in the US. There, the manifestations of rising financial profitability simultaneous with relative manufacturing decline are varied, beginning with the past few years of massive deficit spending by the US, a form of military Keynesianism. But so too is consumer-Keynesianism via credit increasingly crucial, with household debt as a percentage of disposable income rising steadily from below 70 per cent prior to 1985, to above 100 per cent 15 years later.[3] On the one hand, there is no doubt that financial product innovations and especially new debt instruments associated with new information, communications and technology simply permit a greater debt load without necessarily endangering consumer finances. On the other hand, however, during the same period, household savings rates fell from the 7–12 per cent band to below 3 per cent.

Moreover, consumers and other investors are also more vulnerable to larger financial shocks and asset price swings than at any time since 1929. Although there were indications from around 1974 that major financial institutions would be affected by the onset of structural economic problems, few predicted the dramatic series of upheavals across major credit and investment markets over the subsequent quarter century: the Third World debt crisis (early 1980s for commercial lenders, but lasting through the present for countries and societies); energy finance shocks (mid 1980s); crashes of international stock (1987) and property (1991–3) markets; crises in nearly all the large emerging market countries (1995–2002); and even huge individual bankruptcies which had powerful international ripples. In 2006, South Africa, Turkey and Colombia suffered currency crashes against the euro of 25–33 per cent. Names of busted investors caught in financial-speculative gambles gone very sour (or simply corrupt) in derivatives, exotic stock market positions, currency trading, and bad bets on commodity futures and interest rate futures include Enron, Anderson Accounting, World Com, Tyco, LTCM, I G Metallgessellschaft, Orange County and Barings Bank.

In the biggest single crash till date, the US stock market built up an enormous bubble until early 2000, culminating in the bursting of the Dot Com bubble which wiped $8.5 trillion of paper wealth off the books from peak to trough. Optimists point to the Dow's increasing re-inflation since 2003 thanks to the return of household investors and mutual fund inflows, possibly rising further in future years if the Bush regime or a neo-liberal successor succeeds in privatizing social security. The implications of the 2000–2 crash are still important, however, because combined with the demographic trend towards baby-boomer retirement, the US financial system was left with substantial pension shortfalls. Moreover, household asset values also crashed when the share bubble burst, although fast-rising housing prices temporarily kept overall asset levels at a respectable level, at least for the wealthiest 60 per cent of US households who own their homes. This particular bubble was enhanced by the 1998 drop in interest rates – the Fed's response to the Asian and LTCM crises – which spurred a dramatic increase in mortgage re-financings. As a result of the huge rise in property prices that followed, the difference between the real cost of owning and of renting soared to unprecedented levels. The fact that the housing sector has contributed to roughly a third of US GDP growth since the late 1990s makes the real estate speculative bubble particularly worrisome. As the WB (2006, Chapter 1, p. 24) noted, 'By the third quarter of 2006, the contribution to growth of residential investment had swung from a strong 0.5 percentage points in 2005 to a strongly negative 1.1 percentage points'.

Another market that has taken off in a spectacular manner, and which may form the basis for more speculative investment in future, is energy derivatives.

The numbers of options and futures traded has risen steadily, but does not seem to have created a mature market in fields like electricity, gas and oil, as reflected in huge price fluctuations. A market in carbon emissions is also nascent but potentially enormous, given the ratification of Kyoto Protocol by Russia, which is aiming to convert its 'hot air' allowance of emissions into trades with the world's major polluters. Although the market for carbon crashed in May 2006 when emissions measurements in the European Trading System proved severely flawed, the amount of trade during the previous quarter reached $7.5 billion, up from an average $2.7 billion per quarter during 2005 (WB, 2006, p. 159).

Given the US dependence on imported oil, which rose in price from $12/barrel to more than $70/barrel over seven years following 1998 lows, the implications of this scale of speculation-driven price swing are devastating to the US trade deficit, which was already vast at 5 per cent of GDP. Moreover, the US current account deficit – trade plus financial inflows – meant much more penetration by foreign capital. As recently as the early 1980s, the US net asset position against the rest of the world was 5 per cent of GDP, but this reversed to negative 30 per cent within two decades.

Ironically, the power of the US to manipulate the economies of other countries, and lower the value of their exports, has not changed these ratios for the better. The US was the main beneficiary of East Asian countries' 50 per cent currency crash in 1997–8, as enormous capital flows entered the US banking system and as imports from East Asia were acquired at much lower prices, thus keeping in check what might otherwise have been credit-fuelled inflation. After the Dot Com boom was over in 2000, the US share of global foreign direct investment (FDI) fell substantially, even further than the declining US-sourced FDI elsewhere.

Where, then, would the US get its needed capital fixes, especially financial inflows to permit the payment of more than $2 billion each work day required for imports and debt repayments? The foreign inflows were quite volatile, but of greatest importance, perhaps, was the rapid rise in foreign – especially East Asian – ownership of aggregate US Treasury bills, from 20 per cent to 40 per cent over the course of a decade between the late 1990s and early 2000s. By 2005, foreign-owned assets within the US had overtaken US assets abroad by a vast 21 per cent (WB, 2006, p. 24).

This is important not because the supply side of capital market funding is in any way constrained, what with mid 2000s resources of $125 trillion to draw upon within global capital markets, and an additional $40 trillion in GDP each year contributing ongoing surpluses to the markets. The distribution of these funds in 2004 was notable, reflected by four major blocs of funds: the European Union (EU) ($43 trillion), the US ($41 trillion), Japan ($19 trillion) and the Asian emerging markets ($9 trillion). The stock of capital is invested in stock markets ($31 trillion), public bonds ($20 trillion), corporate securities ($31 trillion), and banks ($41 trillion), as well as foreign exchange reserves ($3 trillion). It should be evident that there is no shortage of liquid capital in the global markets, only a question of what rate of return will be required to maintain foreign interest in the US position.

All of this is especially interesting because of the recent stock market turmoil that, as noted above in the case of the US, devastated small investors and pensioners. From early 2000 through the first quarter of 2003, the global share index fell dramatically. The overall index for emerging markets did not fall as far as that of the Global North, given crashes not only on the Dow Jones but also declines of at least 33 per cent during 2002 alone in Finland, Germany, Greece, Ireland, the Netherlands and Sweden. Taken together with the 9/11 terrorism, these processes resulted in large-scale flows of mutual funds back to US corporate funds.

These financial dynamics, mainly measured in local currencies (and sometimes converted to purchasing power parity (PPP)), must also be considered in light of the extreme swings in the dollar's price against other currencies over the past decade. The $/yen appreciation from mid1995 to mid1998 was 82 per cent, and the subsequent crash was 30 per cent; the equivalent figures for the euro were a 63 per cent rise (mid1995 to late 2000) and a 36 per cent fall from late 2000–early 2004 (and indeed, a 57 per cent fall through late 2004). From 2004–6, another 15 per cent decline was recorded.

Indeed, as former US Labour Secretary – Robert Reich – predicted in September 2004, 'I see at some point a tipping point where East Asian banks that have been trying to prop up the dollar, maintaining their exports, because at some point it becomes a lousy investment' (Baxter, 2004). Former Treasury Secretary – Robert Rubin – accused the Bush administration of 'playing with fire' through its policies of dollar weakening alongside continuing federal deficit spending – a combination which would generate 'serious disruptions in our financial markets' (Simon, 2004).

These currency uncertainties remain crucial at the time of writing (the end of 2006). It is worth noting that new international debt securities issued in dollars have been substantially lower than those denominated in euros. The same trends appeared in 2001 in syndicated credit facilities. The July 2005 decision by the Chinese and Malaysian central banks to shift from the dollar as peg to a basket of currencies, while initially resulting in a minor (2.5 per cent) revaluation, may set the stage for the oft-heralded run. In the meantime, severe volatility has affected other markets, such as interest rate futures and options as well as over-the-counter trading, which have seen volume increase by up to 50 per cent, to levels in the tens of trillions of dollars during the early 2000s. Although the dollar will remain the preferred central bank reserve currency, the euro – which came into being only in January 2002 – is racing ahead in cash terms, surpassing the $760 billion in circulation in December 2006.

Because the US is not only vulnerable on its own monetary terms but also dangerous to those countries, like China, with increased dollar reserves, the devaluation of the dollar and the rise of US interest rates will reverberate far. According to the WB's *Global Development Finance* report in 2005:

> Historically, virtually every cyclical monetary policy turn in the United States over the past two decades has been accompanied by heightened volatility in emerging financial markets, with direct implications for the level and price of capital flows. The 1994 tightening cycle, which raised the Fed funds rate from 3 to 6 percent in just over a year, had particularly severe consequences, causing turmoil in financial markets and reducing global liquidity. On the other hand, the global monetary easing that began in the fall of 1998 helped end the 1997/98 round of crises (WB, 2005a, p. 53).

Extreme unevenness has adversely affected the middle-income emerging markets, with capital inflows falling during the 1997–8 Asian crisis, resulting in a net outflow of financial capital started in 1999, as $550 billion flooded out from 2000–3. The switch from mutual funds to far more speculative hedge fund interests in the emerging markets in 2001 was indicative of post-crisis financial market sentiment. Some countries – China, India and Malaysia – maintained stronger currency controls and hence, did far better during this period. But given the outflow, many emerging market economies themselves suffered extreme currency and stock market crashes during 2001–2, like Argentina, Venezuela, Brazil, South Africa, and Brazil especially hard hit.

There were particularly tumultuous sectors within the emerging markets, with energy, materials and luxury consumer goods growing rapidly, financial sector shares fluctuating, and telecommunications losing ground. Emerging market bonds have required high returns to attract foreign buyers, especially in Nigeria, Bulgaria, Ecuador, Panama, Peru, Russia and Venezuela. As for local bond returns, the interest rate spreads are sometimes stratospheric, such as in high-risk sites like Argentina, the Ivory Coast and the Dominican Republic. The dollar rates of return on general emerging market debt during the early 2000s, in international markets, were highest in Uruguay and Argentina, and lowest – indeed negative – in Brazil, Peru and the Dominican Republic. Naturally, the vast GDP growth and financial market expansion of China dominate the data and complicate maters. In the wake of a dramatic FDI decline in nearly all other developing countries during the early 2000s, China continued to attract $40–50 billion each year.

Hence we find amplified uneven development reflected in divergent patterns of financial stability and volatility in these emerging markets. One figure that signals perhaps the greatest danger for the Third World is capital outflow via unofficial routes, an especially severe problem since the mid 1990s in Asia (peaking at $100 billion in 1998), the Middle East ($50 billion in 1999) and Africa ($10 billion in 1998). Another factor reflecting potentially high risks is foreign indebtedness. Third World debt rose from $580 billion in 1980 to $2.4 trillion in 2002, and much of it is un-repayable. In 2002, there was a net outflow of $340 billion in servicing this debt, compared to overseas development aid of $37 billion. As Eric Toussaint (2004, p. 3) remarked, 'since 1980, over 50 Marshall Plans (over $4.6 trillion) have been sent by the peoples of the Periphery to their creditors in the Centre' (see also Toussaint, 2003). The 'Highly Indebted Poor Countries' debt relief concessions were small and came at the expense of deepened neo-liberal conditionality.

By 2005, Argentina and Nigeria represented compelling cases of, respectfully, a successful partial (70 per cent) default on international bonds and threatened repudiation of foreign debt driven by parliament and debt activists. By October 2005, Nigeria had 'won' debt cancellation following an agreement with Paris Club countries who owed $30 billion: Austria, Belgium, Brazil, Denmark, Finland, France, Germany, Italy, Japan, the Netherlands, the Russian Federation, Spain, Switzerland, the UK and the US. But there was a huge price: Nigeria, $6.3 billion in arrears, would first pay $12.4 billion in upfront payments. According to the leader of Nigeria's Jubilee network, Rev. David Ugolor:

> The Paris Club cannot expect Nigeria, freed from over 30 years of military rule, to muster $12.4 billion to pay off interest and penalties incurred by the military. Since the debt, by President Obasanjo's own admission, is of dubious origin, the issues of the responsibilities of the creditors must be put on the table at the Paris Club. As desirable as an exit from debt peonage is, it is scandalous for a poor debt distressed country, which cannot afford to pay $2 billion in annual debt service payments, to part with $6 billion up front or $12 billion in three months or even one year (Jubilee, USA, 2005).

In some cases, like Nigeria, emerging market countries' foreign reserves grew substantially so as to permit this extraordinary incident. But even in Mexico, which increased reserves from $6 billion in late 1994 at the peak of crisis to $60 billion a decade later, the reserves/GDP ratio remained relatively low at 9.4 per cent, near Brazil's. Emerging market countries with extremely healthy reserves during the mid 2000s included Malaysia (42 per cent of GDP), the Czech Republic, Thailand, China and South Korea. Malaysia did, however, suffer a raid on its reserves in 1998, which led to the government's prohibition of foreign trade in its local currency, proving that once hedge markets and other speculators turn against a country, no amount of reserves can help withstand a raid. The governments of Thailand and Korea lied about their reserves in the period prior to their crises, with the former buying forward dollar contracts and the latter keeping dollars in bankrupt banks. Only state intervention to define trading prerogatives – in the form of exchange controls – will staunch the flow.

Likewise, it is important to again raise the alternative to debt repayment: sovereign default. In prior epochs of financial globalization – the 1830, 1880s and 1930s – the prevailing conditions of international volatility and the Third World over-indebtedness led to sustained defaults, with a third of all debtor countries refusing to repay. The situation today is different insofar as centralized creditor cartelization via the Bretton Woods Institutions, make defaults against individual lenders or investors more difficult. Yet, given the failure in many Third World countries to undergird the ongoing rise in foreign debt with FDI (or local investment), the repayment problem may become severe once again, as US interest rates are forced upwards.

Finally, by way of reflecting on how financial volatility generates uneven development, it is worthwhile to consider a 1999 confession of Jeffrey Sachs (and co-author Steven Radelet), given his role in promoting financial liberalization in several Third World countries a decade ago:

> A final, and humbling lesson from the Asian predicament is that the world simply still does not understand financial crises very well. This crisis was almost completely unpredicted, even after all the research and commentary that followed the Mexico/Argentina crisis of 1994/95. We do not fully understand the preconditions for a crisis or the dynamics of capital withdrawals once they start taking place. The rapid development of new financial instruments, such as hedge funds, complicate the situation, since there is only a basic understand of systemic risks from these transactions. The best evidence of these dangers comes from the sudden collapse of LTCM in the United States. Unfortunately, financial crises in emerging markets are likely to be a recurring phenomena in coming years, the only questions being exactly where and when (Radelet and Sachs, 1999).

Is it time to more explicitly ask the same kinds of questions on the Left? To be sure, Panitch and Gindin (2004, p. 74) are correct that 'We must dispense with a notion of "crisis" as something that leads capitalism to unravel on its own; our theories of crisis must be politicized to integrate the responses of both states and class actors'. Hence, within this crisis-ridden context of uneven financial power and vulnerability, a crucial issue for progressive strategists and activists is whether the political balance of forces might adjust to permit the sorts of national-sovereign defaults, influenced by popular anti-capitalist forces, which were in previous epochs central to the task of resisting imperial financial power, followed by a broader agenda of decommodifying resources and, to the extent that it is logical to deglobalize capital.

Resistance via Decommodification/Deglobalization

What, finally, are the strategic implications for contemporary anti-capitalist activism? To the extent to which capitalist crisis displacement, financial volatility and accumulation by dispossession in the eco-social spheres, as described above, are based upon commodification and globalization, struggles for decommodification and deglobalization of capital should have our attention. Will Karl Polanyi's (1957) 'double movement' reassert itself, both through the rejection of market power in many areas of life and nature, and in the reduction of the scope and scale – globalization – through which capital exerts itself?

Here, we can turn to activism in the Global South for guidance, in part because it is in especially middle-income, semi-peripheral countries that commodification and capitalist globalization are most fiercely experienced, and most actively resisted. Consider – in no particular order – the recent waves of labour strikes, popular mobilizations for AIDS-treatment and other health services, illegal reconnections of water/electricity, land and housing occupations, anti-genetically modified organism (GMO) and pro-food security campaigns, women's organizing, municipal budget campaigns, student and youth movements, community resistance to displacements caused by dam construction and the like, anti-debt and reparations movements, environmental justice struggles, immigrants' rights campaigns, political movements to seize state power, etc, etc. These are not purely scenes that occur outside the realm of state politics, for in many Latin American sites, mass-popular initiatives have changed governments through votes and protests. Overall, the last quarter century since the onset of neo-liberalism, and especially the last decade, witnessed a formidable upsurge of unrest: 1980s–1990s IMF riots, high-profile indigenous people's protests since Zapatismo in 1994, global justice activism since Seattle in 1999, the Social Forum movement since 2001, globally coordinated anti-war demos since 2001, autonomist protests and the Latin American left's revival. In the process, the most serious activists are crossing borders, races, classes and political traditions in sector after sector: land (Via Campesino), health care (International Peoples Health Council), free schooling (Global Campaign for Education), water (the People's World Water Forum), energy/climate change (the Durban Declaration), debt (Jubilee South), democratic development finance (International Financial Institutions (IFIs)-Out! and WB Bonds Boycott), trade (Our World is Not for Sale) and so on.

What we encounter on the global stage, in my opinion, are roughly five coherent ideological actors which we can term, from left to right: (i) Global Justice Movements, (ii) Third World Nationalism, (iii) the Post-Washington Consensus, (iv) the Washington Consensus, and (iv) the Resurgent Right-wing. These correspond, respectively, to traditions of socialism and anarchism; *national* capitalism; a lite version of social democracy; neo-liberalism; and neoconservatism. Table 1 considers their agendas, institutional bases, internal contradictions and disputes, and some exemplary personalities associated with the five ideologies.

For activists, what strategies are most appropriate given the circumstances and this array of forces? Some in the Global Justice Movements insist that autonomist independence is the objective; some posit that this is the era of global governance influenced by global civil society; while others consider these as seed-bed struggles for socialism, starting locally but building to national, regional and international scales when the power relations are less adverse (my own position). Although this is not the optimal site for such a debate, it is fairly obvious that in Chiapas, Zapatismo has ended its localist project and moved to a national agenda, in alliance with other indigenous and progressive movements. Argentine factory occupations appear to have hit their maximum autonomist strength at the stage of roughly 200 sites and 15,000 participants. Brazilian landless activists are reformulating critiques of the national state, in the wake of the betrayal by the Workers Party, but making yet more militant demands for state services such as interventions against major landowners and grid connections to water and electricity services for their occupied lands. Johannesburg's Anti-Privatization Forum and its affiliates — sometimes identified as autonomist because of their reconnection of electricity — have recently debated the adoption of an explicitly socialist manifesto. Autonomism may, hence, be at the point of exhaustion as a scale politics, potentially to be renewed by more national-scale political initiatives.

In contrast, for those who would posit a global-reform project, the main hope appears to be the Millennium Development Goals (MDGs) in particular, and the United Nations (UN) as a vehicle for global governance more generally. Yet the UN's drift away from serving the interests of poor people, into the circuit of global neo-liberal power, is obvious. The UN's 1991–2003 sanctions against Iraq and its endorsement of the illegal US occupation on 22 May 2003 were also a source of great concern to peace activists. Subsequent attempts to democratize the UN Security Council (UNSC) appear stalled, or watered down to the point of uselessness. Most striking is the list of mid 2000s multilateral system managers, who fuse neo-liberalism and neoconservatism as in no other period in modern history:

- The EU chose Spanish neoconservative – Rodrigo Rato – as IMF managing director in mid 2004.
- The new head of United Nations Children's (Emergency) Fund (UNICEF), chosen in January 2005, was Bush's agriculture minister Ann Veneman, although the US and Somalia are the only two out of 191 countries which refused to ratify the UN Convention on the Rights of the Child.
- For another key UN post in February 2005, the outgoing neo-liberal head of the WTO, Supachai Panitchpakdi from Thailand (who served the US and the EU interests from 2003–5), was chosen to lead the United Nations Conference on Trade and Development (UNCTAD).
- Paul Wolfowitz – the architect of the illegal US/UK/Coalition of the Willing war against Iraq – was appointed by Bush to head the WB in March 2005.
- The EU's hardline trade negotiator – Pascal Lamy – won the directorship of the WTO a few weeks after that; and
- To ensure that Washington's directives to the UN continued to be as explicit as possible, Bush appointed John Bolton as US Ambassador in mid 2005, and although he departed in December 2006, his replacement will have the same bullying mandate.
- Neo-liberal former WB spokesperson – Mark Malloch-Brown – took up a central job in Kofi Annan's office.
- Neoconservative US State Department official – Christopher Burnham – became UN undersecretary-general for management.
- Another State Department official and former *Washington Times* editor – Josette Sheeran – was made director of the UN World Food Programme in spite of dubious links for 20 years with Rev. Sun Myung Moon's Unification Church.

In sum, it appears that multilateral institutions – not just the Bretton Woods and WTO but also the UN System – are incapable of moving to a reform agenda, given the power of hard-right forces. In this context, the UN MDGs as a campaigning handle require detailed consideration, because of their 2005 adoption by global campaigns such as – Make Poverty History, Live 8 rock concerts and the Global Call for Action Against Poverty (GCAP). No one would object to the broad goals, of course: eradicate extreme poverty and hunger; achieve universal primary education; promote gender equality; reduce child mortality; improve maternal health; control HIV/AIDS, malaria and other diseases; ensure environmental sustainability; and develop a global partnership for development. Yet, the MDG process and the concrete strategies for achieving these objectives – including privatization of basic services such as water and electricity – may do more harm than good.

To be sure, there may be some benefits associated with the globally-constituted, universal objectives. As Peggy Antrobus (2003) the founder of Development Alternatives with Women for a New Era (DAWN) remarks, 'Viewed within the context of "the new aid agenda", the MDGs provide a common framework agreed to by all governments with measurable targets and indicators of progress, around which governments, UN agencies, International Financial Institutions and civil society alike could rally'. They permit at least notional accountability for donor agencies and states, which civil society activists are already pointing to – adorned with white wrist and headbands – as a guilt trip reminder. However, speaking the language of many feminists and social justice activists, Antrobus is blunt:

> I do not believe in the MDGs. I think of them as a Major Distraction Gimmick. To the extent that all the goals relate to the role of the state, one must ask how feasible it is that states weakened by the requirements of policy frameworks of neo-liberalism and whose revenues are reduced by privatization and trade liberalism can be expected to achieve the goals and targets of the MDGs?

Central to MDGs political economy is that the Bretton Woods Institutions and WTO – acting mainly for G8 governments and corporations – appear intent upon bringing ever more aspects of life under the rules of commodification, attributing market values to society and nature. Hence, as the UN itself admits, 'International Monetary Fund program design has paid almost no systematic attention to the goals when considering a country's budget or macroeconomic framework'. A 2005 UN report complains that 'In the vast number of country programmes supported by the IMF since the adoption of the goals, there has been almost no discussion about whether the plans are consistent with achieving them'. The report documents how budget constraints prevent scaling up sectoral strategies for some of the MDGs, and that in some cases, 'countries are advised not to even to consider such scaled-up plans' by the Bretton Woods Institutions (Waruru, 2005). UN Habitat's (2005) website also admits 'the common criticism of MDG as a "top-down" process, which excludes Local Authority and other stakeholders' involvement... There is, thus, an inherent danger that even if the targets are achieved, the inequalities within a nation across people and places would still persist'.

In short, the MDGs are not an optimal site for serious activism, in part because they are subject to both the processes identified earlier as central to capitalist crisis-displacement, commodification and globalization. Indeed, given the power structures, the militarism and the neo-liberal processes that are continually reinforced in the UN, why not let it instead 'go the way of the League of Nations', as Tariq Ali (2003) advocates?

That would leave two other mutually-reinforcing approaches to try at this present stage, ahead of a future effort to rebuild genuine democratic global governance when the conditions are more amenable: 'decommodification' and 'deglobalization' (Bello, 2002). It should not require pointing out that by use of this latter word, no one intends the revival of autarchic experiences (last century's Albania, Burma or North Korea) or corrupt Third World chaos (contemporary Zimbabwe) or authoritarianism (Malaysia). The strategic formula which, amongst other movements, South African progressives have broadly adopted – internationalism combined with demands upon the national state to 'lock capital down' (Bond, 2003) – could begin by removing the boot of the Bretton Woods Institutions from Third World necks, as an example of what must be done. The WB Bonds Boycott is having remarkable success in defunding the institution that is most often at the coalface of neo-liberal repression across the Third World (Bond, 2006a, Chapter 12). In addition, South Africans and other activists have won dramatic victories in deglobalizing the Trade Related Intellectual Property Rights (TRIPS) regime, by demanding and winning generic anti-retroviral medicines instead of branded, monopoly-patented drugs. Similar struggles are underway to deglobalize food, especially transnational corporate GMOs, to halt biopiracy, and to kick out the water and energy privatizers. These are typically 'non-reformist reforms' insofar as they achieve concrete goals and simultaneously link movements, enhance consciousness, develop the issues and build democratic organizational forms and momentum. If properly constructed, they would have explicitly liberatory gender/race/nation components, and incorporate both red and green values so as to assure the connectivity and mutual reinforcement of 'militant particularist' struggles.

As for the scale of the non-reformist reform struggles, the most important challenge is achieving 'subsidiarity': i.e., determining whether local community, subnational, national or regional strategies can best mitigate and reverse global economic tyranny for particular issues. This, too, is crucial for a 'web of life' bio-social understanding of where interventions have to occur. Some eco-political interventions – such as contesting global warming – will have to be internationally coordinated, but many can and must first be addressed within national and regional scalar contexts. Overall, the main reason to deglobalize is to gain space to fight neo-liberal commodification.

To illustrate, the South African decommodification agenda entails struggles to turn basic needs into genuine human rights, and invariably there are international corporations or the WB/IMF/WTO standing squarely in the way. Recent and ongoing campaigns which both decommodify and deglobalize include: free anti-retroviral medicines to fight AIDS (hence disempowering Big Pharma); 50 litres of free water per person per day (hence ridding Africa of Suez and other water privatizers); 1 kilowatt hour of free electricity for each individual everyday (hence reorienting energy resources from export-oriented mining and smelting, to basic-needs consumption); extensive land reform (hence de-emphasizing cash cropping and export-oriented plantations); prohibitions on service disconnections and evictions; free education (hence halting the General Agreement on Trade in Services (GATS)); and the like. A free 'Basic Income Grant' allowance of $15/month is even advocated by churches, non-governmental organizations (NGOs) and trade unions. All such services should be universal (open to all, no matter income levels), and to the extent feasible, financed through higher prices that penalize luxury consumption. This potentially unifying agenda – far superior to MDGs, in part because the agenda reflects real, durable grassroots struggles across the world – could serve as a basis for wide-scale social change, in the manner that Gosta Esping-Andersen (1991) has discussed with respect to the Scandinavian social policy.

It is impossible to say where and how far these initiatives and movements will proceed before they either accomplish their goals or are defeated. But because the commodification of everything is still underway, this could provide the basis for a unifying agenda for a wide-scale movement for fundamental social change, if linked to the demand to 'rescale' many political-economic responsibilities that are now handled by embryonic world-state institutions under the influence of neo-liberal US administrations. The decommodification principle could become an enormous threat to imperial capitalist interests, in the form of a denial of private intellectual property (such as AIDS medicines), resistance to biopiracy, the exclusion of genetically modified (GM) seeds from African agricultural systems, the nationalization of industries and utilities, or the empowerment of African labour forces. To make any progress, delinking from the most destructive circuits of global capital will also be necessary, combining local decommodification strategies and tactics with the call to de-fund and then close the WB, IMF and WTO. Beyond that, the challenge for progressive forces, as ever, is to establish the difference between 'reformist reforms' and reforms that advance a 'non-reformist' agenda. The latter would include generous social policies stressing decommodification, and capital controls and more inward-oriented industrial strategies allowing democratic control of finance and ultimately of production itself. These sorts of reforms – which follow from the fight against degradation and destruction associated with neo-liberalism – would strengthen democratic movements, directly empower the producers, and, over time, open the door to the contestation of capitalism itself.

Five International Ideological Currents, 2007

Political Current	Global Justice Movements	Third World Nationalism	Post-Wash. Consensus	Washington Consensus	Resurgent Right-wing
Tradition	socialism, anarchism	*national capitalism*	(lite) social democracy	neo-liberalism	neo-conservatism
Main agenda	'deglobalization' of *capital* (not of *people*); 'globalization-from-below' and international solidarity; anti-war; anti-racism; indigenous rights; women's liberation; ecology; 'decommodified' state services; radical participatory democracy	increased (but fairer) global integration via reform of inter-state system, based on debt relief and expanded market access; reformed global governance; regionalism; rhetorical anti-imperialism; and Third World unity	fix 'imperfect markets'; add 'sustainable development' to existing capitalist framework via UN and similar global state-building; promote a degree of global Keynesianism; oppose US unilateralism and militarism	rename neo-liberalism (PRSPs, HIPC, PPPs) with provisions for 'transparency', self-regulation and bail-out mechanisms; co-opt potential emerging-market resistance; offer financial support for US-led empire	unilateral petro-military imperialism; crony deals, corporate subsidies, protectionism and tariffs; reverse globalization of people via racism and xenophobia; religious extremism; patriarchy and bio-social power
Leading institutions	Social movements; environmental justice activists; indigenous people; autonomists; radical activist networks; leftist labour movts; liberation theology; radical think-tanks (e.g., Focus on the Global South, Global Exchange, IBASE, IFG, IPS, Nader centres, TNI); radical media (*GreenLeft Weekly*, Indymedia Pacifica, Pambazuka, zmag.org); semi-liberated zones (Bolivaran projects, Kerala); sector-based or	Non-Aligned Movement (NAM), G77 and South Centre; self-selecting regimes (often authoritarian): Argentina, Brazil, China, Egypt, India, Indonesia, Kenya, Libya, Malaysia, Nigeria, Pakistan, Palestine, Russia, South Africa, Turkey, Uganda, Zimbabwe with a few – Bolivia, Cuba, Ecuador and Venezuela – that lean left; *AlJazeera*, supportive	some UN agencies (e.g., UNICEF, Unifem, Unrisd, Wider); some INGOs (e.g., Care, Civicus, IUCN, Oxfam, TI); large enviro. groups (e.g., Sierra and WWF); big labour (e.g., ICFTU and AFL-CIO); liberal foundations (Carnegie, Ford, MacArthur, Mott, Open Society, Rockefeller); Columbia U. economics department;	US state (Fed, Treasury, USAid); corporate media, IT and financiers; WB, IMF, WTO; elite clubs (Bilderburgers, Trilateral Commission, World Economic Forum); some UN agencies (UNDP, UNCTAD, Global Compact); universities and think-tanks (U. of Chicago economics, Cato, Council on Foreign Relations, Adam Smith Inst., Inst. of International Economics, Brookings); BBC,	Republican Party populist and libertarian wings; Project for a New American Century; right wing think-tanks (AEI, CSIS, Heritage, Manhattan); Christian Right institutions and media; petro-military complex and industrial firms; the Pentagon; right-wing media (Fox, *National Interest*, *Weekly Standard*, *Washington Times*); proto-fascist European parties - but also

Political Current	Global Justice Movements	Third World Nationalism	Post-Wash. Consensus	Washington Consensus	Resurgent Right-wing
	local coalitions in the World Social Forum	NGOs (e.g., Seatini, Third World Network)	the Socialist International; Norway	CNN and Sky; most of G8	Zionism and Islamic extremism
Internal disputes	role of state; party politics; fix-it vs nix-it for int'l agencies; gender and racial power relations; divergent interests (e.g., Northern labour or environment vs Southern sovereignty and indigenous rights); tactics (e.g., merits of symbolic property destruction)	degree of militancy versus the North; divergent regional interests; religion; large vs small countries; internecine rivalries	some look left (for alliances) while others look right to the Wash. Consensus (in search of resources, legitimacy and deals); which reforms are optimal	Differing reactions to US empire due to divergent national-capitalist interests and domestic political dynamics	Disputes over US imperial reach, religious influence, and how to best protect culture, patriarchy, and state sovereignty
Exemplary proponents	**POLITICAL SOCIETY:** R Alarcon, F Castro, H Chavez, R Correa, E Morales **CIVIL SOCIETY:** C Abugre, Z Achmat, E Adamovsky, M Albert T Ali, S Amin, C Augiton, D Barsamian, A Ben-Bela, M Barlow, H Belafonte, W Bello, A Bendana, M Benjamin, P Bennis, F Betto, H Bonafini, A Boron, J Bove, J Brecher, R Brenner, D Brutus, N Bullard, A Buzgalin, L Cagan, A Callinicos, L Cassarini, J Cavanagh, C Chalmers, N Chomsky, T Clarke, K Danaher, M Davis, D Dembele, A Dorfman, A Escobar, L Flanders, R Fisk, E Galeano, G Galloway, S Gill, S George, D Glover, A Goodman, M P Giyose, A Grubacic, M Hardt, D Harvey D Henwood, J Holloway, W Kaara, B Kagarlitsky, J Kelsey, N Klein, J LeCarré, S Longwe, M Lowy, M	**POLITICAL SOCIETY:** J Aristide, M Gaddafi, J N Kirshner, R Mugabe, D Ortega, V Putin **CIVIL SOCIETY:** Y Akyuz, Y Graham, M Khor, Y Tandon	**POLITICAL SOCIETY:** M Bachelet, G Brundtland, S Byers, J Fischer, W Maathai. T Mkandawire M Robinson G Verhofstadt K Watkins **CIVIL SOCIETY:** A Adedeji, N Birdsall Bono B Cassen, P Eigen, B Geldof, A Giddens, W Hutton, P Krugman, K Naidoo, D Rodrik, J Sachs, W Sachs, A Sen, G Soros, N Stern, J Stiglitz, J Sweeney	**POLITICAL SOCIETY:** B Bernanke, T Blair, G Brown, M Camdessus, E Cardoso, J Chirac, H Clinton, K Dervis, L daSilva, V Fox, S Fischer, A Greenspan, A Krueger, P Lamy, M Malloch-Brown, T Mbeki, A Merkel, H Poulson, R Prodi, S Royal, M Singh, P Supachai. **CIVIL SOCIETY:** B Clinton, T Friedman, W Gates, H Kissinger, K	**POLITICAL SOCIETY:** E Abrams, K Adelman, G W Bush, D Cheney, R Gates, N Gingrich, J Haider, S Harper, J Howard, Z Khalilzad, B Ki-moon, I Paisley, J M le Pen, J Negroponte, E Olmert, R Rato, O Reich, C Rice, K Rove, A Scalia, R Tobias, A Veneman, P Wolfowitz **CIVIL SOCIETY:** Z Brzezinski, P Buchanan, A Colter, J Falwel, H

Political Current	Global Justice Movements	Third World Nationalism	Post-Wash. Consensus	Washington Consensus	Resurgent Right-wing
	Mamdani Marcos, A Mittal, G Monbiot, M Moore, L Nacpil, R Nader, V Navarro, A Negri, T Ngwane, N Njehu, A Olukoshi, O Ongwen, G Palast, L Panitch, M Patkar, J Perkins, J Pilger, A Roy, E Sader, D Sari, J Sen, C Sheehan, V Shiva, I Shivji, J Singh, B Sousa Santos, W Soyinka, A Starr, J Stedile, H Sumnono, T Teivainen, A Traoré, V Vargas, H Wainwright, N WaThiong'o, L Wallach, I Wallerstein, P Waterman, M Weisbrot, R Weissman, C Whitaker, E Wood, H Zinn			Rogoff, M Yunus	Kissinger, W Kristol, R Limbaugh, R Murdoch, G Norquist, M Peretz, R Perle, R Scaife

Notes

1. http://www.redefiningprogress.org.
2. Brenner (2004) insists that such statistics cover merely short-term fluctuations, and the more rigorous indicators of overaccumulation are not yet available in any data series. For a study of Zimbabwe, I constructed a proxy based on inventory stocks drawn from the manufacturing sector in the annual (quite reliable) Census of Industrial Production series, and thus documented overaccumulation problems emerging during the 1970s (Bond 1998, Chapters 5–6).
3. Unless otherwise noted, all statistics in this section are from the International Monetary Fund's *World Economic Outlook* reports, various issues.

References

Ali, T. 2003. 'Business as Usual', *The Guardian*, May 24.
Altman, D. 2006. 'As the Dollar Falls, Some Dominoes Don't', *The New York Times*, December 10.
Altvater, E. 2003. 'Is there an Ecological Marxism?' Lecture at the Virtual University of Consejo Latinoamericano de las Ciencias Sociales, http://www.polwiss.fu-berlin.de/people/altvater/Aktuelles/EcologicalMarx.pdf.
Antrobus, P. 2003. 'Presentation to Working Group on the MDGs and Gender Equality', UNDP Caribbean Regional Millennium Development Goals (MDGs) Conference, Barbados, July 7.

Arrighi, G. 2003. 'The Social and Political Economy of Global Turbulence', *New Left Review*, March-April.
Bakker, I. and Gill, S. (eds.), 2003. *Power, Production and Social Reproduction*. Basingstoke: Palgrave.
Bank for International Settlements. 2006. *75th Annual Report*, Basel.
Baxter, J. 2004. 'US Dollar Heading for a Collapse, Ex-Clinton Adviser Says', *Vancouver Sun*, September 25.
Bello, W. 2002. *Deglobalization: Ideas for a New World Economy*. London: Zed Books.
Biel, R. 2000. *The New Imperialism*. London: Zed Books.
Bond, P. 1998. *Uneven Zimbabwe: A Study of Finance, Development and Underdevelopment*. Trenton, Africa: World Press.
—. 2003. *Against Global Apartheid*. London: Zed Books.
—. 2005. *Elite Transition: From Apartheid to Neoliberalism in South Africa*, Afterword to the 2nd edition. Pietermaritzburg: University of KwaZulu-Natal Press.
—. 2006a. *Talk Left, Walk Right: South Africa's Frustrated Global Reforms*. London: Merlin Books and Pietermaritzburg: University of KwaZulu-Natal Press.
Brenner, R. 2003. *The Boom and the Bubble*. London: Verso.
—. 2004. Personal communication, November 9.
Clarke, S. 1988. *Keynesianism, Monetarism and the Crisis of the State*. Aldershot: Edward Elgar.
Duménil, G. and Lévy, D. 2003. 'Costs and Benefits of Neoliberalism: A Class Analysis', Unpublished paper, Cepremap, Paris.
Eichengreen, B. 2006. 'The Blind Men and the Elephant', *Issues in Economic Policy* 1, Washington: The Brookings Institution, January.
Elson, D. 1991. 'The Impact of Structural Adjustment on Women: Concepts and Issues', in Onimode, B. (ed.), *The IMF, the World Bank and the African Debt*. London: Zed Books.
Epstein, G. and Power, D. 2002. 'The Return of Finance and Finance's Returns: Recent Trends in Rentier Incomes in OECD Countries, 1960-2000'. University of Massachusetts Political Economy Research Instiute Research Brief 2002-2: Amherst, November.
Esping-Andersen, G. 1991. *The Three Worlds of Welfare Capitalism*. Princeton: Princeton University Press.
Felix, D. 2003, 'The Past as Future? The Contribution of Financial Globalization to the Current Crisis of Neo-Liberalism as a Development Strategy,' Paper presented to the conference New Pathways for Mexico's Sustainable Development, Mexico City: El Colegio de Mexico Department of Economics, September 2.
Foster, J. B. 1998. 'The Scale of our Ecological Crisis', 'Rejoinder to Harvey', *Monthly Review* 49, April 11.
Gill, S. 2003. *Power and Resistance in the New World Order*. Basingstoke: Palgrave Macmillan.
Grossmann, H. 1992 [1929]. *The Law of Accumulation and Breakdown of the Capitalist System*. London: Pluto Press.
Harvey, D. 1998. 'Marxism, Metaphors, and Ecological Politics', *Monthly Review* 49, April 11.
—. 1989. *The Condition of Postmodernity*. Oxford: Basil Blackwell.
—. 1999 [1982]. *The Limits to Capital*. London: Verso.
—. 2003a. 'The "New" Imperialism: On Spatio-temporal Fixes and Accumulation by Dispossession' in Panitch, L. and Leys, C. (eds.), *The New Imperial Challenge: Socialist Register 2004*, London: Monthly Review Press.

—. 2003b. *The New Imperialism*. Oxford and New York: Oxford University Press.
Hilferding, R. 1981[1910]. *Finance Capital*. London: Routledge and Kegan Paul.
International Monetary Fund. *World Economic Outlook*, various issues, Washington, http://www.imf.org.
Jubilee USA. 2005. 'Nigerian Threat to Repudiate Helps Force Paris Club to Deliver Debt Cancellation', Press Release, Washington, October 20. http://www.jubileeusa.org/index.php
Longwe, S. 1991. 'The Evaporation of Policies for Women's Advancement,' in Heyzer, N. et al. (eds.), *A Commitment to the Worlds Women*, New York: UNIFEM.
Luxemburg, R. 1968 [1923]. *The Accumulation of Capital*. New York: Monthly Review.
Mandel, E. 1989. 'Theories of Crisis: An Explanation of the 197482 Cycle', in Gottdiener, M. and Komninos, N. (eds.), *Capitalist Development and Crisis Theory: Accumulation, Regulation and Spatial Restructuring*, London: Macmillan.
Martinez-Alier, J. 2003. 'Marxism, Social Metabolism and Ecologically Unequal Exchange', Paper presented at Lund University Conference on World Systems Theory and the Environment, September 19–22.
McGown, J. 2006. 'Out of Africa: Mysteries of Access and Benefit Sharing', Edmonds Washington, the Edmonds Institute and Johannesburg, the African Centre for Biosafety.
O'Connor, J. 1988. 'Capitalism, Nature, Socialism: A Theoretical Introduction', *Capitalism Nature Socialism*, 1, 1.
Panitch, L. and Gindin, S. 2003. 'Global Capitalism and American Empire' in Panitch, L. and Leys, C. (eds.), *The New Imperial Challenge: Socialist Register 2004*, London: Merlin Press.
—. 2004. 'Finance and American Empire', in Panitch, L. and Leys, C. (eds.), *The Empire Reloaded: Socialist Register 2005*, London: Merlin Press.
Parikh, J. K. 1995. 'Joint Implementation and the North and South Cooperation for Climate Change, International Environmental Affairs, 7, 1.
Perelman, M. 2000. *The Invention of Capitalism: Classical Political Economy and the Secret History of Primitive Accumulation*. Durham: Duke University Press.
Polanyi, K. 1957. *The Great Transformation: The Political and Economic Origins of Our Time*. Boston: Beacon.
Pollin, R. 2003. *Countours of Descent: US Economic Fractures and the Landscape of Global Austerity*. London: Verso.
Radelet, S. and Sachs, J. 1999. 'What Have We Learned, So Far, From the Asian Financial Crisis?' Cambridge: Harvard Institute for International Development CAER II Discussion Paper 37.
Rude, C. 2004. 'The Role of Financial Discipline in Imperial Strategy', in Panitch, L. and Leys, C. (eds.), *The Empire Reloaded: Socialist Register 2005*. London: Merlin Press.
Shutt, H. 1999. *The Trouble with Capitalism*. London: Zed Books.
Simon, E. 2004. 'Weak Dollar Boosts Some Corporate Growth', *AP Business News*, November 11.
Tandon, Y. 2000. 'FDI, Globalization, UNCTAD and Human Development', Malaysia, Third World Network, http://www.globalpolicy.org/socecon/develop/devthry/well-being/2000/tandon.htm
Tett, G. 2004. 'The Gospel According to Paul', *Financial Times*, October 23.
The Economist (2006) 'The Falling Dollar', November 30.

Toussaint, E. 2003. *Your Money or Your Life. The Tyranny of Global Finance.* London: Pluto Press.
—. 2004. 'Transfers from the Periphery to the Centre, from Labor to Capital', Unpublished paper, Brussels: Committee for the Abolition of the Third World Debt.
Tskikata, D. and Kerr, J. 2002. *Demanding Dignity: Women Confronting Economic Reforms in Africa.* Ottawa: The North-South Institute.
UN Habitat, 'Urban Management Programme', Website http://hq.unhabitat.org/cdrom/ump/CD/about.html accessed 7 July 2005.
Waruru, W. 2005. 'IMF, World Bank Come Under Heavy Criticism', *The East African Standard* (Nairobi), January 18.
Wood, E. 2003. *Empire of Capital.* London: Verso.
World Bank. 2005a. *Global Development Finance 2005.* Washington.
—. 2005b. *World Development Report 2006.* Washington.
—. 2006. *Global Economic Prospects 2007.* Washington.

Chapter 7

THE EROSION OF NON-CAPITALIST INSTITUTIONS AND THE REPRODUCTION OF CAPITALISM

David M Kotz

Introduction

More than 150 years ago, in *The Communist Manifesto*, Marx and Engels observed that capitalism has a powerful tendency to destroy pre-capitalist relations and institutions:

> The bourgeoisie, wherever it has got the upper hand, has put an end to all feudal, patriarchal, idyllic relations. It has pitilessly torn asunder the motley feudal ties that bound man to his 'natural superiors'... (Marx and Engels, 1848, p. 475)

Since those words were written, the continuing history of capitalism has borne them out. The vigorous accumulation process that capitalism gives rise to has continued to erode non-capitalist institutions. Feudal and semi-feudal relations throughout the world have, over time, dissolved under the pressure of capitalist penetration. Relations of independent commodity production, while not entirely eliminated, have been gradually reduced and increasingly marginalized.

However, capitalism has not eliminated all pre-existing non-capitalist institutions. In certain instances it reshaped them to suit its needs while retaining them as non-capitalist in form. Three examples that have been essential to capitalist reproduction are states, families and educational institutions. Such institutions are able to play a role in the reproduction of capitalism, not in spite of their internally non-capitalist form, but because of it, as will be explained below.

The tendency of capitalism to erode non-capitalist institutions potentially clashes with the need for non-capitalist institutions to be maintained in their supportive role in capitalist reproduction. A social system made up entirely of institutions that operate on capitalist principles and embody capitalist relations would not be viable. As capitalist development erodes key non-capitalist institutions, partly by injecting capitalist principles into them and partly through the pressures that capitalist development exerts upon them, the continued reproduction of capitalism is threatened.

This chapter applies the above line of analysis to the three institutions mentioned above: states, families and educational institutions. It argues that, in recent times, as capitalist development has both injected capitalist principles into those three non-capitalist institutions and also put pressure on their ability to function effectively, the capacity of these non-capitalist institutions to contribute effectively to the reproduction of capitalism has tended to be undermined. The examples given will be drawn from recent developments in the US capitalism, although it seems unlikely that the trends identified here are exclusively found in the US.

Section two of this paper explains what is meant by non-capitalist institutions and discusses their role in the reproduction of capitalism. Sections three, four and five consider, in turn, the erosion of the ability of each of three key non-capitalist institutions to effectively contribute to the reproduction of capitalism: (i) the state, (ii) families and (iii) educational institutions. Section six offers brief concluding comments.

Non-capitalist Institutions and the Reproduction of Capitalism

By institutions that are non-capitalist in form is meant institutions that do not operate according to capitalist principles or embody capitalist relations. Such institutions do not follow the capitalist principles of pursuit of profit; the treatment of everything including human labour-power as a commodity to be sold to the highest bidder or purchased at the lowest possible price; the drive to cut costs; the acceptance of market valuation as the measure of social worth; the drive to expand output or sales; or the accumulation drive. Non-capitalist institutions do not embody such capitalist relations as the appropriation of surplus value from wage labour or competition among producers.

When capitalism first arose historically, it coexisted with feudal and semi-feudal institutions, which operated according to different principles from those of capitalism. For example, landlord-peasant relations still existed that had elements of feudal obligation on the part of both landlord and peasant, in contrast to the impersonal market relationships that characterize capitalism. While capitalism tended to abolish such relations, as Marx and Engels stated in the quotation at the beginning of this paper, capitalism could not eliminate all non-capitalist institutions. Capitalism is an incomplete system which cannot exist without having, associated with it, a set of non-capitalist institutions. Certain functions essential to capitalist reproduction cannot be effectively performed by institutions that operate according to capitalist principles. These functions include the protection of capitalist property rights, the enforcement of contracts, the provision of means of exchange and the reproduction of the working class.[1]

The most obvious case is the reproduction of the working class. Suppose that new workers were conceived and raised to working age by organizations that operated on capitalist principles. This would mean that the worker-raising organization would undertake this task solely for the purpose of gaining profits. This would require that the worker-raising organization will be able to sell the 'completed' new workers. To do so, it would have to own the newly produced workers. After sale, the workers would become the property of the enterprise that purchased them. That is, the workers would be slaves rather than the free wage labourers that are an essential feature of capitalist relations of production.[2] Free wage labourers can be conceived and raised only by means of non-capitalist institutions which leave the new workers as free human beings. Of course, the family has been the primary institution that has performed this function under capitalism, although educational institutions and some other non-capitalist institutions also play an important role in this process.[3]

Human beings have always lived in families. Capitalism, which arose out of peasant societies in most cases, inherited a family that operated as a productive unit. Capitalism reshaped the pre-capitalist family, largely removing production from the family and turning it into an institution for the reproduction of the wage labouring class.[4] In early capitalism an extended family performed this role. In the mid-twentieth century the single-wage-earner nuclear family developed, in which mothers specialized in raising children and other domestic labour while fathers specialized in wage labour. Recently the single wage earner nuclear family has been largely replaced by a form in which both parents, or a single present parent, engage in substantial wage labour.

The working class family in the capitalist era, in the various forms it has taken over time, has always been a non-capitalist institution. Families do not operate based on any of the capitalist principles, such as pursuit of profit, treatment of family members as commodities, or the acceptance of market valuations as measures of social worth. There may be some tendency to economize on expenditures, to increase family income, and to accumulate savings, but these are pale echoes of the related capitalist drives. The adults in the family may provide a money allowance to the children, but they do not appropriate surplus value from them. On the contrary, parents devote substantial labour time to meeting the needs of dependent members of the family. Families do not compete with one another like capitalist firms, although there is an effort to maintain a 'normal' living standard.

Families are a different kind of social entity from the capitalist firm. Operative principles include patriarchal power of husband over wife and of parents over children, the provision of 'caring labour' for others without monetary compensation, and the sharing of economic resources.[5] It is the non-capitalist character of the family which makes it suitable for reproducing the working class under capitalism.

There is one relation within the working class family which some analysts view as involving appropriation of a surplus, which is that between a husband and a wife. However, those who interpret the husband-wife relation as based on exploitation have not considered that relation as one of *capitalist* exploitation.[6] In any event, it is not necessary here to consider the nature of the husband-wife relation, since we are concerned with the family as an institution for the reproduction of the working class. For this purpose, it is the relation between parents (and other child-raisers in the family) and children that matters.

Educational institutions have played an increasingly important role over time in the reproduction of the working class in the capitalist era. In the feudal era, schools served as institutions for reproducing the religious section of the ruling class as well as certain subsidiary functions. Capitalism reshaped them into institutions for training and socializing the wage-earning class.[7]

Like families, schools differ from capitalist institutions. Majority of schools are, however, state-run or are private non-profit institutions. In primary and secondary public schools, the aim is provision of a service to all local residents of the appropriate age without charge. Evaluation and graduation are supposed to be based on performance, not wealth or willingness to make payments. Private non-profit schools also seek to operate by the merit principle, in their admissions policies as well as their policies regarding evaluation and graduation.[8] Those who teach in schools are engaged in a craft process rather than capitalist wage labour.[9] Efficiency does not play a large role in the production process in schools; rather, the main aim is to achieve a certain standard for the product.

In some capitalist countries, such as the US, there are some schools organized as for-profit firms. However, this form of school is not well suited to reproducing the working class. The most serious deficiency of capitalist schools is that capitalist principles conflict with the enforcement of reasonable educational quality standards, which require that students and their families not be allowed to purchase admission, grades, or diplomas. In the US, scandals involving departures from defensible academic standards are common in for-profit schools.

There is also a problem concerning who will pay for the necessary education of the working class if it is to be delivered by capitalist schools. The prospective employer of a worker is not motivated to pay for basic education because, once educated, the worker is free to work for whatever the employer he/she chooses. If the prospective employer will not pay for a worker's education, neither is it practical to expect the family of the individual worker to pay for his/her education. A sizeable proportion of working class families lack the capital to pay for an education that requires many years. Only the state has the resources and motivation to provide basic education for the working class as a whole, and if the state must pay for it, then the need for acceptable educational standards mentioned above runs counter to contracting with for-profit schools for this purpose.

The protection of capitalist property rights also requires a non-capitalist institution for its effective enforcement. Protecting such rights requires a mechanism of coercion. While ideology is a powerful support of the sanctity of capitalist property, an organization is needed that can use overwhelming force to protect against any threat to capitalist property in case ideology proves insufficient. Such an organization must represent the interests of the capitalist class as a whole in carrying out this function. It must be dedicated to preserving the existing property rights of all capitalists. If such an organization was based on capitalist principles, it would sell its services to individual capitalists, and presumably would be ready, for a fee, to use its coercive power to redistribute property from one capitalist to another. Even worse, the group of officials who ran such a state would have an interest in stealing from the capitalists, and if they followed the capitalist principle of pursuing maximum profits, that is just what they would do.

A capitalist system needs a state that operates based on principles quite different from those of capitalism. The state arose historically with the earliest class society. When capitalism first developed, it reshaped the pre-existing feudal or semi-feudal state into a form suitable for capitalism. Eventually it gave rise to the modern bourgeois-democratic nation state.

The bourgeois-democratic nation state operates by different rules from those of a capitalist enterprise. There is at least the form of popular sovereignty rather than the rule of money, and the form has some substance.[10] However, popular sovereignty is limited by a commitment to protecting 'private property', which is interpreted to include capitalist property.[11] Individuals are held to be equal before the law, regardless of their wealth or their ability to generate profits for a capitalist.[12] Efficiency is sacrificed to other aims in the operation of the state, such as dispensing justice or achieving political compromise. The direct compulsion available to the state is contrary to the free contract and free choice that characterize capitalist institutions.[13] These features of the capitalist state make it suitable for effectively carrying out the function of protecting capitalist property.

The enforcement of contracts is also essential to capitalism, since capitalism is a form of market economy. The exchange process cannot proceed smoothly unless the contracts on which exchange is based are effectively and impartially enforced. As in the case of protection of capitalist property, so to in the case of enforcement of contracts an institution organized according to capitalist principles would be unfit for the job. If the contract enforcement agency was organized on capitalist principles, market participants would have the opportunity to purchase the result they wanted, reneging on contracts for a fee when it was advantageous. Such a system would seriously inhibit the development of exchange. The bourgeois-democratic state, with the features described above, is well suited to the kind of enforcement of contracts that capitalism requires.

Finally, capitalism necessitates a state that can effectively organize the creation and regulation of means of exchange, that is, money. Capitalism cannot exist based on barter, contrary to the conception of capitalism found in neoclassical economic theory. But money cannot be created or properly regulated by institutions that follow capitalist principles. Money as a means of exchange is a social convention, an entity that must be accepted in exchange for goods and services by all sellers. If a capitalist organization was free to create money based on the usual capitalist principle of pursuit of maximum profit, there would be no reason for all sellers to accept such money. Sellers would rightly suspect that such money might operate as a means to transfer wealth to the issuer of the money. This was indeed the situation at times in the nineteenth century US west, where banks issued their own money with little state supervision. Such money circulated at a steep discount and was sometimes simply not accepted.

In modern capitalism the creation of means of exchange has substantially been delegated to a kind of capitalist institution – the commercial bank. However, these institutions operate under strict supervision and regulation by the state, without which they could not effectively perform that function. The overall regulation of the money supply is directly undertaken by the state through a central bank. State guarantees and regulations ensure that, within the borders of each capitalist state, its money must be accepted by all sellers at face value in exchange for goods and services.

The crucial role of the state in providing and regulating money becomes clear in exchanges across state boundaries. Since there is no international state in the capitalist era, there is no true international money. Various systems have been devised over the centuries to facilitate exchange between parties in different countries, but all of them have been problematic and at times have ceased to function effectively, leading to international monetary crises.

The State

During the post-World War II era of regulated capitalism in the US in 1948–73, the state not only effectively performed the functions of protecting capitalist property relations, enforcing contracts, and issuing and regulating money, it also actively intervened in the economy in ways that facilitated the accumulation of capital. One example of such intervention was the federal government's programme to encourage home ownership, which spurred a huge wave of home-building by means of the creation and close regulation of a special set of financial institutions (saving banks, or savings and loan associations) that funneled cheap credit into home construction and home mortgages plus a large tax subsidy to enable working class families to afford home mortgages. Other examples included Keynesian macro-stabilization through counter-cyclical fiscal and monetary policy; regulation of certain naturally unstable prices in agriculture and primary products; and government promotion of peaceful collective bargaining between labour and capital.

The regulated form of capitalism in the US succeeded in promoting rapid capital accumulation, producing the highest rate of growth in real gross domestic product (GDP) of any period for which data are available for the US. From 1948–73 real GDP grew at 4.0 per cent per year. The regulated form of capitalism was dismantled during approximately 1973–9, and by the latter year the neo-liberal era had begun. Economic growth has been slower since the end of the regulated capitalist period. GDP growth averaged 3.0 per cent during the period of transition from regulated capitalism to the neo-liberal form during 1973–9; then rose slightly to 3.1 per cent per year during the neo-liberal era of 1979–2000 (US Bureau of Economic Analysis, 2006, Table 1.1.6).[14]

Since the beginning of the neo-liberal era at the end of the 1970s, the state in the US has significantly reduced its formerly active role in the economy in several respects. There has been deregulation of formerly regulated sectors in transportation, power, communication, finance and agriculture. In addition to the state's withdrawal from micro-regulation, it has also withdrawn from Keynesian-type macro-regulation. The Federal Reserve – the central bank in the US – has remained interventionist, but its focus in the neo-liberal era has shifted entirely to control of inflation. The state's former commitment to using both fiscal and monetary policy for stabilizing real output and stimulating aggregate demand growth was renounced in the early 1980s. It was not reintroduced even during the Clinton Presidency despite Clinton's promise to do so when he first ran for that office in 1992.[15]

The welfare state has been sharply reduced since the late 1970s, when President Carter first called for cutbacks in social spending. All state income maintenance programmes have been pared back, including the overwhelmingly popular social security retirement pension programme, although the current Bush administration's effort to privatize it was overwhelmingly defeated. Public support for meeting the housing needs of the population practically disappeared in the neo-liberal era. Under a Democratic President in 1996, the 1930s-era federal commitment to support those without a means of income was rescinded. Federal taxes on business and the rich have been reduced sharply over this period, although in the 1990s the top personal income tax rates were raised somewhat and an income tax credit was introduced that benefits low-income working people. Even public spending for building infrastructure, one of the most essential state contributions to the reproduction of capitalism, was reduced over this period, even during the Clinton administration which had argued strongly for more spending for this purpose.[16]

Sometimes individual episodes capture the character of an era better than data series. One episode involved a US Supreme Court decision, the US versus Lopez, on 26 April 1995. In a 5-4 decision overturning a ban on gun possession within 1,000 feet of a school, the Supreme Court questioned, for the first time in 60 years, the scope of the inter-state commerce clause of the US Constitution. A broad interpretation of that clause had formed the basis for all federal regulation of business since 1937, when the court shifted course and first began to uphold New Deal regulatory laws (Greenhouse, 1995).

A second episode was the partially successful drive to weaken the Internal Revenue Service (IRS) that culminated in a new law in June 1998. One area in which the US has long been a world leader is in the collection of taxes. The US government has historically collected a relatively high proportion of taxes owed by law. Congressional hearings in 1998 presented the IRS as a kind of Gestapo that was terrorizing citizens (Cropper, 1998). Had the bill introduced by the Republicans passed unaltered, payment of taxes would have become more voluntary than mandatory. Even the amended bill that became law significantly weakened the ability of the IRS to collect the taxes necessary for a functioning state.

Thus, in the current era the effectiveness of the US state as regulator of the capitalist economy has been significantly reduced. Efforts to weaken the IRS have threatened the ability of the state to function effectively at all. The most ambitious of the anti-government advocates have admitted that their ultimate aim is to make the federal government as weak as possible, based on their belief that the state is essentially an enemy of individual freedom. Grover Norquist – an influential tax policy advisor to the Administration of US President George W Bush – stated that his ultimate goal in promoting the large tax-cuts enacted by the Bush administration was 'to reduce it [government] to the size where I can drag it into the bathroom and drown it in the bathtub' (interview with Grover Norquist by Mara Liasson on Morning Edition, National Public Radio, 25 May 2001). The increasingly competitive character of capitalism in the neo-liberal era lies behind the resistance of capital to paying the taxes needed to maintain an effective state (Kotz, 2002).

While the substantial dismantling of the regulatory state and the reduction in its ability to collect tax revenues in the US have greatly reduced the state's effectiveness at promoting rapid capital accumulation, this process has not so far undermined the state's ability to perform its core responsibilities under capitalism. That is, the US state is still effective at protecting capitalist property, enforcing contracts, and issuing and regulating money. However, the trends which have so far only reduced the state's ability to promote capital accumulation, as well cutting back state programmes that benefit working people, may, if they continue, eventually threaten these core functions as well.

State corruption plays an important role here. While corruption of state officials has always been a part of political life in the US, it appears that its scope has increased significantly in recent times. State corruption represents the penetration of capitalist principles into the state, since it involves the purchase of state actions and policies by wealthy interests. Currently Washington is awash in corruption scandals, which so far have primarily involved Republican members of Congress. However, many political analysts suggest that corruption has come to reach deep into both major political parties. The rising cost of running political campaigns has been one factor driving this development. Candidates for high office find they must solicit funds from various capitalist groups, and such funds are not free gifts. It has become common to read that 'K Street', where many corporate lobbying firms in Washington DC, have their offices, has become the real power behind the government (Birnbaum, 2005; Drew, 2005).

Another example of the penetration of capitalist principles into the state is the widespread privatization of state functions and responsibilities in the neo-liberal era. State functions that have been privatized include not just such peripheral functions as provision of meals to state employees but also the operation of prisons and recently even military functions. In Iraq private US security firms provide armed agents to perform many functions previously handled by the US armed forces, including guarding officials and running supply convoys (Priest and Flaherty, 2004). Recently the Bush administration proposed farming out part of the job of collecting unpaid federal taxes to private companies, which would get to keep a share of the collections. Critics pointed out that the government would not derive any financial benefit from such a plan and would in fact lose financially. This proposal is a throwback to the pre-capitalist practice of tax farming, which played an important role in some pre-capitalist modes of production.

At this time one can only identify tendencies in capitalist development that put pressure on the state or that inject capitalist principles into the state which might eventually threaten the ability of the state to perform the core state functions required by capitalism. Even today one can get an idea of where this could lead by looking at the example of post-Soviet Russia.

One can actually observe today – in post-Soviet Russia – what happens when a state in a capitalist system is organized on more or less capitalist principles. The neo-liberal model, which has been applied only partially so far in the US, was fully applied in Russia starting in 1992 (Kotz and Weir, 1997, Chapter 9). A result has been that the post-Soviet Russian state, under both the Yeltsin and Putin regimes, has been organized primarily to enrich the top officials of the state and their relatives and associates.[17] The Russian state preys upon individual capitalists, as well operating some of its own wealth-generating enterprises for the benefit of state officials. Capitalist property is not safe in Russia, from the state or from non-state criminal organizations that operate with the purchased connivance of state officials.[18]

The Russian state neither effectively protects capitalist property nor enforces contracts impartially. As a result, smaller capitalists must pay large bribes to organized criminal groups to protect their property and enforce their contracts, while the wealthier Russian capitalists maintain their own expensive armed bodies ('security departments') for these purposes. The presence of a state that operates on more-or-less capitalist principles in Russia is the major reason why capitalism has not developed very fully in that country (Kotz, 2001). The capitalist means of accumulating wealth is not a very profitable one in Russia, compared to other means of accumulating wealth such as appropriating raw material rents, collecting land rent, pursuing speculative gains and various forms of extortion and theft.

The neo-liberal understanding of the nature of the state is essentially a version of the kind of state that exists in Russia today. That is, neo-liberalism sees the state as an agency that steals from the wealth creators (the capitalists). The reason they hold this view is that their simplistic assumption of 'economic man' leads them to assume that state officials will naturally act according to capitalist principles. They cannot believe that a major institution in society can be organized on quite different principles. The neo-liberals' success in turning Russia into their experiment ironically ended up creating a state that corresponds rather closely to their conception of how a state should be expected to function – although of course they have decried the result that flowed from their experiment.

However, neo-liberal theory has made an exception to its usual assumptions in the case of money. In this case the neo-liberals forget their deep belief that every agent pursues material self-interest. Instead they assume an 'impartial' central bank that will, or should, regulate the supply of money so as to optimize the functioning of the capitalist economy. Contrary to the neo-liberal view, unlike in the case of state protection of capitalist property and enforcement of contracts, the central bank's role is normally a somewhat contested one in capitalist society. The central bank's regulatory actions affect different segments of the capitalist class differently. These segments, particularly financial capital and industrial capital, struggle to affect central bank policy. Even working class organizations sometimes participate in this political struggle.

Families

The single wage-earner family predominated among working people in the post-World War II decades in the US. Although it was based on a patriarchal relation in which the husbands dominated wives it was an effective institution for reproducing the working class. This form was well suited to the requirement for an increasingly mobile labour force, since having only a single wage-earner facilitated relocation when it was needed. In 1950, the labour force participation rate for married women with children under age six was only 11.9 per cent and for those with children between six to 17 years was only 28.3 per cent.[19] Mothers devoted their labour time primarily to raising children and other domestic labour.[20] A majority, although not all, of the married male part of the working class had achieved a 'family wage', sufficient to support a working class family at the accepted living standard.

In the 1950s the labour force participation rate of married women with children in the US began to rise, and by 1980 it had reached 45.1 per cent for those with children under age six and 61.7 per cent for those with children between the ages six to 17.[21] After World War II, the previous main source of new wage labourers, simple commodity producers in agriculture, had been largely exhausted in the developed capitalist countries. Adult female domestic labourers in the traditional family represented the last large potential pool of new wage labourers. It was capitalism's never-ending hunger for new supplies of wage labour to exploit that has been the primary force drawing female domestic labourers into wage labour (Kotz, 1994).

The spread of capitalist relations to a new sector of the economy – the restaurant industry – also played a role in the transformation of the family. Capitalist penetration of the restaurant industry – long a stronghold of petty commodity production – created the fast food industry, which contributed to the entrance of women into the paid labour force by providing a cheap source of prepared food.

As married women with children entered the paid labour force, the ability of the working class family to effectively raise children came under great pressure. The availability of high-quality daycare in the US is far short of what the new family configuration requires. The new family configuration also conflicts with capital's need for labour to be mobile, since husbands and wives are likely to often have different locational requirements connected with their jobs. The new family creates serious strains both for capitalist employers and for the family itself.

The previous version of the family was relatively stable, with a low divorce rate, due to the economic dependence of wives on their husband's paycheck, as well as the cultural expectations that accompanied that system. As women increasingly gained access to income through their own paid work, and as cultural expectations changed along with this, the divorce rate rose rapidly. While women have benefited from the independence of earning an income and from the ability to escape from oppressive marriages, the effect on the reproduction of the working class has not been beneficial, both because children receive less parental attention under the new system and they grow up under less stable family conditions.[22]

Furthermore, the pressure this system places upon parents has contributed to a drop in fertility rates that poses a very direct threat to the reproduction of the working class. Another factor contributing to the rapid drop in fertility has derived from the increasing influence of individualist ideology in the neo-liberal era. Potential parents may be deciding whether to bear and raise children based on an individualistic cost-benefit analysis, which will never justify having children. Today no country in the European Union (EU) has a fertility rate above 2.1, the level required to reproduce the population (*The New York Times*, 2006, p. A3).

Educational Institutions

The working class is not reproduced by families alone. In the post-World War II decades the school system in the US underwent a great expansion at the primary and secondary levels and also at the post-secondary level. New schools were built throughout the country, the number of teachers grew rapidly, and public higher education was transformed from a system primarily for a small elite into a mass system that served a significant part of the working class.[23] The public schools experienced large infusions of funds into their budgets, enabling them to significantly improve education in this period. The educational level of the working population rose rapidly, which is believed to be a major contributing factor for the rapid labour productivity growth of that period in the US.[24] Output per hour in the non-farm business sector grew at 2.8 per cent per year during 1948–73, compared to only 1.2 per cent per year in the crisis-ridden period 1973–9 and 1.7 per cent per year in the neo-liberal era during 1979–2000 (US Bureau of Labour Statistics, 2006).[25]

During the past several decades there has been a campaign to persuade the public that the US school system is in a crisis. Critics complain that American schools have been turning out a growing proportion of graduates who lack even a minimal level of competence in reading, writing and mathematics. The problem is not seen as one that concerns the upper part of the academic performance distribution – it is believed that America's top students continue to receive an excellent education and perform well academically. The problem is presented as one involving those in the middle and bottom of the academic distribution.

There is some uncertainty whether this story of educational decline is fact or fiction: Similar warnings of a decline in public education, compared to some presumed past golden age, have recurred in US history since the late nineteenth century.[26] However, it does appear that influential capitalists regard the US school system as failing to produce graduates with the skills it requires for its workers. This has been demonstrated by the calls for educational 'reform' that have issued from a series of high-profile 'educational summit meetings' hosted by the last three US presidents starting with the first Bush administration. 48 corporate chief executive officers' (CEO) attended the second meeting in 1996, with a prominent role played by former International Business Machines (IBM) CEO – Louis Gerstner (Doyle, 1996).[27]

One can cite several factors that have put stress on the educational system in the US and may be undermining its effectiveness at reproducing the working class. One factor stems from changes in the family discussed above. Today, most school children live in families with either two working parents or a single working parent.[28] In either case, the availability of a parent to aid in the children's education, which is an important determinant of school success, appears to have decreased over time.

Secondly, the erosion of barriers to women pursuing any career they desire, including such previously all-male professions as law and medicine, has affected the public schools. Before these barriers were demolished, the public schools could draw upon a pool of highly qualified female teachers willing to work for low pay because they had few other career options. This supply is no longer available today, which has caused the school system to face a choice between improving the pay and working conditions of teachers or suffering a decline in the number of highly talented teachers.

A third factor, shrinking budgets for education in recent decades, has probably been the greatest threat to the quality of the schools. In the neo-liberal era a tax-cutting drive hit the funding sources for public schools particularly hard, as voter initiatives in many states set ceilings on the local property taxes that have traditionally been the main source of public school financing. This started in California, where the famous Proposition 13, passed in June 1978, drastically reduced school funding. California used to have one of America's best, and most generously funded, public school systems, but in recent decades its system has been decimated by funding cuts. In November 1980, the voters of Massachusetts, the birthplace of free public education in the US, passed a similar tax-cutting ballot proposition, known as 'proposition two and a half', which undercut the tax base for public education in the state. Rising costs of incarceration in the US have also squeezed state and local budgets, reducing the funds available for education. From 1980–2000 education's share of state and local spending dropped by 21 per cent while the share of prison spending doubled (Western, Schiraldi and Ziedenberg, 2003, p. 4).

More recently further damage has been done to the schools' ability to reproduce the working class as a result of the 'reforms' sponsored by corporate interests that have been decrying the decline in skills of American high school graduates. These reforms, designed by neo-liberal educational analysts, diagnose the problem as one of declining standards, unsound 'liberal' pedagogical methods, and the diversion of school revenues into the salaries of 'greedy' unionized teachers. Their solutions have involved introducing capitalist principles and relations into the educational system. These have included the privatization of education through voucher programmes that would put public funds into private schools; the injection of competition into the school system through merit pay for teachers and the creation of semi-private charter schools with non-unionized teachers that compete with regular public schools for funds; and centering the educational process around standardized tests produced and graded by private for-profit testing companies. These standardized tests are used to both determine students' 'competency' and their right to receive a diploma and also to determine 'teacher competency'. There has also been an expansion of federal funds going to for-profit trade schools and 'colleges' under legislation passed by the US Congress. Finally, public schools have been pressured to spend a growing share of their budgets on computer technology that, while enormously profitable for the computer industry, is of doubtful efficacy as an educational tool.

One more capitalist development has had a negative influence on education in the US. In recent decades capitalist marketers uncovered a previously fallow market among teenagers, who in earlier times had been a relatively commodity-free part of the population. In short order advertisers were able to turn teenagers into a major segment of consumer demand, for products ranging from brand name clothing to electronic gear. At the same time, the beckoning fast food establishments provided teenagers with a means to earn the cash to buy the new youth-oriented commodities. This drove one more spike into the educational system, as high school students regularly fall asleep in class after working at McDonald's the previous evening to enable them to purchase expensive commodities that the previous generation of teenagers never required/desired.[29]

While this helps to keep the wheels of capitalist production and commerce humming, it contributes to undermining the reproduction of the working class, upon which capitalism's long-term survival depends.

Thus, in a wide variety of ways, capitalist development in the US appears to have been eroding the ability of educational institutions to effectively reproduce the working class. The sources of this development include both the penetration of capitalist principles into the schools and the indirect effects of capitalist development on the schools.

Concluding Comments

This chapter has identified recent tendencies for capitalist development, at least in the US, to erode the ability of three key non-capitalist institutions – the state, families and educational institutions – to contribute effectively to the reproduction of capitalism. The very feature of capitalism which underlay its rapid spread around the world – capitalism's tendency to destroy non-capitalist institutions – now seems to have turned against the underpinnings of capitalism itself. This represents one more contradiction of contemporary capitalism which potentially undermines its ability to continue to form a viable basis for human society. However, social systems do not simply pass away as a result of their internal contradictions. Class struggle and political action are necessary to bring about the replacement of one mode of production by another. An understanding of the particular contradiction of contemporary capitalism discussed in this paper may be helpful to popular movements in the struggle to supersede capitalism.

Notes

1. By the term reproduction of the working class in this paper is meant its inter-generational reproduction through conceiving and raising the next generation of wage workers. The term reproduction of the working class is sometimes intended to include the daily reproduction of the current generation of workers.
2. Alternatively, one might imagine capitalist-like enterprises that produced and then rented out new workers. In that case, the producers in the system would remain the property of the worker-producing enterprises and hence would still be slaves rather than free wage labourers. In the slave system of the pre-Civil War US South, some planters rented out slaves who were skilled labourers.
3. Religious and social organizations also have played a role in reproducing the working class.

4. The family plays a different role in the capitalist class, serving as a means of reproducing that class and passing property on to the next generation.
5. Such operating principles are not always followed, but they nevertheless serve as a widely accepted norm for the family.
6. Fraad, Resnick, and Wolff (1994) view the husband-wife relation as entailing a feudal mode of surplus appropriation.
7. Schools serve other functions as well under capitalism, including aiding in the reproduction of the capitalist class and various professional and managerial groups.
8. Schools do not always hold to their non-capitalist principles. Local financing of public schools creates a significant departure from the principle of equal access to education, while financial pressures on private non-profit schools lead to privileged access to such schools by the children of wealthy families.
9. One does not find wage-workers in capitalist enterprises donating their own money and time to make sure that the product turns out well in the face of financial shortages, yet this is commonplace in schools.
10. Of course the capitalist class can influence state policies and the selection of state officials through a variety of means beyond the votes of individual capitalists. Nevertheless, such means of special influence must work around the disjuncture between the principles of operation of states on the one hand and the capitalist process on the other. A wealthy capitalist can legally purchase shares of stock in a capitalist firm, entitling the capitalist to select its directors, but capitalists cannot legally purchase the right to select government officials. The principle of popular sovereignty is critical to the legitimation function of the state under capitalism. Without it, capitalist society could not be represented as 'democratic society'.
11. Marx pointed out that capitalist property is the negation of individual private property. Capitalist property is normally accumulated through appropriating the labour of wage workers. Capitalist property also arises from the confiscation, through various means, of the individual property of independent producers, as is recounted in detail in Capital volume 1 on primitive accumulation (Marx, 1887, part VIII). In the corporate stage of capitalism, the corporate form of capitalist property requires legal recognition as a form of private property with all the rights of individual property owners accorded to corporate property owners, although without all of the former's obligations.
12. As in the case of selection of state officials, justice is not legally for sale. Large corporations can purchase talented lawyers, giving them an advantage in defending their legal interests. However, they often still find themselves in the position of having an expensive lawsuit against them decided by a jury of ordinary working people.
13. Capitalists dominate and exploit workers, yet this takes place by means of economic pressure rather than direct coercion, at least in principle.
14. The GDP growth data for the neo-liberal era is carried only through 2000, so that every beginning and ending year of the three periods is a business cycle peak year, which is the best way to compare long run growth rates of different periods. The GDP growth rate for 1979–2005 is 3.0 per cent per year.
15. A large public spending programme to lower unemployment was part of Clinton's 1992 campaign. It was the first campaign pledge upon which he reneged. A jobs-creation bill was introduced into Congress, but the new administration did not make even a pretense of seeking to get it passed.

16. Investment in structures by all levels of government, which is an approximation of public investment in infrastructure, fell from 3.25 per cent of GDP in the 1960s to 2.62 per cent in the 1970s, 2.04 per cent in the 1980s, and 1.92 per cent in the 1990s, before rising slightly to 2 per cent in 2000–5 (U S Bureau of Economic Analysis, 2006, Tables 3.9.5 and 1.1.5).
17. A survey found that state corruption has actually increased in Russia in recent years, as the total value of bribes paid by businesses rose tenfold from 2001 to 2005. By the latter year, this figure exceeded the official budget revenue of the state (Lee Myers, Steven, 'Pervasive Corruption in Russia is "Just Called Business"', *The New York Times*, 13 August 2005, p. A3, reporting the results of a study conducted by the Indem Foundation – a Moscow research group).
18. See Kotz and Weir (2007), Chapters 12 and 14.
19. US Bureau of the Census (1970), Table 331, p. 223.
20. Mothers also bore the primary responsibility for caring for their own and their husband's retired parents, which, given the socially accepted standard that retired workers must be supported, represents part of the cost of the reproduction of the working class over the entire life-cycle.
21. US Bureau of the Census (1993), Table 633, p. 400. By 1992, the two figures were 59.9 per cent and 67.8 per cent respectively.
22. These observations do not justify a call to return to the single wage-earner patriarchal family. The entrance of women into wage labour was a progressive development, leading to the weakening of patriarchy and a move in the direction of equality between the sexes. However, under capitalist conditions this development has created serious social problems. The solution is not to drive women back into the home, but to transform the economy and society to fit in with an egalitarian family structure.
23. Over the course of the 1960s, the number of teachers in primary and secondary education in the US increased by 43 per cent while educational spending at those levels doubled in real terms. The number of students enrolled in institutions of higher education more than doubled in that decade (National Center for Education Statistics, Tables 26, 63, 170).
24. Labour productivity growth reflects not only accumulation and technological innovation by individual capitalists. State-funded improvements in educational levels produce productivity increases from which capitalists reap higher profits. The working class was sufficiently well organized in this period to share these productivity gains.
25. The slower growth rate of labour productivity in the neo-liberal era is also probably a result of the slower rate of capital accumulation in that period, which was noted above.
26. In the late nineteenth century some warned that large numbers of non-English speaking immigrants' children were threatening America's schools. This charge has echoes today.
27. Also attending were CEOs from AT&T, Bell South Corporation, Kodak, Proctor & Gamble and Boeing.
28. In 2002, 42.9 per cent of children in the US lived in families with two working parents and another 21.6 per cent in a family with one parent only and that parent working. The two types of families encompassed almost two-thirds of all children (Fields, 2002).
29. A *New York Times* article recounted the experience of high school students who worked 30 hours a week, impinging on their ability to study for school (*The New York Times*, 29 January 2001, pp. A1, A22).

References

Birnbaum, J. H. 2005. 'The Road to Riches is Called K Street', *The Washington Post*, June 22.
Cropper, C. M. 1998. 'Spending It; Tangled Tale Of the Oilman Vs. the I.R.S', *The New York Times*, August 2, Late edition – Final, Section 3, Page 1, Column 1.
Doyle, D. P. 1996. 'A Personal Report from the Education Summit: What Does It Mean for Education Reform?' Heritage Lecture #564, May 21, from website http://www.heritage.org/Research/Education/HL564.cfm.
Drew, E. 2005. 'Selling Washington', *The New York Review of Books* 52 (11), June 22.
Fields, J. 2002. 'Children's Living Arrangements and Characteristics: March', US Census Bureau, Current Population Reports, June 2003. Website http://www.census.gov/prod/2003pubs/p20-547.pdf
Fraad, H., Resnick, S. and Wolff, R. 1994. 'For Every Knight in Shining Armor, There's a Castle Waiting to be Cleaned: A Marxist-Feminist Analysis of the Household', in Fraad, H., Resnick, S. and Wolff, R. (eds.), *Bringing It All Back Home*. London and Boulder: Pluto Press, pp. 1–41.
Greenhouse, L. 1995. 'High Court Kills Law Banning Guns in a School Zone', *The New York Times*, April 27.
Greenhouse, Steven. 2001. 'Problems Seen for Teenagers Who Hold Jobs', *The New York Times*, January 29, p. A1, p. A22.
Kotz, D. M. 2002. 'Globalization and Neoliberalism', *Rethinking Marxism*, 14, 2.
—. 2001. 'Is Russia Becoming Capitalist?' *Science and Society*, 65, 2.
—. 1994. 'Household Labor, Wage Labor, and the Transformation of the Family', *Review of Radical Political Economics*, 26, 2.
Kotz, D. M. and Weir, F. 2007. (forthcoming). *Russia's Path from Gorbachev to Putin: The Demise of the Soviet System and the New Russia*. London: Routledge.
—. 1997. *Revolution from Above: The Demise of the Soviet System*. London: Routledge.
Marx, K. 1887. *Capital: A Critical Analysis of Capitalist Production*, vol. I. Moscow: Foreign Languages Publishing House (year unstated, a reproduction of the 1887 text).
Marx, K. and Engels, F. 1848. *Manifesto of the Communist Party*, in Tucker, R.C. (ed.), *The Marx-Engels Reader*, 2nd edition. New York: Norton, 1978.
National Center for Educational Statistics. 2006. *Digest of Education Statistics*, Website http://nces.ed.gov/programs/digest/.
Priest, D. and Flaherty, M. P. 2004. 'Iraq: Security Firms Form World's Largest Private "Army"', *The Washington Post*, April 8.
Rosenthal, Elisabeth. 2006. 'European Union's Plunging Birthrates Spread Eastward', *The New York Times*, September 4, p. A3.
US Bureau of Economic Analysis. 2006. *National Income and Product Accounts*. Website http://www.bea.gov., revision of September 28.
US Bureau of Labour Statistics. 2006. Major Sector Productivity and Costs Index, Series Id PRS85006093, data extracted October 10, website http://www.bls.gov.
US Bureau of the Census (Various Years) *Statistical Abstract of the United States*, Washington DC: US Government Printing Office.
Western, B., Schiraldi, V. and Ziedenberg, J. 2003. *Education and Incarceration*, Washington DC: Justice Policy Institute, August 28, website http://www.justicepolicy.org/reports/EducationandIncarceration1.pdf.

Chapter 8

THE TRANSFORMATIVE MOMENT[1]

Julie Matthaei and Barbara Brandt

We are living in one of the most exciting times in history. It is a time of crisis and breakdown, and a time of potential transition to a new and more evolved economic and social stage. Diverse and vibrant movements for social transformation are springing up all around the world. The US, while playing a reactionary role through its imperialist state policies and globalizing corporations, is also a locus of significant post-modern transformation. We call this time in the US 'the Transformative Moment', to emphasize its potential for paradigmatic and systematic economic and social change.

The Transformative Moment can be understood as a deep-seated and many-faceted response to the imbalances, inequality and lack of freedom created by the reigning economic and social paradigm, a paradigm that we call the Hierarchical Polarization Paradigm. In the first part of this paper, we will analyse the core elements of the Hierarchical Polarization Paradigm. In the second part, we will discuss the seven transformative processes that various US social movements are participating in now; processes, which are beginning to construct a new, more balanced, free and equal paradigm of economic and social life.

Our goal in this paper is to provide the reader with a new conceptual framework, which will help them understand the transformative potential of the present historical conjuncture in the US – the Transformative Moment. The conceptual framework presented here builds on the fundamentals of Marxian economics, particularly as interpreted by David Levine (1977; 1978; 1981). It also builds on over 40 years of anti-oppression/anti-discrimination action and research by civil rights, feminist, anti-racist, lesbian/gay and other scholars, especially hooks (1984), Nelson (1996) and Folbre (2001). We have stood gratefully on their shoulders as we have created this overarching analysis. Our conceptual framework is also built on our own histories: we have each been researching and writing about gender, race and economics for over 30 years (Matthaei 1982; 1996; 2000; Brandt, 1995; Amott and Matthaei, 1996), and we have been working together on this conceptual framework for seven years (Matthaei and Brandt, 2001; forthcoming). Finally, we have both been active participants in the movements we are describing: Barbara, in the civil rights, feminist, ecology and new economics movements; Julie in the anti-war, feminist, lesbian/gay, anti-racist and ecology movements.

The Hierarchical Polarization Paradigm

To understand the present historical conjuncture in the US, we have created the concept of the 'Hierarchical Polarization Paradigm', building on the concept of hierarchical dualism developed in the work of John Hodges, Donald Struckmann, and Lynn Trost (1975); Rhonda Williams (1993); and Ann Jennings (1993). We use the word 'polarization' instead of 'dualism' here to emphasize that the Hierarchical Polarization Paradigm polarizes universal dualisms such as male and female, masculine and feminine, light and dark, parent and child into extreme and rigidly opposed and mutually exclusive categories.

The Hierarchical Polarization Paradigm pre-existed capitalism, and was built into the US capitalist economic system in the eighteenth and nineteenth centuries. It still undergirds US economic and social values, practices and institutions today; and is so deeply engrained in our ways of thinking, being and acting that it is difficult for us to even see it.

The Hierarchical Polarization Paradigm divides people and life itself into a number of distinct, purportedly independent, 'hierarchical polarities'. Each hierarchical polarity is composed of two polarized, mutually exclusive and unequal groups. Most of the hierarchical polarities create divisions among people: men vs and over women, whites vs and over blacks, heterosexuals vs and over homosexuals, US citizens vs and over foreigners, etc. Another set of hierarchical polarities divide realms of life: man vs and over nature, God vs and over man, materialism vs and over spirituality. We summarize some of the various key hierarchical polarities in US and European history in Figure 1. In this paper, given space limits, we will focus our discussion on two key hierarchical polarities: gender and race.

THE TRANSFORMATIVE MOMENT

Figure 1: Hierarchical Polarities Present in the US and Europe

\	\	\
Hierarchical Polarities between Groups of People		
	Superior, Dominant Group	*Inferior, Subordinated Group*
Authoritarian Parenting	Parents	Children
Gender	Men (people with male sexual organs)	Women (people with female sexual organs)
Aristocracy	Aristocrat (parents are aristocrats)	Commoners (parents aren't aristocrats)
Nationalism	Citizens of our country	Citizens of another country, or group of other countries
Colonialism	Colonizer	Colonized
Religious Intolerance	Christians	Heathens or Pagans or Muslims or Jews
Race	Whites (people of European 'blood')	Blacks (people with any African 'blood') OR Native American 'savages' OR Non-White/Colored People, etc.
Sexuality	Heterosexuals	Homosexuals
Ability	Normal	Disabled
Other Hierarchical Polarities		
	Superior, Dominanting Group/ Principle	*Inferior, Subordinated Group/ Principle*
Religion	God (white man in the sky)	Man (all human beings)
Man/nature	Man (all human beings, especially men)	Nature (non-human beings and life; to some extent, women)
Secularism	Material life	Religion, Spirituality

While there are many differences between the various hierarchical polarities, we believe it is helpful to discuss them together, analytically. Such an analysis helps us:

- Understand the commonalities among the various, distinct hierarchical polarities.

- Understand the ways in which the different hierarchical polarities reinforce one another as part of the Hierarchical Polarization Paradigm.
- Identify the underlying processes, which create each hierarchical polarity.
- Recognize the similarities in the transformative processes undertaken by the various, identity-based and other social movements against the different hierarchical polarities.
- Understand the ways in which these various movements are increasingly coming to support one another and are beginning to undermine the Hierarchical Polarization Paradigm itself.
- Begin to envision a world, which is free from inequality, oppression and violence inherent in the Hierarchical Polarization Paradigm.

Hierarchical Polarization Processes

The Hierarchical Polarization Paradigm views the process of domination and subordination, and the various hierarchical polarities through which it is played out, as inevitable and God-given. However, the various hierarchical polarities are actually economic and social constructs. We call the social concepts, values, practices and institutions, which produce and reproduce hierarchical polarities, 'hierarchical polarization processes'.

Here we will focus on the hierarchical polarization processes which create, polarize, and 'un-equalize' groups of people. We have identified nine such processes, which are present in nearly all of the various hierarchical polarities, which have occurred in US history. In order to discuss the essence of these processes, we refer to past forms of gender, race and other polarities, forms which had not yet begun to be broken down by transformative processes. The nine hierarchical polarizations processes are as follows:

(i) *Categorization*: The Hierarchical Polarization Paradigm creates mutually exclusive categories of people, along a variety of different criteria- white or black, man or woman, colonizer or colonized, heterosexual or homosexual, American or foreigner, etc.

(ii) *Ascription*: Each person is assigned to one category in each hierarchical polarity at birth, based on some aspect of their being that they cannot control, such as biological sex, disability, skin colour, sexual orientation, or parents' group assignment/s (race, religion, nationality, aristocracy). Each of these group assignments is made integral to the social identity of the person, for example, a gay white disabled US man.

(iii) *Polarization*: Within each hierarchical polarity, the two categories of people are treated differently. They are assigned different personality traits and different, mutually exclusive, work and social activities, and in this way, are made to be socially different and opposite.

(iv) *Hierarchization*: Within each polarity, one group of people is viewed as superior to the other, in terms of its way of being, its traits and its work.

(v) *Domination/Subordination*: Within each polarity, the group of people that is seen to be superior is given political and economic power over the other group, in terms of citizenship, civil rights, property rights and pay.

(vi) *Violence*: The dominant group uses violence, both overt and institutionalized, to create, maintain and reproduce its domination; the subordinated group often rebels violently against its subordination, only to be 'put down' with more violence.

(vii) *Rationalization*: Each hierarchical polarity is justified by religious dogma (as 'God-given') or by science (as 'natural').

(viii) *Internalization*: Authoritarian parenting, education and other social institutions cause people to internalize each hierarchical polarity, i.e., accept its dictates and expectations of them and of others. In this way, groups that are oppressed can come to 'internalize their oppression'.

(ix) *Stigmatization*: Social stigmatization, such as teasing, ostracism, and in extreme cases, group violence, punishes those who do not conform, i.e. who do not behave according to their assigned roles.

Based on a belief that people are naturally different and unequal, these processes indeed make people different and unequal, according to a variety of different socially created categories.

Figure 2: The Nine Hierarchical Polarization Processes, as Applied to Race and Gender

	Race (white/black)	*Gender*
Categorization	Two mutually exclusive racial categories are created: 'whites' (people of European heritage with less than 1/16 African heritage), and 'blacks' (people with 1/16 or more African heritage)	People are separated into two groups: 'men' (those with penises) and 'women" (those with vaginas)
Ascription	At birth, people are assigned to one category or the other based on their parents', grandparents', or great grandparents' race, or on their skin colour and features. People are assigned a racial identity, white or black; mixed heritage people are assigned as above	At birth, people are assigned a gender identity based on their sexual organs, as per above; people who cannot be easily categorized in this way are assigned as parents/medical authorities see fit
Polarization of People, Traits, and Work	Whites are the opposite of blacks, have different traits, and do different work	Men are the opposite of women, 'opposite sex'; men are masculine, women are feminine; sexual division of labour
Hierarchization	Whites and white abilities and traits are viewed as superior to blacks and black abilities and traits	Men are household heads; represent household as citizens;
Domination/ Subordination	Whites are given legal and economic power over blacks, in terms of citizenship, civil rights, property rights, pay for work	Men are given legal and economic power over women, in terms of citizenship, civil rights and property rights, pay for work
Violence	Beating and killing of slaves; lynching; imprisonment, and threats of above	Wife-beating, rape, murder, and threats of above

	Race (white/black)	*Gender*
Rationalization	Racial theories which racialize people, and claim that whites are superior to blacks and other peoples of colour	Religions teach gender roles and men's dominance as head of family; science claims women lack brain capacity, are overly emotional
Internalization	Parents, schools and religious institutions teach children (and adults) the above, and train them into their prescribed Hierarchical Polarization Paradigm roles	
Stigmatization	Parents, siblings, authority figures, and peers stigmatize and 'make an example of' anyone who doesn't conform, that is, of anyone who deviates from their prescribed Hierarchical Polarization Paradigm roles, as delineated above	

How do the hierarchical polarization processes relate to class? A key part of the Hierarchical Polarization Paradigm is the economic exploitation of the subordinated group by the dominating group. Economic relationships and processes are organized to transfer property and output from the subordinated group into the hands of the dominating group, and to protect these accumulations from being redistributed back to the needier, subordinated group. Some examples of economic domination/subordination include slavery (whites/African – Americans), land grab and displacement (whites/Native Americans), non-payment for their work (white men/white women) and segregation into the lowest paid jobs (white men/white women, and men and women of colour). Economic power feeds political power, and hence cements systems of domination, especially in terms of race and colonization, for it can finance the weapons and prison system to enforce domination/subordination. Marx called such processes and the struggles than ensued from them – 'class'. However, in order to distinguish between the ascribed aspect of hierarchical polarizations and the potential freedom of upward mobility present in capitalism, we use the term 'class' only to refer to the latter.

Interdependence of the Various Hierarchical Polarizations

While the various hierarchical polarizations appear to operate independently, they in fact coexist and co-determine the economic and social values, practices and institutions of our country. They also coexist within each individual, whose social status is co-determined by the various hierarchical polarizations, according to his or her assignment to one or the other pole of each. Most individuals are dominators in some hierarchical polarizations, and subordinated in others.

Finally, the different hierarchical polarizations tend to support one another, in that they embody and rationalize the larger Hierarchical Polarization Paradigm's logic of polarization, domination/subordination, and so on.

The Hierarchical Polarization Paradigm treats and talks of its constructs – woman, man, white, black – as universal categories. However, the coexistence of the various hierarchical polarizations and their co-determination of economic and social life is such that the meaning of each category of hierarchical polarization varies according to a person's position within the others. What it means to be a woman, for example, varies, according to whether one is white or black, aristocrat or commoner, heterosexual or lesbian, rich or poor (Spelman, 1988, Mohanty, 2003). Nevertheless, the category remains, and has social significance.[2]

Transformation of Hierarchical Polarization

Because hierarchical polarities restrict freedom, and cause deprivation and inequality, they usually engender resistance in many forms, from slave revolts to anti-colonial struggles to women's liberation movements to consciousness-raising groups and therapy. This resistance to particular hierarchical polarizations is usually initiated by members of the group oppressed by that hierarchical polarization – although people from the oppressor group sometimes join them.

Often, the oppressed are drawn into violent struggle as a reaction to violent domination by their oppressors, and their movements for freedom and self-determination also take a violent form. This, in turn, can intensify – and be used to justify – the violence of the dominating group. Each group views the other as its enemy, and as a threat. This tense situation creates a pervasive sense of insecurity and fear for both oppressors and the oppressed that can intensify the polarization and domination/subordination process.

Starting in the nineteenth century, and growing rapidly over the last 50 years, new, non-violent approaches to resistance to hierarchical polarization have been developing, approaches which reject violence in favour of other modes of social power and transformation. We call these new types of resistance to hierarchical polarities, and to the Hierarchical Polarization Paradigm, 'transformative processes'. The remainder of this paper is devoted to exploring the different transformative processes, which are at work in the US today.

The Seven Types of Transformative Processes

We have identified seven distinct types of transformative processes currently at work in the US, healing a variety of individual hierarchical polarizations and the Hierarchical Polarization Paradigm itself. These transformative processes are creating the basis for an economy and society based on solidarity, cooperation, freedom, democracy, economic and social justice, diversity and sustainability. We will discuss each process briefly here, putting more emphasis on the latter processes, which are more recent and less understood.

These transformative processes are at work both in organized social movements, and in individuals' everyday, personal and work lives. Civil rights, feminist, gay and lesbian, children's rights, anti-colonial, anti-racist, ecology and other movements all embody one or more of the transformative processes discussed below. At the same time, peoples' individual struggles for healing, wholeness, connection and liberation from the restrictive dictates of the Hierarchical Polarization Paradigm are also an important part of these transformative processes, as we will see. Individual transformation and organized movements for social and institutional transformation complement one another.

The different transformative processes have emerged more or less sequentially, each process building on the preceding ones. The first five transformative processes focus on healing particular hierarchical polarizations; the last two begin to integrate the issues raised by the different hierarchical polarizations, and through their transformative actions, to replace the Hierarchical Polarization Paradigm with a new, non-hierarchical, more just and sustainable paradigms We summarize them in Figure 3.

Figure 3: The Seven Transformative Processes

TRANSFORMATIVE PROCESSES	ASPECT OF HIERARCHICAL POLARIZATION PARADIGM CHALLENGED	BASIC THRUST OF TRANSFORMATIVE PROCESS
Transformative Process that Challange the Various Hierarchical Polarities		
Questioning	View of social identities and relationships as natural or God-given, i.e. ascription (can also challenge Hierarchical Polarization Paradigm itself)	Why are things this way? Isn't that particular social practice or institution unfair? Are people naturally different as categorized? Are people inevitably unequal and violent?
Equal Opportunity	View that certain people are naturally superior to others; resultant restriction of rights, privileges and occupations of subordinated group	All are created equal; members of a devalued group should have the rights and privileges that the valued group has, including access to the higher-paid higher-status occupations

TRANSFORMATIVE PROCESSES	ASPECT OF HIERARCHICAL POLARIZATION PARADIGM CHALLENGED	BASIC THRUST OF TRANSFORMATIVE PROCESS
Valuing the Devalued	Devaluation of subordinated peoples, along with their traits and activities	The values, traits and works of the devalued group are important and valuable, and need to be recognized and revalued
Integrating	View that certain kinds of people, ways of being, values, character traits, and works cannot/should not be combined; polarization/segregation of people, traits, and types of work	It is healthy and balanced to integrate social spaces and relationships; to combine the two poles of a hierarchical polarity in a person and in an activity; and to combine in one's life activities that previously were polarized, such as active parenting and paid work
Discernment	Negative aspects of ways of being, values, character traits, and works resulting from hierarchy and/or polarization	Critical re-examination of the basic building blocks of our social order – including masculinity, femininity, spirituality, materialism, whiteness, nature, success – so as to free them from their distortion by hierarchization and polarization
Transformative Process that Challange Multiple Hierarchical Polarities and the Entire Hierarchical Polarization Paradigm.		
Combining	Assumption that hierarchical-polarity-created groups are homogeneous, and disconnected from one another	Expansion of social movements beyond single-issue, identity-politics-based awareness and organizing; expansion of one's sense of solidarity in standing against the oppressions suffered by others
Diversifying/ Unifying/ Globalizing	Inevitability of polarization, domination, and violence; fragmentation of individuality and of social movements; the Hierarchical Polarization Paradigm itself	Solidarity amidst diversity; globalization from below; socially responsible economic behaviour, constructing a new paradigm

Questioning Processes

The questioning process challenges the rationalizations, and internalization of these rationalizations, that undergird the Hierarchical Polarization Paradigm, by asking questions about aspects of a hierarchical polarity that are taken for granted. Questioning processes are supported by self-conscious reflection, and by true scientific investigation and education.

Here are a few examples of transformative questions:

Are women, blacks, gays, poor people naturally inferior in their abilities, or have they been made such by our economic and social institutions?

Do we all experience equal opportunity, regardless our gender or skin colour?

Are white women, and men and women of colour, or even white men, really rewarded according to their productivity?

Are gay people biologically and morally inferior to heterosexuals?

Is US culture really the highest stage of civilization or could we learn from 'underdeveloped' societies?

And, above all, do innate differences among people make them naturally unequal and in conflict, or would it be possible to construct a diverse, harmonious and cooperative country and world in which everyone could live in safety and peace?

Questioning processes are the *sine qua non* for the transformation of hierarchical polarities, and of the Hierarchical Polarization Paradigm. For this reason, the ability to think for oneself, and to think critically about social roles, values, practices and institutions, is the key to the Transformative Moment.

Equal Opportunity Processes and the Capitalist Class System

Equal opportunity processes are struggles by members of the subordinated groups, and their allies, to gain political and economic rights, social treatment and economic opportunities equal to those of the dominating group. Equal opportunity processes challenge every hierarchical polarization process, and are a key force in breaking down the injustices, the imbalances and the lack of freedom of the Hierarchical Polarization Paradigm.

The US itself was established as part of an equal opportunity process. With their famous, liberatory claim that 'all (white) men are created equal', the Founding Fathers not only declared political independence from their British colonizers, but also formally overturned the aristocrat/commoner hierarchical polarization.

With historical hindsight, the 'all men are created equal' statement can be understood as an assertion of equal opportunity for white men. This assertion forcibly rejected one pillar of the then current Hierarchical Polarization Paradigm – aristocratic political and economic domination – while accepting all of the others. In particular, the hierarchical, domination/subordination view of economic and social life, along with the race, gender, God/man and man/nature polarities, were maintained and built into the developing emerging capitalist economy. However, the hierarchy among white men, instead of being based on ascription and aristocratic privilege, was replaced by a flexible, semi-meritocratic hierarchy.

The developing capitalist economy became a competition among white men to dominate or 'better' each other in their struggle for wealth, a process called 'breadwinning'. A white man's wealth, and his ability to support a full-time homemaker, became the measure of his worth or level of success, rather than his pedigree. The true winner in this new system was seen to be the 'self-made man': The man who, through his own effort, earnings, savings and investments in expanded production, worked his way up the economic hierarchy from entry-level worker to head of a large and powerful firm (Matthaei, 1982, Chapter 5).

The new flexibility in the economic hierarchy – that is, the freedom of white men to increase their economic status and power through their own efforts as workers and entrepreneurs – let loose a flurry of effort and invention which, coordinated by the market, fueled a new, dynamic economic system we call capitalism. The competition of white men to dominate one another in the market was institutionalized in capitalist firms. By the end of the nineteenth century, this process had created a new, immortal individual – the corporation – that abstractly embodied this competitive struggle for profits and growth, and, in turn, harnessed self-interested, competitive white men to its service, as managers and workers, in complex internal labour markets.

White women and people of colour, of course, were excluded from this declaration of equality, and from the economic competition based on it. They were segregated into subordinate non-capitalist forms of labour like slavery, and/or into lower paid work and unpaid reproductive work. However, white women and black men and women, participated in their own equal opportunity processes over the course of the nineteenth and twentieth centuries. Black men and women (with some white allies) fought for the abolition of slavery in the nineteenth century, and against educational and employment segregation in the twentieth century. White women fought for (white) women's suffrage and property rights, and then (with some women of colour) for the right to enter the higher paid higher status white men's jobs (Amott and Matthaei, 1996). In the second half of the twentieth century, the gay and lesbian and disability rights movements also participated in equal opportunity processes against discrimination and for equal opportunity in the labour force.

Each of these equal opportunity movements has made major strides in eliminating the particular discrimination it is targeting. All continue their fights today, because discrimination and segregation persist.

All of these equal opportunity movements are based in 'identity politics' in the sense that their members are overwhelmingly members of a particular subordinated group – i.e. they are blacks, women, gays, or disabled people – fighting for equality with a particular dominant group – i.e. with whites, men, heterosexuals, or able-bodied people. Finally, each of these identity-politics equal opportunity movements tend to give rise to a counterbalancing processes, which we call 'valuing the devalued'.

Valuing-the-Devalued Processes

Valuing-the-devalued processes tend to accompany, or come on the heels of, equal opportunity processes. A key part of the Hierarchical Polarization Paradigm is the devaluation both of the people placed in the subordinate group and of the traits and activities associated with them. A central aspect of civil rights, feminist, gay and disability movement has been the fight against this devaluation. The black-is-beautiful movement, including the celebration of one's African heritage with holidays like Kwanzaa, is an example of this process. The wages for housework movement and organizing for paid maternity leaves are also examples of the valuing-the-devalued process, because they work to achieve financial compensation for unpaid work in the home. Native American nations' movements to recuperate and maintain their languages and cultures are a third example.

These and many other examples of the valuing-the-devalued process both respond directly to the devaluation created by the Hierarchical Polarization Paradigm, and compensate for imbalances created by the equal opportunity process. In the equal opportunity process, as we have seen, subordinated groups struggled for equal rights and opportunities. However, the equality they struggled for was equality with white, able-bodied, heterosexual men. Thus, in their very nature, equal opportunity struggles tended to set their sights upon gaining what the dominant group had, or becoming like the dominant group. For this reason, the equal opportunity process, as embodied by processes of individual transformation and different social movements, has tended to implicitly accept and even reinforce the reigning socio-economic devaluation of people and work that are located in the subordinated category. As Martin Luther King once commented about the civil rights movement: 'We're integrating into a burning house' (Belafonte, 2006).

For example, when second-wave feminists fought for access to and success within high-status, male-dominated jobs, they implicitly or explicitly accepted and reinforced the reigning devaluation of the work of mothering and of full-time homemakers as 'just housewives' (Matthaei and Brandt, 2001).

The valuing-the-devalued process redresses this problem, by noting how crucial reproductive work is to our economy and society, and advocating for public support of it through paid parental leaves, parental education, and the like. One prominent example is feminist economist Nancy Folbre's thorough and convincing analysis of the need to value caring work in *The Invisible Heart* (2001).

Integrative Processes

Integrative processes bring together people, characteristics, or activities that were polarized and made opposite by the Hierarchical Polarization Paradigm. As we have seen, US economic and social values, practices and institutions separate and differentiate people, human traits and ways of being, and spheres of life. We are supposed to be different from, and do different things than, those in the opposite categories. We are supposed to be either masculine or feminine, white or black, heterosexual or homosexual. 'Man' is seen as different from and in control over 'Nature'. Our economic decisions are supposed to be ruled by financial, materialistic considerations; however, while in our religious institutions, spiritual values take over. People and social movements engaged in integrative processes, individually and/or in groups, reject one or more of these polarities as restrictive, unbalanced and unhealthy; and set out to combine things, which were previously seen to be mutually exclusive.

Equal opportunity processes often set in motion integrative processes in two ways. First, they 'integrate' previously all-white or all-male enclaves with blacks and women, respectively. This integration breaks down race and gender polarization, and disproves the assertion that the races or genders have inherently different abilities and traits. Second, equal opportunity processes, especially feminist ones, have led to the combining of types of work that had been mutually exclusive under the Hierarchical Polarization Paradigm. For example, when feminists won access into white men's jobs, many of them sought to continue women's traditional mothering and homemaking work as well – to be traditionally masculine and feminine at the same time. And in couples where both husband and wife are employed full-time, many husbands have begun to take on women's traditional mothering and housekeeping work along with their masculine work.

Whenever we see what was previously polarized being combined, we have the integrative process at work. When people marry across race, and interracial people acknowledge their complete heritage, the integrative process is at work. When consumers, workers and managers bring their spiritual values – values like justice, equality, sustainability – into their economic decisions, the integrative process is at work. By transforming the way, people are and act, integrative processes begin to qualitatively restructure social values and institutions (Matthaei and Brandt, 2001).

Discernment Processes

Whereas integrative processes combine what was polarized, discernment processes subject each pole of each hierarchical polarity, and the values, practices and institutions constructed around that those polarities, to serious critical evaluation. In particular, the discernment process involves identifying and redressing the distortions and injustices caused by polarization and domination/subordination.

The polarization of people, work and traits into mutually exclusive categories distorts and unbalances humanity. As feminist economist Julie Nelson has shown, the combination of previously polarized traits allows more positive forms to emerge (1996, Chapter 2). For example, when polarized between men and women, the basic human traits of directivity and receptivity degenerate into arrogance, insensitivity and domination, for men; and self-effacement, oversensitivity and subservience for women. These distorted traits are then built into unbalanced and dysfunctional economic and social institutions. The integrative process, which we discussed above, combines poles and transcends polarization; the discernment process follows up as we redefine ourselves and our work, free from restrictive polarizations. A key current area of the discernment process is occurring as a result of work/family integration; efforts to combine the two are leading to the redefinition of both.

The second major type of discernment addresses the distortions and injustices caused by domination/subordination. Those who belong to dominant groups have been actively or passively involved in unjust and oppressive economic and social institutions, which they have benefited from. In the past, they were able to rationalize their actions and privileges, because of the racism, sexism and other forms of bigotry, which they had internalized. However, the many-faceted identity-based organization of subordinated groups through the first four transformative processes has changed the experience of people in dominator groups. Knowledge about the various oppressive and unjust hierarchical polarization processes has been expanded dramatically. Further, personal experiences with members of subordinated groups in equal opportunity workplaces and desegregated schools have also eroded dominator group members' beliefs in their natural superiority. The family is also a site of discernment for members of dominator groups, as their children come out, and/or marry people of colour, and/or adopt children of colour, and as men's dominance is challenged by their wives and daughters.

For these reasons, more and more people are rejecting the dominator roles, which they have been assigned to by the Hierarchical Polarization Paradigm, and becoming active in the feminist, anti-racist and GLBT (Gay Lesbian Bisexual Transsexual) movements. Many of these changes are on a very personal level, in everyday actions, which acknowledge and reject one's special privileges, treat members of subordinated groups as equals, and challenge others in the dominated group who do not. White feminist Peggy McIntosh's widely circulated article, 'Unpacking the Invisible Backpack' (1989), about her realization of the privileges she enjoyed by virtue of being white, has educated scores of whites about their unjust racially-based privileges. Also, across the country, white people have been actively involved in organizing and giving anti-white racism training, as part of grassroots anti-racism groups, academic institutions and religious organizations (Groot, 2006).[3] Many men are renouncing male privilege, and confronting sexist men. For example, the White Ribbon Campaign: Men Working to End Violence Against Women was started by Canadians in 1989 in response to an anti-feminist man's massacre of 14 women. Today, there are Men who are against Violence Against Women with 'White Ribbon' groups in 52 countries around the world, including the US (Minerson, 2006). PFLAG (Parents, Families and Friends of Lesbians and Gays) organizes actively against homophobia and for gay rights; it has over 200,000 members and supporters and over 500 affiliates in the US.

One final and important set of examples of discernment by members of a dominator group is the new anti-class privilege movements. For example, wealthy people are working in a group called Responsible Wealth against the widening class divide by organizing against the repeal of the estate tax (www.responsiblewealth.org). In cities and towns across the US, the non-poor have joined their low-income neighbours in successful campaigns to provide all workers with Living Wages (www.livingwagecampaign.org), and in the November 2006 elections, voters in six states passed increases in the minimum wage.

Discernment takes different forms for people in subordinated groups. A person in a subordinated category tends to be more critical of the hierarchical polarity that oppresses them, and more active in struggles to transform it, than those in the dominator group, as we have seen in our discussions of previous processes. However, people in subordinated groups cannot escape internalizing the hierarchical polarity, which oppresses them, in subtle ways. For example, for millennia, femininity has been intertwined with subordination, and women have internalized this as active self-subordination. The valuable feminine activity of caring for others, structured as unpaid and devalued work done under the control of one's husband to fulfill social mandates of 'proper behaviour', has become equated with self-sacrifice and self-subordination to the needs of others.

Mothering has been defined as the unquestioning socialization of children into the oppressive dictates of Hierarchical Polarization Paradigm.

For women (and men expressing their feminine sides), the discernment process here means developing and expressing a positive sense of femininity, both through individual behaviour and through institutional changes. For example, positive femininity defines the feminine activity of caring for others as a valuable social activity, which requires support through public policy. Positive feminine caring heals and empowers both others and oneself. Finally, positive femininity, expressed in mothering, rejects the unquestioning transmission of ones' cultural heritage, replacing it with a critical awareness, which evaluates reigning social mores. Thus, positive feminine mothering (and fathering) affirms and transmits to one's children those values and practices which one finds to be healthy, just and life-affirming; and rejects and reshapes values, practices and identities which are oppressive. An excellent concrete example of the latter is the work by the Center for a New American Dream to help parents resist the hyper-materialism that is being cultivated in their children by advertising.

The first five transformative processes seek to heal the various hierarchical polarities both within individuals, and as they are manifested within economic and social institutions. These transformative processes also support one another in key ways. These represent a huge step forward in economic and social development.

However, the first five transformative processes tend not to challenge the separations among specific hierarchical polarities, and so the various movements, which embody these processes tend to be based in single-issue, single-identity politics, such as anti-racist, or feminist, or pro-worker, or environmental, or gay rights, or disability, etc. To be fully effective, transformative social movements need to incorporate the last two processes, the combining and diversifying/unifying/globalizing processes.

The Combining Process

The combining process connects and combines consciousness-raising and social action vis-à-vis two or more hierarchical polarities. In this way, it begins to break down the compartmentalizing aspect of the hierarchical dualist system, laying the foundation for the systematic transformation of our economy and society into a higher stage. The combining process is a natural outcome of the other processes, because the various hierarchical polarities are all interconnected as intertwined aspects of the Hierarchical Polarization Paradigm. We will present the combining process briefly here, using the example of second-wave feminist organizing starting in the 1970s.

Women of different classes, racial-ethnicities, and sexualities came together in the grassroots 'women's movement' that swept the US in the 1970s. However, when women came together to raise their consciousnesses, fight sexism and liberate 'WOMEN', women who were working class, and/or of colour, and/or lesbians were marginalized, and their political issues were downplayed or ignored. These excluded groups of women reacted with anger and disaffection. Many felt the need to split from the white-heterosexual-middle class-dominated mainstream feminist movement, forming groups of their own, and creating feminist theory and practice that spoke to their issues (Moraga and Anzaldua, 1981; Joseph and Lewis, 1981; Hull, Scott and Smith, 1982; hooks, 1984).

This set the stage for the complicated, many-faceted combining process, which began to extend feminist movement beyond the compartmentalization of polarities, issues and identities created by the Hierarchical Polarization Paradigm. For example, the combining process taught many white middle class heterosexual feminists (ourselves included) about racism, classism and homophobia. Based on this learning, many feminist groups have subsequently become multi-issue movements that truly aspire to address the issues of all women. Indeed, the National Organization of Women now lists on its platform of key issues 'racism, lesbian rights, and economic justice'.[4] Julie has participated in a similar combining process in the class-centred Union for Radical Political Economics. Groups which have expanded their focus as a result of the combining process also actively seek to work in coalition with other groups working on issues which affect their constituency.

A second source of the combining process is the coming together of movements because they have a shared goal or 'enemy'. The economic dislocation and environmental destruction brought about by corporate globalization, with its neo-liberal agenda of Free Trade and new institution, the World Trade Organization (WTO), has brought together diverse, grassroots movements from around the world. For example, the famous Seattle anti-WTO protest of 1999 brought together for the first time organized labour and environmental groups, who have usually been in conflict into what has become a 'blue-green coalition'. This marked the coming of age of a vibrant anti-globalization movement, which unites a broad range of groups around the world against corporate abuses, a process, which has been called 'globalization from below' (Brecher, Costello and Smith, 2000).

In these ways, the combining process has been creating ties of understanding and solidarity among people involved in different social movements, across the globe, laying the groundwork for the last process, the diversifying/unifying/globalizing process.

The Diversifying/Unifying/Globalizing Process

The diversifying/unifying/globalizing process is building on all of the other six processes to give birth to a new kind of person, and new types of political and economic organizing. These new people are capable of directing and coordinating all of the other processes in a wonderful symphony of systemic personal-and-social healing and transformation. The diversifying/unifying/globalizing process is the newest of all the transformative process, so it is only beginning to be expressed. Nevertheless, it has already spawned entirely new concepts and forms of movement capable of achieving the transition to a post-Hierarchical Polarization Paradigm country and world.

The first six processes have begun to create a new kind of person, a person who is deeply committed to transcending all of the hierarchical polarities in his or her life. Such a person resists the ways in which society tries to subordinate him or her (for being of colour, working class or poor, gay, not American, not Christian, female, and/or disabled). Equally importantly, as we have seen, this new kind of person refuses the privileges accorded to him or to her of being a dominator or exploiter (because of being white, upper-class, heterosexual, American, able-bodied and/or male).

This new kind of person – a person who tries, in all of his or her actions, to live according to the principles of equality, justice, democracy, mutual respect and freedom – is the force behind the diversifying/unifying/globalizing process. This process expresses calls for and works towards a socially responsible 'citizen of the world' consciousness, which is based on unity or a sense of oneness with all human beings, and indeed, with all of life. People involved in this process acknowledge and defend civil and human rights, economic justice, freedom and democracy for every human being in the world, while acknowledging and embracing the diversity of ways to construct free and equitable people and institutions. Such people actively seek balance, connection, integration, equalization – of the parts within themselves, and of all the rich diversity of people and life forms on earth.

Such a consciousness does not flow from a sense of self-sacrifice, but rather out of an understanding that one will not be fully healed, whole, and fulfilled if he or she is not positively engaged in living his/her larger life in such a manner. Such a person embodies the questioning process, listening to her inner voice, the voice of conscience, the voice, which rejects any or all social mandates and structures which go against his or her core inner values. He or she listens to all who are protesting, evaluates their concerns, and, if she finds them to be justified, takes them on as her own. Rather than fitting into and furthering the global capitalist economy, such a person embodies positive economic transformation.

At the root of our current globalizing economic system, with all its wonders and its deadly destructiveness, is the Hierarchical Polarization Paradigm. The US economy has been structured on the super-exploitation of subordinated groups and of non-human nature, and on narrowly self-interested, materialistic and exploitative competition among white men and any others who can compete their way into the game and play by its rules. In this capitalist class system, money – and the material goods and power over people and non-human nature which it buys – is the ultimate goal of life, and striving for domination over polarized 'others' is seen as the inexorable way of life. However, the diversifying/ unifying/globalizing process is leading people all over the world to reject these prevailing values and say 'no' to business as usual in all that they do. As the Zapatistas say, '*Un solo no, un million de si*': a shared, unified 'no' to the global capitalist economic system, and a million 'yeses' to the multiplicity of different positive alternatives that people all over the world are constructing.

What are the yeses? As the diversifying/unifying/globalizing process develops and extends across our country, and the world, it is inventing new economic and social values, practices and institutions, which can heal the individual and social wounds and imbalances created by the Hierarchical Polarization Paradigm. We will discuss a few key examples here.

One example of the diversifying/unifying/globalizing process is the new economic concept of stakeholders. Traditional, profit-motivated firms are expected to serve their stockholders, period. The interests and well-being of many other people who have a stake in what the firm does are ignored, such as workers, suppliers, the local community, government and non-human life. The stakeholder concept challenges managers, and boards of directors, to find win-win solutions that benefit all of their firm's stakeholders, not just the stockholders (Kelly, 2001; Blair and Stout, 2001).

A related economic concept, which has emerged in tandem with the stakeholder concept, is the concept of socially responsible economic behaviour. Socially responsible decision-making has come to mean making decisions that are good both for the narrow self-interest of the decision-maker AND for others and society at large. The concept of socially responsible decision-making represents an alternative economic value system to narrowly self-interested, money- and profit-maximizing decision-making, which motivates our Hierarchical Polarization Paradigm economy. This new value system charges and empowers not just the managers of firms, but ALL who engage in economic activity, to help make our economy more just and sustainable through their decisions as consumers, workers, investors, citizens and entrepreneurs. This trend includes the continually growing movements for socially responsible investment (Social Investment Forum), for corporate social responsibility and social impact management (Gentile, 2006),[5] for socially responsible work (Graduation Pledge Alliance; Idealist.org) and for socially responsible consumption (Co-op America, Center for a New American Dream).

A third example of the diversifying/unifying/globalizing process is a new form of political organizing for peace, justice, democracy and sustainability, exemplified by the annual World Social Forum, and the hundreds of other similarly-organized forums that now take place yearly throughout the world. These forums build on the combining of groups in response to the many destructive, oppressive and life-threatening aspects of our global capitalist economic system, discussed above. People working in the vast diversity of social and political movements have begun to come together, to work together to begin to envision and create new economic and social structures. Under the motto, 'Another World is Possible,' experienced progressive activists created the World Social Forum, a type of 'movement of movements'. This movement of movements is bringing together people of all ages, classes, genders, sexual preferences, race-ethnicities and nations who are engaged in socio-economic justice, environmental, peace and democracy activism. The focus is on listening to one another, learning from one another, forming cross-country alliances, and creating and advocating for new values, practices and institutions, which respect all of life. The World Social Forum is committed to non-violence. The underlying assumption for the meetings is a shared commitment to eradicate any injustices and to preserve the beautiful planet, which we inhabit together. In particular, the World Social Forum connects together feminist, anti-racist, worker, disability, ecological, spiritual, gay and peace movements, who are sharing their knowledge and experience with the goal of building institutions which serve us all (www.forumsocialmundial.org.br; Fisher and Ponniah, 2003). A jointly written book, *Alternatives to Economic Globalization: A Better World is Possible*, has emerged from these meetings, and the groups which they have catalyzed, which lays out what is becoming a growing consensus around the necessary direction for economic transformation out of global capitalism into a post-Hierarchical Polarization Paradigm economy (Cavanagh and Mander, 2004).

In these and similar ways, the diversifying/unifying/globalizing process holds out the promise of what Martin Luther King called 'the beloved community'. Beloved community is a 'society in which every person [is] valued and where all conflicts [can] be reconciled in a spirit of goodwill and mutual benefit…where all of us can live together in a climate of understanding, cooperation and unity' (Coretta Scott King, 2004).

The seven transformative processes, developed and honed through over a century of struggles, provide us with the tools to dismantle the Hierarchical Polarization Paradigm, and build more egalitarian, peaceful, loving, free, and democratic economic and social values, practices and institutions. We are blessed to have been born into such an historic, transformative moment, and it is up to each of us to do what we can to help guide our world to this possible future.

Notes

1. Heartfelt thanks to Donna Bivens, Janice Goldman and Germai Medhanie for their help. A shorter version of this article was presented at the Rethinking Marxism conference in Amherst, October 2006.
2. Brien (2006, p. 272) employs the notion of a 'concrete universal' to understand the existence of socially meaningful categories that do not, however, describe a shared experience.
3. Some examples are The Center for the Study of White American Culture in New Jersey (www.euroamerican.org), Challenging White Supremacy in California (www.cwsworkshop.org), European Dissent in New Orleans (www.pisab.org), and Community Change in Boston (www.communitychangeinc.org) (Groot, 2006).
4. http://www.now.org/history/history.html, accessed 26 October 2006.
5. See caseplace.org for an excellent collection of journal articles and cases in the fields of corporate social responsibility and social impact management.

References

Amott, T. and Matthaei, J. A. 1996. *Race, Gender, and Work: A Multicultural Economic History of Women in the United States*, Boston: South End.

Belafonte, H. 2006. 'Politically Incorrect', Bill Maher Show, October 27.

Blair, M. and Stout, L. 1999. 'A Team Production Theory of Corporate Law,' *Virginia Law Review*, 85, 2.

Brandt, B. 1995. *Whole Life Economics*. Philadelphia: New Society Publishers.

Brecher, J., Costello T. and Smith, B. 2000. *Globalization from Below: The Power of Solidarity*. Cambridge, Mass: South End Press.

Brien, K. M. 2006. *Marx, Reason, and the Art of Freedom*, 2nd edition. New York: Prometheus Books.

Cavanagh, J. and Mander, J. (eds.), 2004. *Alternatives to Globalization: A Better World is Possible*. San Francisco, CA: Berrett-Koehler.

Center for a New American Dream, www.newdream.org

Fisher, W. F. and Ponniah, T. (eds.), 2004. *Another World is Possible: Popular Alternatives to Globalization at the World Social Forum*. London: Zed Books.

Folbre, N. 2001. *The Invisible Heart: Economics and Family Values*. New York: The New Press.

Gentile, M. C. 2006. Social Impact Management, www.caseplace.org, accessed 20 November.

Graduation Pledge, www.GraduationPledge.org

Groot, Meck. 2006. Co-Director of Women's Theological Center. Interview on November 20.

Hodges, J., Struckmann, D. and Trost, L. 1975. *Cultural Bases of Racism and Group Oppression: An Examination of Traditional 'Western' Concepts, Values and Institutional Structures Which Support Racism, Sexism and Elitism*. Berkeley, CA: Two Riders Press.

hooks, b. 1984. *Feminist Theory: From Margin to Center*. Boston: South End Press.

Hull, G. T., Scott, P. B., and Smith, B. (eds.), 1982. *All the Women are White, all the Blacks are Men, but Some of us are Brave: Black Women's Studies*. Old Westbury, NY: Feminist Press.

Jennings, A. L. 1993. 'Public or Private? Institutional Economics and Feminism,' in Ferber, M. A. and Nelson, J. A. (eds.), *Beyond Economic Man: Feminist Theory and Economics*. Chicago: University of Chicago Press.

Joseph, G. and Lewis, J. 1981. *Common Differences: Conflicts in Black and White Feminist Perspectives*. New York: Anchor Press/Doubleday.

Kelly, M. 2001. *The Divine Right of Capital: Dethroning the Corporate Aristocracy*. San Francisco: Berrett-Koehler.

Levine, D. P. 1977. *Contributions to the Critique of Economic Theory*. London: Routledge & Kegan Paul.

—. 1978. *Economic Theory, vol I. The Elementary Relations of Economic Life*, London: Routledge & Kegan Paul.

—. 1981. *Economic Theory, vol II. The System of Economic Relations as a Whole*. London; Routledge & K. Paul.

Matthaei, J. A. 1982. *An Economic History of Women in America: Women's Work, the Sexual Division of Labor, and the Development of Capitalism*. NY: Schocken Books.

—. 1996. 'Why Marxist, Feminist, and Anti-Racist Economists Should be Marxist-Feminist-Anti-Racist Economists', *Feminist Economics*, 2, 1.

—. 2000. 'Beyond Racist Capitalist Patriarchy: Growing a Liberated Economy,' in Baiman, R., Boushey, H. and Saunders, D. (eds.), *Political Economy and Contemporary Capitalism: Radical Perspectives on Economic Theory and Policy*. Armonk, NY: M.E. Sharpe.

Matthaei, J. A. and Brandt, B. 2001. 'Healing Ourselves, Healing Our Economy: Paid Work, Unpaid Work, and the Next Stage of Feminist Economic Transformation', *Review of Radical Political Economics*, 33.

—. (forthcoming). The Transformative Moment.

McIntosh, Peggy. 1989. 'White Privilege: Unpacking the Invisible Backpack', available at http://stickyrice.itgo.com/whiteprivilege.html

Minerson, T. 2006. 'From Canada, Some Thoughts on Organizing against Femicide', *Peaceworks*, November.

Mohanty, C. 2003. *Feminism Without Borders: Decolonizing Theory, Practicing Solidarity*. Durham: NC: Duke University Press.

Moraga, C. and Anzaldua, G. (eds.), 1981. *This Bridge Called My Back: Writings by Radical Women of Color*. Watertown, Mass: Persephone Press.

Nelson, J. 1996. *Feminism, Objectivity and Economics*. London: Routledge.

— 2006. *Economics for Humans*. Chicago: University of Chicago Press.

Parents, Families and Friends of Lesbians and Gays, www.pflag.org

Scott King, C. 2004. 'Building the Beloved Community', www.jewishpost.com/jp1001/jpbr1001e.htm

Social Investment Forum, www.socialinvest.org.

Spelman, E. 1988. *Inessential Woman: Problems of Exclusion in Feminist Thought*. Boston: Beacon Press.

Chapter 9

FRONTIERS OF CADRE RADICALIZATION IN CONTEMPORARY CAPITALISM

Kees van der Pijl

Introduction

In this chapter, I argue that in the current phase of social development, a crisis of exhaustion of the biosphere may be beginning to radicalize segments, or 'fractions' of what I call the class of managerial *cadre* – the auxiliary, executive arm of the capitalist class properly speaking.

The capitalist ruling class is the owner of capital, who by its restless quest for high-yield assets decides the direction of social development. The cadre are the paid functionaries overseeing that development in the economy and society at large, integrating all its technical, educational, and other aspects, and as organic intellectuals, providing ideological cohesion to the consequences of this particular course. Thus, when capitalist discipline is effectively imposed on a global scale, the cadre will be involved in managing globalization in all its aspects, from actual transnational business operations and training other managers, via propaganda praising the blessings of free trade and payments, to organizing forms of 'global governance'. In the process, certain fractions of the cadre are in a position to observe, at close range, current developments from a different angle than that of the stock market operator. And what they see is not necessarily encouraging. Indeed as Anthony Hopkins playing Nixon in Oliver Stone's movie says to his First Lady, 'It's not pretty, Buddy! It's not pretty!'

The effect of the world-embracing operation of capital creates complex webs of interaction, a socialization of labour on a planetary scale. Socialization of labour is a key concept from the Marxist critique of capital, but not so prominent in critical thinking today. Yet, it remains the key to understanding both the development and the moment of transformation of contemporary capitalism. 'The socialization of labor by capitalist production', Lenin wrote in one of his early articles, 'does not at all consist in people working under one roof (that is only a small part of the process), but in the concentration of capital being accompanied by the specialization of social labor, by a decrease in the number of capitalists in each given branch of industry and an increase in the number of separate branches of industry – in many separate production processes being merged into one social production process' (*Collected Works*, 1, p. 176). The reality of socialization, therefore, requires a range of integrative activities, be they straightforward planned integration, indirect 'programming', or merely the standardization of production and market conditions. What counts is that in capitalism, economic activity is continuously being broken up *and* reintegrated.

The cadre, as I have argued elsewhere (van der Pijl, 1998, Chapter 5), are the *class of socialization*; they embody one particular strand in 'the specialization of social labor' referred to. Thanks to their education, the cadre is ideologically under the hegemony of the capitalist ruling class and often relatively well paid. Yet, ultimately, they simultaneously constitute, as a salaried and functionally property-less social category (never mind that they may have some stocks or other capital savings), a fraction of the working class. It is on this central fracture that the broad sociological stratum of which we speak here, may split, and it depends on how well capital is doing, whether this split will have political consequences.

A New Era but No New Social Forces

The collapse of the Soviet Union (USSR) and its bloc, and the parallel demise of the Third World as a tentative coalition of those states seeking to play off East and West for the purpose of their own stability and betterment, in combination have allowed capital to recapture the entire globe as its terrain of operations. It has done so under an evolving neo-liberal concept of control, discarding the class compromises with organized labour of post-war corporate liberalism. The globalization of market discipline along neo-liberal lines was a way of undermining the corporate entities of which society was made up in the prior era. It has turned negotiated Keynesian macro-economy for the heavily institutionalized 'social partners', into naturalized Hayekian micro-economy for everybody individually. But as socialization of labour necessarily accompanies capital accumulation, capital's global profitability drive necessarily entails the proliferation of rules and norms throughout the global political economy, to ensure the compatibility of accumulation conditions (see the papers in Giesen and van der Pijl, 2006).

The sovereign state – as Braithwaite and Drahos (2000, p. 31) note – in the process mutates into a force 'constituted by and helping to constitute webs of regulatory influences comprised of many actors wielding many mechanisms'. Politics becomes increasingly divorced from the domestic mobilization and interest articulation of 'national' social forces. Politicians, being part of the managerial cadre of capitalist society, must seek to carve out positions primarily in these 'webs of regulatory influences'. Mark Duffield in this connection speaks of a 'shift from hierarchical and territorial relations of government to polyarchical, non-territorial and networked relations of governance' (2001, p. 2).

The main parameters of the current field of forces affecting these relations are twofold. First, all social development is based on the exploitation of nature yielding a historically definite set of productive forces. In our epoch, however, this process is beginning to affect social development negatively: productive forces are being destroyed at a growing rate without adequate replacement. This may seem a somewhat convoluted way of saying that we are experiencing an exhaustion of the biosphere. But the phrasing allows us to see that the contradiction between the productive forces and the relations of production, which in a Marxist perspective engenders social transformation, in the current period is not based on new productive forces spawning new social forces. Instead, the transformative momentum is being generated by a falling away of productive forces straining the existing pattern of social relations, without a novel social force making its appearance and pressing political demands to adjust society to its needs. This would mean, in the existing circumstances, that new profit opportunities for the capitalist class will tend to diminish, whilst the demands on the cadre to sustain the existing order by integrative action will increase, and with it, the social weight of the cadre relative to the class of owners.

The second assumption is that no socio-political transformation is based on new economic interests alone. The radical revision of the overarching cosmology and world view of an epoch, say, Protestantism in the coming of bourgeois society displacing feudalism, is equally important. True, that transformation too was anchored in a contradiction between productive forces and relations of production becoming acute; in Braudelian terms, the 'limits of the possible' allowed society to move to a stage of greater individual freedom contradicting the hierarchies of the feudal order (cf. Braudel, 1981). But a revolutionary class is always first of all a class of a new consciousness, and only when its world view has been firmly implanted, will narrower economic interests become attuned to it. If today, therefore, the 'limits of the possible' are becoming narrower (assumption one), that will not change in itself that a new cosmology and world view will be the unifying element in a social transformation. The radicalizing cadre is, in my view, in the process of producing such a new ideology as the glamour of neo-liberalism is wearing off in the face of the crises referred to earlier.

The Cadre in Corporate Liberal Capitalism

The cadre in corporate liberalism operated almost as an aspirant ruling class, the protagonists of a much-debated 'managerial revolution' curtailing some key prerogatives of the capitalist class such as making private investment decisions. As a concept of control, corporate liberalism combined nationally organized, Fordist mass production, Keynesian demand management, and a social contract organized around the exchange of welfare for the support of Cold War and imperialist policies (along the lines of Robert Cox's 'welfare-nationalist state', 1987). In each of these areas, complex collective bargaining structures (including parliamentary structures of government) relied on solid bureaucracies of cadre who shared with the workers the commitment to job security and bona fide welfare arrangements.

However, in the late sixties, a range of signals that the corporate liberal concept of control was unravelling also began to suggest that the life cycle of the 'managerial revolution' had reached its final phase. The cadre actually played a key role in making this public. Thus the 1972 *Limits to Growth* report to the Club of Rome – a bulwark of progressive managerial thinking – highlighted that the growth of world population under the prevailing conditions of production and consumption would exhaust the world's natural resources within a century. However, as Annemieke Roobeek argues, these conclusions tended to overlook that such equations cannot be calculated without taking the relations of production into account, and these pointed to other problems such as declining productivity growth. The real limits were hidden in these relations, what she calls the *inherent control problems of Fordism* (Roobeek, 1987, p. 137).

The cadre in corporate liberalism was a key part of these control problems. As I have shown elsewhere, their relative presence had significantly increased over the post-war period, and the new recruits of the baby-boom generation tended to carry the echo of the May 68 radicalism into the structures of the welfare state, capital/labour compromise and the political arena itself (van der Pijl, 2002). But its political outlook was not monolithic. Even Samuel Huntington and two co-authors in a gloomy report to the Trilateral Commission dealing with the 'Crisis of Democracy' noted that whilst there was a problematic influx of 'value-oriented', 'adversary' intellectuals, a parallel growth was occurring of 'technocratic and policy-oriented intellectuals' (Crozier et al., 1975, p. 8).

To reinforce this latter strand of cadre as part of a comprehensive reorientation of the structures through which capitalist discipline is imposed on society, it is necessary that the structures of socialized labour are reorganized to begin with. Now, here we are dealing with patterns of middle-class formation that have a logic and history of their own. As we saw in the definition of socialization of labour given by Lenin (cf. above), there are two sides to the process. One is the organization of labour under an explicit discipline, as in a factory; the other is a process at the social level, involving separate capitals, and referring to a 'social production process' which is not as such organized as a single entity. In the former, socialization assumes the form of planning, so we can speak of planned socialization of labour; in the latter, this is not as clear-cut. We are rather looking at a context of socialization that is mediated by competition, market relations.

Two Forms of Socialization of Labour, Two Types of Cadre

On the basis of the foregoing, we may distinguish between two forms of socialization of labour: *market socialization*, in which the units in which labour is brought together under a single command, are not able to extend their jurisdiction to the economy as a whole; and *planned socialization*, where this is potentially the case. Here, to say it in German, the objective *Vergesellschaftung* (*Gesellschaft* meaning 'society') may become *Sozialisierung* – a nuance not available in English.

Sociologically, market socialization originated in a society of relatively small producers (the type of society Adam Smith had in mind) whose collaboration is realized blindly, across market exchange. The market 'spontaneously' connects the producer of chairs and the supplier of timber etc., into a chain of production. In the normative sphere, the state and the legal apparatus critically assist this process of socialization by providing overall cohesion and guaranteeing the right to private property (Weber, 1976, p. 383). The range of tasks required to have all these functions performed involves self-employed 'notables' such as notaries and lawyers, as well as public dignitaries like town clerks and others associated with certain state functions. In addition to these intermediaries, there is the stratum of traditional intellectuals from priests and journalists to novelists and philosophers who contribute in one way or another to shaping and/or upholding the normative structure of society. Self-employment is the hallmark of this class. *Market socialization in other words (re-) produces a cadre of self-employed dignitaries overseeing a capitalist system revolving around private property rights.*

Planned socialization of labour begins when the first boss tells the first employee what to do. Within the firm, the market is transcended and replaced by *flow* processes, logistical input/output configurations, as concentration and centralization of capital proceed. A specialized cadre handling these processes within and between corporations, entrusted with tasks of direction and conception as well as normative unification emerges in this context. They are typically salaried employees (Bihr, 1989; Duménil and Lévy, 1998). This cadre would include company managers, engineers, and all kinds of 'knowledge workers' taking the places of the priest and novelist of old: public relations (PR) managers, soap opera writers, 'spin doctors', university lecturers and so on. The self-employed, 'notable' status for the greater part has been left behind here and is replaced by state or corporate employment. *Planned socialization of labour, then, (re-) produces a salaried cadre-oriented towards the integration of flow processes in the context of an advanced division of labour involving the application of science to production and communication.*

Politics was one area branching off from the set of tasks handled by the old notables. The workers brought together in their tens of thousands in the mass factories of the second Industrial Revolution (IR) of the early twentieth century, not only required (scientific) management on the factory floor, but also in politics. Gaetano Mosca described this political cadre at the turn of the century as 'the second stratum of the ruling class', whose task would be to provide the 'political formulas' by which the challenge of electoral majorities facing the numerically small ruling classes, have to be met (Mosca, 1939, p. 410).

In the crisis of the 1930s, when James Burnham coined the notion of the managerial revolution, the willingness to leave ever-larger areas of organizing the economy to the cadre transpires in Keynes's recommendation that even the tasks of the private investor, whom he proposed should be subjected to euthanasia, should be passed on to specialists 'harnessed to the service of the community on reasonable terms of reward' (Keynes, 1970, pp. 376–7). After World War II, the outward push of the American political economy provided a new, if still limited terrain for exporting this Keynesian order abroad, and the new cadre were prominent in the process. The public international governance structure of the United Nations (UN) in this period shared the Keynesian assumptions that underlay the International Monetary Fund (IMF) –World Bank(WB) – General Agreement on Tariffs and Trade (GATT) nexus, broadly speaking. As Pierre de Senarclens (1990) reminds us, the post-war multilateral governance infrastructure was to a considerable extent populated by a cadre for whom national welfare was the priority consideration. Thus, Dag Hammarskjöld had been a pupil of Keynes; he had been involved in the development of the Swedish welfare state and the execution of the Marshall Plan, before moving on to becoming the Secretary General of the UN. In development matters, the UN fostered a broad school of thought of its own, with Furtado, Kaldor, Kalecki, Myrdal and many others committed to development of the Third World in a broad Keynesian perspective. Arthur Lewis and Jan Tinbergen, future Nobel Prize winners, and Raul Prebisch too, are associated with the corporate liberal – the UN-mediated development effort.

Of course, the cadre, deployed by the UN organizations and the Bretton Woods Institutions were technocrats first of all. This had a background in political sensitivities of the Cold War and Third World non-alignment, but more fundamentally reflected the fact that their knowledge is obtained in the characteristic managerial way, as something appropriated from a more complex human context, abstracted, and 'technicized' (cf. Saurin, 1994, p. 56). The managerial revolution that had emanated from the socialization of labour nationally, thus came to characterize the international order as well, and in the 1970s Keynesianism began to spill over to the international sphere irrespective of the Cold War dividing lines, through deficit-financed industrialization of both the Soviet bloc and the strongest Third World states. This would culminate in the drive(s) for a New International Economic Order (NIEO) in the 1970s. Even more importantly, the growth of large corporations and their close imbrication with states in this period appeared to crowd out market relations altogether, and in combination with various schemes of profit socialization with trade union participation, restrict property rights. The thesis of 'state monopoly capitalism', originally coined by Lenin, and developed into theory by the Communist Party intellectuals in the USSR, the German Democratic Republic and France, elaborated this connection. It held that the cumulative socialization of labour binding the largest corporations, the state apparatus committed to supporting them, and the structures of class compromise with workers and farmers, at some point will tip over into comprehensive social planning. As such, state monopoly capitalism could be seen as the 'complete material preparation for socialism, the threshold of socialism', as Lenin put it on the eve of the Bolshevik Revolution in his article 'The impending catastrophe and how to combat it' (*Collected Works*, 25, p. 363). And whilst the programme of the French United Left to nationalize the country's largest corporations in 1980 was certainly not intended to trigger a revolution, it was based on a comparable argument.

By then, powerful forces were at work derailing what appeared at the time to be developing into an 'impending catastrophe' for the capitalist class. Hayek in the 1940s already warned that the planning aspirations of the cadre were based on an illusion that any planning institution can have the knowledge necessary to manage a complex modern economy (Hayek, 1987, Chapter 4). Such knowledge, he argued, can only be generated by the spontaneous workings of the market, which totalizes the subjective preferences of millions of people. Long marginalized, even ridiculed by the Keynesian mainstream, Hayek's hour struck when the debt crisis triggered by the reduction of the money supply in US dollars effectively bankrupted the states of the Soviet bloc and the Third World and the cumulative structures of class compromise grew around the state-monopoly capitalisms in the West. A policy of aggressive imperialism was simultaneously unleashed against the USSR and NIEO coalition, dismantling the positions they had occupied in the previous era (I discuss this at length in van der Pijl, 2006). Corporations and their owners, the private investor resurrected from the grave Keynes had dug for them, within a decade found themselves in a 'liberated' world market context. In that setting, each corporation, even the largest one, was always at arms' length from any state or bloc of states and hence, from democratically enacted intervention.

The Neo-liberal Property Regime versus the Global Flow Economy

Effectively what has happened in terms of socialization of labour in neo-liberalism has been the recreation, on a world scale, of a 'Smithian' universe of small producers whose private concern is mediated by markets. Even if states back their 'national champions', none of them will be able to impose their will on the world market, although Microsoft of course comes close. The shift to market socialization in a liberalized international context, entailed the new prominence of a cadre which functions like the notaries and town clerks of old. However, they do so not in a quiet atmosphere as provincial 'notables', but as highly dynamic operators in a global arena. Even so, like the nineteenth century professional intermediaries, this cadre, emerging in the context of comprehensive market socialization, also carry certain aspects of state authority even though in principle they are self-employed, or employed in partnerships. In addition, upholding property rights has again become a key element in their interventions. Cutler et al. (1999, p. 10) in their study on private international authority, speak of 'coordination services firms – multinational law, insurance, and management consultancy firms, debt-rating agencies, stock exchanges, and financial clearinghouses'. These are the contemporary equivalents of the provincial dignitaries of the nineteenth century; they are professionals, self-employed, working in partnerships, or otherwise employed in ways allowing them the freedom we associate with self-employment. Like their counterparts in the past, they are bearers of authority although not as officials of states.

However, what happened in the context of national economies is bound to repeat itself on a global scale. The concentration and centralization of capital that at some point imposed the 'flow logic' on the national economy, evoking the notion of state-monopoly capitalism with its transformative associations, also are operative in the liberalized global setting. True, this is happening on a vast terrain, and a planned socialization of the world economy is as remote as anything. But there is no doubt that important changes are underway in the type of socialization of labour between the most advanced economies again. By 1990 already, growth rates of foreign direct investment (FDI) by corporations (albeit often a matter of takeovers); of internationalized production relative to the volume of international trade; and of trade in parts and semi-finished products relative to the growth of trade in finished goods and to manufacturing output as such, prompted Stopford and Strange to conclude that '*a qualitatively different set of linkages among advanced countries*' were being established (1991, p.14, emphasis added). This continued in the 1990s, when growth in manufactures production and growth of trade in manufactures were diverging to a degree not seen before (respectively, 1.1 per cent a year, and 6.3 per cent in the period 1990–6, *Financial Times*, 18 May 1998).

Transnational production chains are now the trend, and the Organization for Economic Cooperation and Development (OECD) countries have become net exporters of parts and components in e.g., transport and machinery, whereas peripheral producers tend to serve as assembly platforms (Lawton and Michaels, 2000, p. 65). Another variety is that while the design is done in the OECD economy, production is subcontracted abroad in its entirety. 'Outward processing traffic' (OPT) involving exports of semi-finished products for finishing and re-import of finished product, is an important aspect of these transnational flows. It is counted as trade but is in fact an intra-corporation flow. The 'flow' logic of the socialization of labour is reasserting itself in the wider OECD economy as it did (until the 1970s) in national economies. 'Enterprise resource planning' (ERP), which is 'an integrated suite of software modules that automates internal "back office" operations for each function within an organization, such as manufacturing, distribution, financials, purchasing, sales and human resources' since the late 1990s is being applied no longer just to companies on their own, but to entire product chains (*Financial Times*, 15 December 1999; cf. Lawton and Michaels, 2000, p. 63). ERP in combination with barcode technology is indeed defying Hayek's claims that only the market can totalize the subjective preferences on which a 'free' economy is supposedly based – never mind the effects of a 24/7 advertising culture shaping these preferences in the first place.

Now by the same logic, the cadre find themselves dealing not just with the protection of private property in a global economy. More and more of them are needed also to ensure that the different links in a product chain are viable, compatible and remain connected; in other words, they are entrusted with managing the flow logic of transnationally socialized labour processes. Hence the product chains that reach into the far periphery, many of them linking consumption in the West to production in Asia, have become sites of struggle, and not just between capital and labour. There is also a struggle between different strands of managerial cadre going on. Industry (product and process) standards, which have become a key vector along which the transnational socialization of labour is being realized, are in case in point. Those involved in standard-setting and the monitoring of compliance with property rights as their main concern, the cadre associated with globalized market socialization, regularly find themselves in conflict with those who seek to expand the domain of rule-based product and process standardization from a point of view of managing the conditions under which the flow logic of transnationalized production can develop. In the words of Jean-Christophe Graz, 'Rather than a public/private, or state/market divide, we are looking at a rift confronting the advocates of further socialization of international standards (that is, bringing standard-setting bodies into a universal legal domain), and advocates of a commodification of technical standards (minimal sector and market-based standards, universally recognized)' (Graz, 2006, p. 119).

Managing a product chain implies the standardization of the conditions under which the successive nodes of such a chain are interlocked, including a measure of ensuring minimum working conditions to avoid reputational risk for the final sellers. It is in these conditions that as Jeroen Merk has argued, codes of conduct regulating the labour process at the point of production, for all their shortcomings, have pushed specific categories of cadre into a role where their concerns converge with those of the actual workers, and in these circumstances a reconstitution of what Marx once called the 'collective worker' is no longer a chimera. Corporate social responsibility departments of large Western firms may even intervene, on the basis of what they perceive to be their task and given that what they see is 'not pretty', with subcontractor operations in a role one would expect from local unions – but these of course are usually outlawed (Merk, 2004).

The Collective Worker in the Global Setting – Dispersion and Division

Now the cadre, much more than the sedentary owners of capital (both property dynasts and the average owner of stock), are a highly mobile and dynamic element in the global political economy. They apply the norms emanating from best practice benchmarks throughout the global political economy, and have to have a presence in the places where these norms are actually being applied. This holds for both the coordination firms that emerged in global market socialization, and the cadre active in the emerging global networks of production expressing the flow logic of the socialization of labour. By their very presence (both the consultants and other 'new notables' and the cadre associated with standardization) they tend to be much more directly confronted with the natural and social consequences of the increasingly exhaustive impact of neo-liberal capitalist discipline on the planet. Are they, therefore, destined to engage in dealing with the dangers to human survival contained in current economic practices?

The novelty of the present era in terms of social change, as argued above, is that there is no obvious 'progressive' way out of the world's crisis, as productive forces are being destroyed rather than produced, and no entirely new class is being formed. But this does not mean that there is therefore no future: we must rather think about it in terms appropriate to the aforementioned 'crisis of regression'.

In *Capital* (vol. 3), Marx outlines the conditions under which what he terms the 'associated' mode of production, might arise from certain inherent tendencies in capitalism. This would involve (i) the re-appropriation of the social labour process by the self-conscious 'collective worker', the various fractions into which the workforce has dissolved over the last century – as technicians, designers, manual labourers of all types, managers, transport and infrastructure regulators, and so on and so forth. Such an emancipation of production from capitalist discipline might take the form of political action (ii) to restore control over the world of finance, which in mature capitalism has a tendency to degenerate into speculation and swindle. To safeguard actual production, Marx argued, financial transactions would at some point have to be curtailed, if not altogether suppressed (*Marx-Engels Werke*, 25, pp. 485–6). As we saw, this already was put into practice as part of the Keynesian reordering of the economy towards its corporate liberal format. But the measures against speculative finance enacted in the US and a number of other countries in the 1930s, were rescinded again in the 1970s as part of the restructuring towards neo-liberal globalization. Meanwhile, the intricacies of global financial flows have become far more complex and difficult to control, the imbalances created by them incomparably more unstable.

The other aspect, the 'collective worker', in Marx's own time initially took the form of cooperatives, but these tended in almost all cases to pass under capitalist discipline again. More generally, the process of socialization of labour on which the notion of the collective worker is based under capitalist conditions remains an alienated form. Work and 'the economy' are reified and re-naturalized in the consciousness of the producers. Foreignness is a key aspect of this alienation and has historically worked against worker mobilization. As Gabriel Kolko has argued, immigrant labour in the US after the Civil War usually landed in communities largely segregated from others. Each immigrant group was desirous, first of all, to return home with money to improve their lot in their country of origin. Different forms of work were routinely assigned to different ethnic groups, often unable to communicate (or read safety instructions) in English; the result was that the hope of return mixed with quasi-tribal foreign relations with other workers into mutual distrust and animosity (Kolko, 1976, Chapter 3).

The neo-liberal restructuring has given a mighty push to migration generally, both in terms of job-seeking by those in the reserve army of labour, and as plain flight from degraded environments. Today, some 25 million people are already on the move fleeing desertification and other forms of exhaustion of the natural milieu, twice as many as there are political refugees; the number of environmental refugees is expected to rise to 200 million in 50 years' time if no major change of policy occurs (*The Independent*, 20 October 2006). Both, for intentional job-seekers and refugees, policies to ensure that 'foreign' dividing lines remain intact, continue to operate in the global context. States play an active role in keeping workers separated even if they end up in the same place. 'State borders', Anderson and Shuttleworth write (2004, p.152), function as regulators which 'serve to cheapen and weaken labour' by stripping workers of their social and political status upon entry.

The territoriality of borders, and their contradictory nature as 'bridges', 'barriers', 'resources' and 'symbols' are a means of allowing migrants in while denying them legal and democratic rights, national and cultural 'belonging', and hence, economic bargaining power.

Incoming labour tends to be directed towards different tasks along ethnic lines by immigration policy, selecting immigrants with transferable skills for permanent residence, whilst allowing in others on a temporary basis. In Canada, Philippine women as domestics are only admitted under highly regulated conditions; these do not apply to workers whose services are in high demand and who are more than proportionally male (Gabriel, 2004, pp.166–7, pp. 174–5). If looked at in this light, the prospect of a collective worker emerging in the contemporary period seems as remote as a political clampdown on the derivatives markets and other forms of speculative finance. It is different if we look at the axes along which socialization of labour develops.

The Collective Worker in Action?

Activists concerned about the dislocations produced by neo-liberal globalization were never far behind the actual transnationalization of capital. The destruction of the environment, the use of pesticides in the Global South, or working conditions in places such as China where the apparel sold in the West by fashionable brands are being produced, each created its own small nodes of activism. The internet in the 1990s offered new ways of actually getting in touch with people in faraway places. The anti-capitalist activists converged into a more or less cohesive movement in the campaign against the Multilateral Agreement on Investment (MAI). The MAI would have been, if enacted, the exact opposite of the NIEO movement of the 1970s. Whereas in the projected NIEO, corporations were to be placed under scrutiny by states and the institutions of the UN, the MAI boldly projected a global sovereignty of capital, from which no state was to be exempt. In the wake of the 1992 Rio Earth Summit, concern over such a framework for investor access and control was articulated notably in France, where a powerful popular protest movement against neo-liberal 'market reform' erupted in the winter of 1995–6. This movement brought down the right-wing Juppé government; it also spawned new forms of trade union organization and the Association for the Taxation of Financial Transactions to Aid Citizens (ATTAC) network, which soon radiated beyond France.

In 1996, the alternative globalizers began to interlock with groups from other countries concerned over the MAI plans. In October 1997, a first consultation between non-governmental organizations (NGOs) and the OECD took place over the issue of a global neo-liberal investment regime that would in effect preclude the turn to a sustainable global economy that had been judged necessary in Rio. The readiness of the OECD to engage in talks showed the degree to which the rising tide of anti-globalizing activism was taken seriously. One year on, a veritable mass movement had erupted over the MAI issue, echoed in resolutions by the European Parliament and many local government bodies (Mabey, 1999, pp. 60–1). Converging on the World Trade Organization (WTO) meeting in Seattle in 1999, more than 40,000 demonstrators sent a shock wave through the world that led one mainstream journalist to conclude that the idea that economic issues could be negotiated in isolation from political and social issues, 'had been dealt a blow from which it will not recover' (William Pfaff quoted in Rupert, 2000, p. 151).

'Seattle' became the undisputed high point of the movement. From there, a summit-hopping phenomenon developed that for a brief period appeared to establish itself as a disturbing force at every meeting of the multilateral and supranational organizations that form the regulatory infrastructure of global capitalism. In the World Social Forum convened in Porto Alegre, Brazil, the movement obtained a key organizational node which initially achieved great publicity successes such as the widely publicized telephone debate with their counterparts, the neo-liberal World Economic Forum in Davos. However, 9/11 and the anti-Islamic backlash it entailed, dealt a massive blow to the playful counterculture of the summit-hopping anti-capitalists. The alternative, 'anti'-globalization movement has subsided, its main form of activism contained by improved policing and the removal of the summits to places difficult to reach. This does not mean that the effort was therefore wasted. Not only did the activist wave publicize the issues of survival of life on the planet and the murderous effects of the WB and the IMF recipes imposed on states the world over; it qualitatively raised the level of awareness of how the world economy combines people in incomparable circumstances, from leisurely consumption to modern slavery. This was the first time a left movement constituted itself not as national first, to grapple with internationalism later, but directly as a movement on the global level. Finally, not unlike May, 68 activists had been absorbed into traditional left-wing parties and expanding state apparatuses in the 1970s, many from the 1990s anti-globalizing generation were recruited into the expanding NGO sector.

The NGO sector, for all its diversity, has become a highly visible channel through which what used to be development aid is being re-routed to emergency assistance in disaster areas, observance of human rights, and various other terrains on which the consequences of neo-liberal globalization are in evidence. In fact they are one, and growing, vehicle of cadre involvement in the functioning of the global political economy. Their auxiliary, executive role (without which we would not be able to define the people working in them as cadre) is defined by the founding and funding of NGOs by the states of the West. Their role increasingly has become one of smoothing the processes through which societies become part of the globalizing economy. The French medical NGO – Médecins sans Frontières (MSF) – is an example of how the activist critique of the established order (in this case a bureaucratized, conservative Red Cross) merges with practical involvement of a cadre nature. There is no doubt that many NGOs, especially the larger ones with a media reputation and enjoying access to states and corporations, have become part of a functional complex smoothing the workings of the global political economy. As Siméant notes (2005, p. 874).

Thus, perversely, the representatives of 'civil society' – held to be antithetical to economic actors – regulate some of their relationships through the use of the same instruments multinational corporations use.

But precisely because of the mixture between activism and functional involvement, the NGO sector has the potential of also contributing to the improvement of working conditions in a way out of reach for local union organizers, and to serve as a channel through which concern over such conditions and other destructive impacts of globalizing capitalist discipline, can pass along product chains to crisis points. Being present at the hot spots where neo-liberal 'best practice' is being applied, increasingly guarantees a front seat in observing how best practices create 'trouble spots'. Of course, here we will not usually find the coordination services cadre and transnational managerial element with their Master of Business Administration (MBA) credentials. But the concerns publicized by the alternative, 'anti'-globalization movement, and practically addressed by the NGOs, have not failed to also activate the potential rifts within other cadre strongholds. As Bob Deacon writes, 'Human resource specialists [of international organizations] have a degree of autonomy... which has increasingly been used to fashion an implicit global political dialogue with international NGOs about the social policies of the future that go beyond the political thinking or political capacity of the underpinning states' (Deacon, 1997, p. 61).

Likewise, the World Bank Environment Department is home to 'heretics', the International Labour Organization (ILO) and to some extent, the European Union (EU), the OECD directorate that deals with human resources and labour, the United Nations Children's (Emergency) Fund (UNICEF), the United Nations Development Programme (UNDP) and the Council of Europe, all in one way or another are working to deflect the outright application of neo-liberal policies, and the cadre active in them in that sense must be considered potential allies of the forces seeking to resist such policies. Deacon argues that the idea that nothing can be gained from engaging with the Bretton Woods Institutions and other international organizations, is mistaken. 'The empirical evidence suggests... that a war of positions... IS being fought within and between international organizations; that through the support given to labor movements and their representatives in ministries of labor... a connection to local social forces can be developed; and that international [NGOs] and their complex connections to local civil society are part of this war of positions' (Deacon, 1997, p. 218). A senior WB official has even made the case for setting up ratings agencies which will monitor state and corporate behaviour as to the observance of those rules that are vital to humanity's survival on the planet (Rischard, 2002).

The socialization of labour has produced a grid of rules with a class committed to upholding these rules in order to maintain the cohesion of the overall political economy. There is no doubt that the infrastructure of public and private authority has reached the point where at first glance, it is merely working to facilitate capital accumulation on a global scale. As 'global governance', this set of rules and the cadre to monitor their observance, are obviously directed towards this end. As André Drainville writes:

> Central to 'global governance' as a hegemonial strategy is a broad attempt to assemble a global civil society in which to embed neoliberal concepts of control. Key here are twinned processes of severance and recomposition. At once, the making of global civil society involves (i) cutting off social forces and organizations willing to work within a global market framework from other social contexts and (ii) re-assembling the lot into a functional and efficient whole that will work to solve global problems and, in the process, fix the terms of social and political interaction in the world economy (Drainville, 2005, p. 889)

But 'fixing the terms', i.e., the enunciation of rules, by a logic of its own produces the interest to uphold them, just as they bind even those who proposed the rules, into implications that occasionally may go against the original intentions behind them. The fact that regulation is so often written by corporations, their business associations, or organizations otherwise under their influence (Picciotto and Mayne, 1999) does not in the end suspend this principle. So, whilst many would rightly consider the WTO to represent a bulwark of neo-liberal capitalist discipline (e.g., Barker and Mander, 1999), the WTO dispute panels which can no longer be vetoed and the conclusions of which cannot be ignored, and the establishment of a permanent court, have greatly enhanced the visibility and legal standing of the WTO compared to the GATT. This has reached the point where the US, one of the strong advocates of an organization committed to globalizing neo-liberalism, finds it often difficult to accept its rulings. The 60 per cent rise in number of cases under the WTO (if compared to the trend line for the last 14 years of GATT) has been explained by the fact that many more obligations have to be observed under the new organization. It is also true that almost half of all the cases were brought by the US, often against poor countries failing to observe the WTO rules which they have to accept en bloc. Even so, there exists according to Judith Goldstein, a perception in the US that the WTO may easily overrule domestic legislation, and hence, threaten its sovereignty (Goldstein, 2000, p. 266).

As the stock market splendour of globalizing capitalism further wanes and the realities of ruthless exploitation become more visible, sections of the cadre may well gravitate into a bloc of forces openly prioritizing the need for human survival and the preservation of the biosphere. There is no point in glorifying this class into a saviour of mankind, or romanticizing it as a quasi-Bolshevik vanguard. But in the specific context of an impending catastrophe defined by the exhaustion of society and nature by capitalist market discipline, their predilection for management may gain the upper hand over their ideological commitment to neo-liberalism. It will then depend on the strength of popular resistance in all its forms, and on the quality of intellectual reflection on what is happening before our eyes, whether a transition to an associated mode of production will proceed as a process of deepening democracy as well.

References

Anderson, J. and Shuttleworth, I. 2004. 'A New Spatial Fix for Capitalist Crisis? Immigrant Labour, State Borders and the New Ostracising Imperialism', in van der Pijl, K., Assassi, L. and Wigan, D. (eds.), *Global Regulation. Managing Crises After the Imperial Turn*. Basingstoke: Palgrave Macmillan.

Barker, D. and Mander, J. 1999. *Invisible Government. The World Trade Organisation: Global Government for the New Millennium*. San Franscisco: International Forum on Globalization.

Bihr, A. 1989. *Entre bourgeoisie et prolétariat. L'encadrement capitaliste*. Paris: L'Harmattan.
Braithwaite, J. and Drahos, P. 2000. *Global Business Regulation*. Cambridge: Cambridge University Press.
Braudel, F. 1981 [1979]. *The Structures of Everyday Life. The Limits of the Possible. Vol. I of Civilization and Capitalism 15th–18th Century*, translated by S. Reynolds, London: Collins.
Burnham, J. 1960 [1941]. *The Managerial Revolution*. Bloomington: Indiana University Press.
Cox, R. W. 1987. *Production, Power, and World Order. Social Forces in the Making of History*. New York: Columbia University Press.
Crozier, M., Huntington, S. P. and Watanuki, J. 1975. *The Crisis of Democracy. Report on the Governability of Democracies to the Trilateral Commission*. New York: New York University Press.
Cutler, A. C., Haufler, V. and Porter, T. (eds.), 1999. *Private Authority and International Affairs*. Albany: State University of New York Press.
Deacon, B. with Hulse, M. and Stubbs, P. 1997. *Global Social Policy –International Organizations and the Future of Welfare*. London: Sage.
Drainville, A. 2005. 'Beyond altermondialisme: anti-capitalist dialectic of presence.' *Review of International Political Economy*, 12 (5), pp. 884–908.
Duffield, M. 2001. *Global Governance and the New Wars. The Merging of Development and Security*. London: Zed.
Duménil, G. and Lévy, D. 1998. *Au-delà du capitalisme?* Paris: Presses universitaires de France.
Gabriel, C. 2004. 'A Question of Skills: Gender, Migration Policy and the Global Political Economy', in van der Pijl, K., Assassi, L. and Wigan, D. (eds.), *Global Regulation. Managing Crises After the Imperial Turn*. Basingstoke: Palgrave Macmillan.
Giesen, K-G. and van der Pijl, K. (eds.), 2006. *Global Norms in the Twenty-First Century*. Newcastle: Cambridge Scholars Press.
Goldstein, J. 2000. 'United States and World Trade: Hegemony by Proxy?' in Lawton, T. C., Rosenau, J. N. and Verdun, A. C. (eds.), *Strange Power. Shaping the Parameters of International Relations and International Political Economy*. Aldershot: Ashgate.
Graz, J-C. 2006. International Standardisation and Corporate Democracy' in K-G. Giesen and van der Pijl, K. (eds.), *Global Norms in the Twenty-First Century*. Newcastle: Cambridge Scholars Press.
Hayek, F. A. 1985 [1944]. *De weg naar slavernij*, translated by H.L. Swart et al, Amsterdam: Omega.
Keynes, J. M. 1970 [1936]. *The General Theory of Employment, Interest and Money*. London: Macmillan.
Kolko, G. 1976. *Main Currents in Modern American History*. New York: Harper & Row.
Lawton, Th. C. and Michaels, K. P. 2000. 'The Evolving Global Production Structure: Implications for International Political Economy', in Lawton, Th. C., Rosenau, J. N. and Verdun, A. C. (eds.), *Strange Power. Shaping the Parameters of International Relations and International Political Economy*. Aldershot: Ashgate.
Lenin, V. I. 1967–. *Collected Works*, 39 vols. Moscow: Progress.
Mabey, N. 1999. 'Defending the Legacy of Rio: The Civil Society Campaign Against the MAI' in Picciotto, S. and Mayne, R. (eds.), *Regulating International Business. Beyond Liberalization*. Basingstoke: Macmillan.
Marx-Engels Werke, 1956–. Berlin: Dietz, 38 vols., (vols. 23–5 contain the three volumes of *Capital*).

Merk, J. 2004. 'Regulating the Global Athletic Footwear Industry: the Collective Worker in the Product Chain' in van der Pijl, K. Assassi, L. and Wigan, D. (eds.), *Global Regulation. Managing Crises After the Imperial Turn.* Basingstoke: Palgrave Macmillan.

Mosca, G. 1939 [1896]. *The Ruling Class,* edited with an introduction by A. Livingston; translated by H. Kahn, 2nd edition. New York: McGraw-Hill.

Picciotto, S. and Mayne, R. (eds.), 1999. *Regulating International Business. Beyond Liberalization.* Basingstoke: Macmillan and New York: St. Martins; in association with Oxfam.

Rischard, J. F. 2002. *High Noon. 20 Global Issues, 20 Years to Solve Them.* Oxford: Perseus Press.

Roobeek, A. J. M. 1987. 'The Crisis in Fordism and the Rise of a New Technological Paradigm', *Futures,* 19 (2), pp. 129–54.

Rupert, M. 2000. *Ideologies of Globalization. Contending visions of a New World Order.* London: Routledge.

Saurin, J. 1994. 'Global Environmental Degradation, Modernity and Environmental Knowledge', *Environmental Politics,* 2 (4), pp. 47–64.

Senarclens, P. de. 1990. 'La transnationalistion des clercs. Essai sur les experts internationaux', *Revue Européenne des Sciences Sociales* 28 (87), pp. 231–49.

Siméant, J. 2005. 'What is Going Global? The Internationalization of French NGOs "without borders"', *Review of International Political Economy,* 12 (5), pp. 851–83.

Stopford, J. and Strange, S. with Henley, J. C. 1991. *Rival States, Rival Firms. Competition for World Market Shares.* Cambridge: Cambridge University Press.

Van der Pijl, K. 1998. *Transnational Classes and International Relations.* London: Routledge.

—. 2002, 'Holding the Middle Ground in the Transnationalisation Process', in Anderson, J. (ed.), *Transnational Democracy. Political Spaces and Border Crossings.* London: Routledge.

—. 2006. *Global Rivalries from the Cold War to Iraq.* London: Pluto.

Weber, M. 1976 [1921]. *Wirtschaft und Gesellschaft. Grundriss der verstehenden Soziologie.* Tübingen: J.C.B. Mohr.

Chapter 10

GREEN MARXISM AND THE INSTITUTIONAL STRUCTURE OF A GLOBAL SOCIALIST FUTURE

Richard Westra

Introduction

The *green* challenge to Marx's socialist vision for its purported commitment to industrial giganticism and the fact that a *green* politics has emerged as a focal point for oppositions to the current world order has spurred Marxists to reconsider the theory and practice of socialism in a *green* light.[1] The present chapter follows in the spirit of that work intent upon defending the potency of Marxist theory – particularly Marxian economics – to expose the roots and modalities of the eco-destructive tendencies of capitalism. And, this work shares in the belief that it is only through the building of a genuine socialism that an eco-sustainable global future for humanity can be realized. However, the chapter maintains the case Marxism makes regarding such paramount questions needs to be strengthened and that there exists a latent power of Marxian analysis waiting to be tapped for precisely this purpose.

Marx's *Capital* has been successfully mined for its elucidation of the class-exploitative, crises-ridden, lop-sided wealth-concentrative nature of capitalism. But only marginally has it been explicitly drawn upon for its exploration of how it is possible for such a society – what Marx referred to variously as an 'upside-down', 'alien', 'fetishistic' social order reducing human socio-economic relations to 'relations among things' – to reproduce human economic life over an extended period in the first place. Yet it was the position of the Japanese Marxist political economist Kozo Uno (1980)[2] that for *Capital* to prove its mettle as an economic theory it necessarily had to demonstrate how capitalism could wield human material life for capital's abstract goal of augmenting value while simultaneously satisfying 'general norms of economic life' required by any viable form of human society. After all, if as Marxists have long held, capitalism is an historically delimited and transitory human society, then according to Uno, it is incumbent upon them and Marxian economic theory to clearly distinguish between the constituents of economic life – economic life, of course, being something without which human society would be impossible – and the peculiar means by which the reproduction of such is guaranteed by capital. And it is a hallmark of the Uno approach to apply this particular apprehension of *Capital* both to the study of capitalist development and theorizing socialism.[3]

The purpose of this chapter then, is fourfold: First, it seeks to draw out the key insights of Marx's work on economic viability and juxtapose these with arguments drawn from Marxian economics for the essential eco-destructiveness of capitalism to provide a metric for assessing economic viability and eco-sanctity of alternative forms of human society. Second, the article will briefly assess the potential inherent in the trajectory of globalization to realize an economically viable and eco-sustainable future. Third, the metric will be applied in summary fashion to new ideas of socialism and the benchmark 'small is beautiful' version of *green* theory. Finally, lessons drawn from the foregoing analysis will be tabulated to suggest an institutional framework for a future socialist society that is economically viable, eco-sustainable and which realizes the overall aim of socialism to offer human socio-material betterment.[4] To be sure, though the purview of this article is quite broad, there are significant benefits to be reaped from an overarching perspective such as this which will play an under-labouring role for more in-depth future work on what is the most paramount issue for Marxism – creative thinking about a genuine socialism for the here and now.

Economic Viability and Eco-sustainability in the Theory of Capital

In building the argument it is worth referring back to economic historian Karl Polanyi's highly instructive and widely cited differentiation between capitalism and pre-capitalist societies in terms of the economy in capitalism tending to become 'dis-embedded' from other realms of the social – politics, religion, ideology – with which it had been intermeshed since the dawn of human society. Less acknowledged, but even more intellectually potent, Marx also has an understanding of this peculiar attribute of the capitalist market. His conceptualizing of the fetishism of capital captured the tendency of capital to 'reify' economic life. That is, for Marx, not only does the economic in capitalist society dis-embed from the social but, though capitalism is a socially and historically constituted order, the economic in capitalism comes to take on a 'life of its own' and wields the social, human beings and the human life-world for its own self-aggrandizement – the augmentation of value.[5] However, it would remain the task of the Japanese political economist Kozo Uno (1980) to draw out the ultimate implications of Marx's work for social science, the analysis of capitalism and study of economic life across varying forms of human society.

It is no accident that economics emerges as a field of study only in the age of capitalism: for it is precisely the reification of economic life or again, the dis-embedding of the economy from its enmeshment among other realms of the social that constitute the ontological condition of possibility for economic theory. That is, as Polanyi, Marx and Uno observe, pre-capitalist societies reproduce their economic life through interpersonal relations of cooperation, dependence, or domination and subordination. Capitalism, however, tends to dissolve all such interpersonal relations of economic existence in its organizing of human material life in impersonal, society-wide integrated systems of self-regulating markets. In this fashion, and I will pursue this point further below, capital converts human relations of material life into what Marx refers to as relations among things, and it is this conversion in the abstract operation of self-regulating markets which then 'objectifies' economic relations rendering them 'transparent' for theory to explore.[6] The key social science implication for the study of capitalism flowing from this is that political economy necessitates a specific cognitive sequence where exposing the deep economic structure of capital not only offers a devastating critique of capitalism in its most fundamental incarnation, but it also provides a window of opportunity for the elaboration of what Uno dubs the general norms of economic life; norms that capitalism as well as all other human societies have to satisfy as conditions of their material-reproductive viability.

Marxists have long decried neoclassical economics' notion of the market reaching a state of 'equilibrium' for its eliding of crises tendencies, which lurk at every turn of the capitalist economy. Notwithstanding his theoretical elaboration and historical evidentializing of these tendencies, Marx also understood that in the course of business cycles capitalism necessarily realizes a phase of 'average activity' marked by the sale of commodities at 'normal' or equilibrium prices. That Marx never completed his three-volume *Capital*, wherein this issue was to be unwrapped, has led to immense confusion. In the most up-to-date Uno approach recasting and completion of Marx's project of *Capital* (Sekine, 1997) as the *theory of a purely capitalist society* (TPCS)[7] there is agreement with neoclassical economics that market forces of supply and demand determine the relative prices of commodities. However, what neoclassical economics does not recognize, and the TPCS so incisively demonstrates, is that for the notion of equilibrating supply and demand to be meaningful in an economically substantive sense, it must be placed within the context of the historical conditions and specific social class relations of capitalist production. That is, all investment decision-making on the part of the capitalist in response to price signals require the commodification of labour-power to bear fruit. For it is only on the basis of the existence of a class of 'free labourers' offering their labour-power on the market for capital to purchase, as but another input into the production process, that it is possible for capital to shift to the production of *any* good as per the changing pattern of social demand and opportunity for value augmentation or profit-making.

In other words, no human society could survive for long if it chronically over-produced or under-produced basic goods relative to the existing pattern of social demand: If, for example, human labour is diverted from production of basic foodstuffs to production of iron leaving the demand for the former unmet, the respective society would eventually collapse. And human history is littered with precisely such examples of societies the material-reproductive modus operandi of which could not ensure this fundamental requirement. Therefore, the key norm of economic life captured by Marxian economics is that, as the basic condition of viability, all human society must have at its core a central operative principle ensuring the social demand for basic goods is met without chronically misallocating social resources and that in this process the direct producers must at minimum receive the product of their necessary labour. In capitalist society, this principle is the *law of value*, which, under the constraints of capitalist social relations of production, works to allocate social resources by ensuring that commodities embody only *socially necessary labour*. Socially necessary labour refers to the peculiar means by which work in the capitalist commodity economy is validated. If capital deploys commodified labour-power in the production of goods that are not in demand or in the production of goods with the operation of redundant technologies, the commodities will not be sold and profits not be made and, from the perspective of capitalist society as a whole, such work will be deemed a waste. In this sense, the law of value 'mediates' between the specifically capitalist commodity economic organization of economic life and the production of use-values that constitute the basis of all human material existence. And conceiving of the formation of equilibrium prices in the capitalist market in the absence of this understanding of the economic viability of capitalism is tantamount to the absurd view that somehow the capitalist market could be de-coupled from the capitalist mode of production.

Let us return, as promised, to an unpacking of the earlier statement that the capitalist market constitutes a domain of impersonal relations among things: For, from here, spring the most profound insights into the eco-sustainability of capitalism. When neoclassical economics adverts to the economic 'efficiency' of the capitalist market it is highlighting the market's 'cost-less' transmitting of economic information to economic actors in the way of market prices such that a purported 'optimal' allocation of resources, captured in the notion of a general equilibrium, will be achieved. Bracketing here Marxian economics exposure of neoclassical occluding capitalist social relations in its model of resource allocation, what the capitalist market is in fact doing is performing a series of abstract 'calculations' based upon value/price or *quantitative* criteria. Through the operation of the integrated system of self-regulating markets of capitalism then, human beings in fact abdicate their responsibility for organizing their economic affairs to what amounts to an 'extra-human' force – the law of value – that reproduces their economic life as a by-product of value augmentation. Recalling the discussion above, this modus operandi of capitalism is what the term reification is intended to capture. And, because value augmentation is an *abstract-quantitative* goal, we can say that at a most fundamental level capital, with its commodity economic material outcomes, is destined to conflict with *concrete-qualitative* human goals to the extent that the latter necessitate respect for the earth and the life-world within which long-term human existence is necessarily embedded. Such is illustrated vividly by the historical record of capitalism that displays how value augmentation can proceed extremely successfully through the production of noxious goods as well as those with the potential to destroy life itself. Paradoxically, therefore, while an unimpeded procedure of abstract-quantitative market calculation is the basis of capital's ability to constitute a viable economic order it is also the root of capital's profaning of the human life-world and the earth.

Economic Viability and Eco-sustainability in the Trajectory of Globalization

While Marx's *Capital* recast as the TPCS exposes the basic conditions of economic viability and true eco-colour of capitalism in its most fundamental incarnation the question remains of the transformability of capitalism with respect to these constituents. The TPCS – following Marx's *Capital* – unfolds its analysis and development of categories of the capitalist economy through the dialectical contradiction between value and use-value.[8] What the TPCS makes explicit here is that the most forceful statement of precisely what capital *is* requires that theory extrapolate to conclusion the neutralizing by value of all use-value opposition. The fact is however, across capitalist history the march of value is resisted in manifold ways ranging from class struggle to the recalcitrance of use-values themselves. Treating this problem places Marxism in the thorniest epistemological thicket. In other words, to refer to a society as capitalist, it is necessary for the reifying logic of value self-augmentation predicated upon commodified labour-power to be present in it as a *constant*. And Marxian economic theory unravels the inner-logic of this constant. On the other hand, the resistances to capital refract this logic in varying ways and degrees (though there are necessary limits to this for a society to remain capitalist, a point that I will revisit below). According to the Uno approach, it is a fact that capital never completely purges human material existence of extra-economic, extra-capitalist forces which foregrounds the study of the capitalist state/superstructure and the latter's role in managing market *externalities* (all those facets of economic life that capital is unable to manage according to its principle of self-regulating market operation).[9] And it is the major world-historic transformations in the interplay between the abstract logical constant of capital and the capitalist management of predominant forms of use-value production with state/superstructure support (to deal with market externalities) that constitute the basis for theorizing stages of capitalist development.

In other words, stage theory as a *level of analysis* entails a 'concretizing' of the contradiction between value and use-value as it theorizes the core capitalist structures and state supports ensuring the economic viability of capitalism as value augmentation proceeds around the production of stage specific use-values.[10] Following Albritton (1991), the argument here in brief is that capitalism is marked by four world-historic stages of development named for the representative state policy supporting capital – mercantilism, liberalism, imperialism and consumerism – with each characterized by a dominant form of commodity production (wool, cotton, steel/heavy chemicals and automobile/consumer durables respectively), a geospatial core (Britain, Britain, Germany and the US respectively) and a stage-specific institutional architecture that constitutes the matrix through which capital accumulation proceeds and extra-economic supports for capital are articulated. From this perspective, if there ever existed a stage of capitalism exemplifying the pattern of competitive price-taking firms and market equilibrating business cycles captured in the TPCS, where the externalities (running the gamut from organized class opposition to environmental destruction) the capitalist state was called upon to manage were minimal, it is the stage of liberalism characterized by capital accumulation of mid-nineteenth century Britain.

On the other hand, the capitalist stage of consumerism typified by US capital in the post-World War II period, and marked by the production of consumer durables (typified by the automobile industry), represents a huge departure from the market equilibrating principles of capitalism captured in the TPCS or approximated by the entrepreneurial capitalism of nineteenth century Britain. To manage the capitalist *mass*-production of such a relatively *complex* use-value cluster, consumerist capital could only at its peril, leave accumulation to the vagaries of the market, and increasingly adopted principles of economic programming and planning. For example, the massive investment costs of consumer durable production led to the refinement of the corporate type of business structure that would vest control of decision-making in a managerial techno-structure, strive to increasingly internalize business transactions, become deeply involved in demand management and cultivate varying types of class accords with organized labour to keep interruptions of production to a minimum. The internationalization of production and finance characterizing consumerism not only intensified such trends but also contributed to corporate capitals' need to coordinate each and every arm of business activity. Paralleling the programming and planning activities of corporate capital was the rise of the consumerist state with a formidable policy arsenal at its disposal to support capital accumulation. The social wage, creation of effective demand (military, transportation infrastructure and so on), monetary, fiscal, labour and trade policy are just a few of the well-known initiatives. The upshot of the foregoing is that the augmentation of value and viable material reproduction of the economic community in the capitalist stage of consumerism becomes more and more dependent upon extra-market principles; a trend setting the course for a peculiar political-economic outcome.

However, to re-focus the argument back on the question of the eco-viability of capitalism, the reasons why the capitalist stage of consumerism emerges as the most environmentally unsound stage of capitalism hardly need any rehearsal. The mass consumption of consumer durables depended upon by corporate accumulation requires that consumer demand for an ever expanding and novel assortment of such goods remains virtually insatiable, thus generating rapid product obsolescence and excreting mountains of waste. Further, the energy profile, mainly that of petroleum but also of nuclear power coupled with the gargantuan energy requirements for electricity and transportation has ravaged the biosphere and contains the spectre of human annihilation. Moreover, global pollution has only been compounded by the increasing internationalization of production, both for the latter's tendency to shift environmental problems around the world as well as the need it promotes to augment hyper-polluting transportation networks for global commodity chains. All this, of course, saddles the consumerist state with the burden of not only managing the aforementioned burgeoning externalities of capital accumulation but also those now involving the very eco-sustainability of the social community and human life-world through which capital operates.

Therefore, globalization – the neo-liberal compelled processes of national deregulation, frenetic world economic financialization, dismantling of social wage structures, abandonment of demand management beyond military outlays – amounts to the fact that the consumerist state is increasingly abdicating its responsibilities for managing those externalities that capital had demanded of it to enable capitalism to continue as a viable economic order. For, though capital depended upon the programming and planning of the capitalist state, as capital accumulation continued to slow across much of the capitalist heartland from the mid 1970s onward (Webber and Rigby, 2001), capital also began to experience its expanded armature of extra-market supports as a constraint, and sought to dismantle it and 'free' itself from them. In opposition to neo-liberal ideology that would have us believe the world economy is in transition to a new stage of market-equilibrating entrepreneurial capitalism, I have argued (Westra, 2003b; 2004b) that given the persistence of the corporate/ consumer-durable production/high energy use/high waste material substructure of the world economy today, without the state performing its historic role as a *capitalist* state (one that manages the market externalities that necessarily encumber such an economy), we are instead witnessing a transition *away* from capitalism; a transition whereby other material reproductive principles, the contours and potential viability of which are not yet completely clear (though, certainly entail authoritarian modes of labour and population control as well as forms of global apartheid), are emerging to fill the void. Nevertheless, in this epochal transitional era, globalization, which, paraphrasing Marx, I maintain constitutes a retreat of capital to the 'interstices' of the globe from whence capitalism originated (Westra, 2003b), is failing human society in terms of material reproductive viability. The burgeoning world economic asymmetries in productivity, resource capacity, commodification of labour-power, and so on, mitigate the rise of a capitalist market-based coordinating economic principle ('perfect competition' in neoclassical terms) to ensure that the variegated global demand for basic goods is met. And, in lieu of the rise of a world capitalist state there is no institution adequate to the task of managing the colossal externalities generated by a global *capitalist* economy.

Such tendencies also portend bleak prospects for the eco-sustainability of the current political economy: the increasing short-term profit horizon and 'off-ground' investment orientation of corporate capital is dispersing marketable productive capacity across the globe where there is less and less inclination on the part of business and host polities to concern themselves with the managing of any externalities. And both national and international regulatory systems for eco-monitoring have never kept in step with this trend of internationalization of production, and that those systems, which were developed, are now being progressively gutted. What is needed, as one analyst puts it (Lipietz, 2004), is not a World Trade Organization (WTO) that exacerbates these tendencies but a World Environment Organization (WEO) to contain them. However, like the emergence of world capitalist state, this is unlikely to materialize given the centripetal tendencies marking the current world order.

Economic Viability and Eco-sustainability of Varieties of Socialist and Green Society

What about the possibility of a form of socialist or green society providing the pathway to an economically viable, eco-sustainable, progressive human future? Without entering the debate over what kind of economy the Soviet-style system was, the oft referred to 'economics of shortage' of its cumbersome centralized state planning apparatus never satisfied the metric for economic viability. It not only failed to meet the demand for basic goods but also chronically misallocated resources generating a huge 'parallel economy' that helped to support human material existence by a welter of extra-planning means. And, with its disintegration, the disgraceful environmental record of the Soviet Union has been vividly exposed.

It is hardly surprising that the discrediting of Soviet-style planning would reinvigorate an old debate over so-called 'market socialism'. However, if, following Schweickart (1998, p. 19), market socialists are seeking a socialism that will 'allow us to get on with our lives without having to worry so much about economic matters', their quest is sheer folly. That is, the abdicating of responsibility for human material reproduction to the reified force of self-regulating markets is predicated upon the commodification of labour-power, which a genuine socialism can never countenance. To restate a point made above, it is impossible to de-couple the capitalist market from the capitalist mode of production. Thus, both material economic and environmental outcomes of so-called market socialism cannot be expected to differ in a fundamental fashion from capitalism. Similar criticism may also be leveled at the project of *socializing* the market (Elson, 1988). Efficiency gains sought here necessarily derive from the abstract quantitative calculation procedure of market allocation. Besides the issue of maintaining labour-power as a commodity to optimally capture these gains, interfering with society-wide market operation by socializing both distributive outcomes and costs of addressing externalities will face the same clash of interests experienced in the worlds' social democracies recently overrun by neo-liberalism.

Though discredited in its Soviet-style form, economic planning has been resurrected in models purporting to surmount the two main deficiencies of their predecessor — authoritarian centralism and allocation inefficiency. To begin with the latter point, these demonstrate how computers may be utilized to perform market calculations and obtain equilibrium solutions combined with redistributive social outcomes (Cockshott and Cottrell, 1997; 2003). Paralleling this work, are models confirming that the information relied upon to arrive at equilibrium allocations of social resources need not emanate from a central plan but could be channeled through decentralized participatory, democratic iterative decision-making bodies (Albert and Hahnel, 1991). The significance of this work is that it defies views that markets remain the only socialist alternative. And, importantly, its equilibrium solution complies with our metric for economic viability. Also, it extends democracy into the economic realm, as micro, meso and macro elected planning bodies coordinate economic decision-making. As well, participatory planning holds out the promise of decommodifying labour-power (I will return to this).

Where such participatory planning models miscarry however is in their conception of socialist planning as a society-wide endeavour of simulating equilibrium calculations of the capitalist market. This reduces the possibility of socialism to an abstract technical question and imports into socialism a mechanism of the capitalist economy at the root of capitalist insensitivity to use-value and nature. Related to this is the problem of co-opting the capitalist division of labour in arriving at an equilibrium allocation of resources. As noted (Gough and Eisenschitz, 1997), this is also not simply a technical consideration as that division of labour was shaped by centuries of capitalist social relations of production. Further, while the proposed expanded democratization and social redistribution serve to partially de-commodify labour-power, it is not clear how far this can proceed when the demands of meeting a society-wide equilibrium require labour-power to be freely available for planning bodies to rapidly shift in response to changing patterns of social demand. Finally, what remains unaddressed in the foregoing is the matter of work alienation, a key facet of socio-material betterment socialists are committed to (Westra, 2002).

In unfurling his 'small is beautiful' argument E F Schumacher (1999 [1973]) reflects the sentiment that it is the element of society-wide *scale* of economic coordination inherent in both the capitalist market and socialist planning, participatory or otherwise, that is the origin of eco-insensitivity of each society and distributive asymmetry of capitalism. What he proposes in the small is beautiful model is the breakdown of current nation state political communities into economic 'districts' consisting of approximately a few hundred thousand people. Districts would deploy so-called 'intermediate technologies' geared at the outset to the support of agriculture and the alleviation of hunger and poverty, and eventually providing for full employment and an adequate living standard. These districts would further generate new ownership structures and an economy that hangs together without plan or market. However, most importantly, so the argument goes, the combination of reduced scale and intermediate technology will consequentially render these districts environmentally friendly.

As socialist critics observe (Pepper, 1993) there is in fact no inexorability of reduced scale engendering sound environmental outcomes; for not only

Schumacher, but the genre of green writing following him has been vague on how communities might coordinate eco-policy to ensure that the results of potentially unsound activities are not blithely passed along to other districts. And, without addressing the subject of social class, there is nothing to prevent green communities from descending into forms of elitist eco-authoritarianism. A criticism of the small is beautiful approach from the perspective of the political economic analysis of globalization presented above is that current eco-degradation exceeds the capacity of even powerful nation states to singularly remedy; hence, it is difficult to comprehend how our environmental morass could be dealt with solely in an autarchic context. But of greatest import from the point of view of this chapter is the question of economic viability. Marx's studies make it clear that modes of production cannot simply be generated *ex nihilo*. And, as the TPCS demonstrates, economically viable forms of human society require at their core an operative principle or set of these to ensure that the general norms of economic life are met. In eschewing both markets and planning as economic principles, it is incumbent upon *green* theory to elaborate a replacement. That they have not been forthcoming with one is a gaping lacuna in their work and a major ramification of their recoiling from Marxism and its wealth of insight in this area, over the mistaken belief that Marxist theory predisposes socialist construction towards industrial giganticism.

New Socialisms for the Global Future

The ultimate revolutionary implication of Marx's work in *Capital* on the economic viability of capitalism is that, in proving how it is possible for the impersonal abstract logic of the capitalist market to satisfy the general norms of economic life, *Capital* confirms the *feasibility* of socialism; a society in which those same general norms will be met by the conscious and concrete activities of freely associated human beings. Working with this assumption let us draw together threads of the above discussion. A key maxim of Marx's thinking about social change across the sweep of history is that all new societies are born in the womb of their predecessor and emerge scarred with its markings. In this regard, the concern with economic scale in the writing of Schumacher is certainly something socialists must seriously consider for future creative redesign of economic life. After all, as capital subsumes the economic life of society with the spread of integrated systems of self-regulating markets operating within the geospatial contours of modern nation states, it sunders the historical links between production and consumption that characterized community existence since its dawn. Thus, capitalism cultivates the disinterest of workers qua producers in what is produced and also creates their indifference as consumers in how goods are produced. World economic globalization exacerbates this trend as not only do value determinations impel the production of the simplest use-values to locales continents away from the point of their consumption (even away from places with available materials and labour-power for their production), but globalization serves to further efface the fact that basic goods on the convenience store shelf of one worker comes 'dripping with the blood' of another.

However, and this is the penultimate revolutionary implication of *Capital's* insight into the economic viability of capitalism, if capital reproduces material life by reifying it, converting social relations into relations among things according to the abstract quantitative criterion of value augmentation, to eviscerate centuries of capitalist impact upon our lives, including that of current globalization, will require institutional vehicles that operate to replace quantitative value considerations with qualitative use-value ones. The issue, therefore, is not small-scale economic units vs large-scale as *green* theory has it, for without crisp clarity over capitalist material reproductive modalities residues of capitalism could easily be imported into Schumacher's districts to infect them with capital's eco and socio-economic pathologies, rather the problem for institutional design is qualitative vs quantitative economic outcomes. And, given how the march of capital in history involves the subsuming of use-value life – including its wellspring human labour-power – to the dictates of value, socialist institutional construction must entail measures for prying use-value life back out of value and capital's reified grip.

One proposal for dismantling existing economic structures and building a material-reproductively viable eco-sustainable socialism (Sekine, 1990; 2004; Westra, 2002; 2004a) consists of breaking economies down into sectors, communities and modes of *socio-material communication* – communal reciprocity, local markets, economic planning – geared to managing the production and distribution of specific use-value complexes. First, a *qualitative* use-value sector community might be formed around rural areas and small towns, and with potentially arable lands and boroughs adjacent to major urban centres. Its production focus, depending on local resources, would be use-values such as foodstuffs, furniture, apparel, household sundries and so forth. However, while such qualitative goods producing communities replicate geospatial aspects of Schumacher's districts, on questions of economic reproduction, they follow Marx. As Marx's historical studies make abundantly clear, markets for face-to-face personal exchange or barter of goods existed as benign supplements to the varying dominant principles of economic life marking pre-capitalist modes of production. Similarly, types of markets such as local exchange and trading systems (LETS), 'need exchanges', community barter and reciprocity for goods and services, all based on a local community currency, may be adopted as benign instruments for viably organizing socialist economic life given socializing of property ownership and extension of direct economic and political democracy.

Second, a *quantitative* goods or state sector would assume responsibility for producing heavy goods both producer and consumer as well as environmentally sound forms of mass transportation, energy delivery and social infrastructure; all forms of use-value production carrying economy of scale requirements transcending capacities of qualitative communities to manage. Potential range of ownership choices for the socialist state sector are quite varied (Roemer, 1994) however a scheme of shareholding predicated on that of contemporary corporations, with shares held by qualitative goods communities linked to the state sector and state sector workers themselves might be adopted. The mode of socio-material communication of this sector would duplicate aspects of the aforementioned iterative participatory planning schemes. However, the requirement of a society-wide equilibrium outcome would be dropped, in part because demand for basic goods is met by more face-to-face exchanges in qualitative communities. As well, like corporations today in transportation and producer goods and many consumer durable sectors, economic programming and planning has already replaced markets in allocating resources. The quantitative goods state sector would have its own currency, exchangeable with the local currencies of the communities with which it interfaces, as well as exchangeable with the currencies of other 'states'; though the issue of whether the construction of a socialist commonwealth of states would utilize the configuring of current states as a template is something that must be dealt with in practice.

Third, for the near future, an administrative sector, interlinked with local communities and quantitative goods sectors through ownership and shared currency may remain the site of governance. Of course, the distinction between these categories is not firm and will necessarily vary according to local and regional geospatial conditions and structures of the pre-socialist economy. The force of this tri-sector model is intended as a means of disrupting global commodity chains shaped by the demands of value augmentation and placing the focus of economic life of socialist society on use-value considerations. The absence of a heavy use-value and administrative sector in green models is a major weakness of the approach as it is through such sectors that elements of cosmopolitan society can be salvaged from capitalism and the material means to clean up capitals' rampage across our biosphere ensured.

In applying the metric for eco-sustainability, the prospective dumping of eco-problems on others inhering in Schumacher's schema of autarchic districts will be averted by the fact that though collectively owned and largely politically independent qualitative goods communities are linked to each other through ownership relations with the quantitative state and administrative urban sectors, thus promoting a broader collective interest in the eco-sanctity of lived environments. Further, and I intend to revisit this issue below, procedures must be established for democratic rotation of working families through each sector. This will offer an incentive to promote eco-sustainability through the entire system of communities. Moreover, with participatory planning in the quantitative goods sector involving both state enterprise stakeholding workers and shareholders from qualitative communities, not only will capitalism's bias toward polluting industrial environments distanced from suburban homes of business owners be reduced, but socialist communities will be empowered to radically transform the energy profile and production process from that under the rule of capital. Also, the adopting of different modes of socio-material communication to satisfy the material requirements of society moves qualitative use-value needs and the sanctity of the human life-world and nature in which material life is embedded to the centre of attention. Finally, the ecopedigree of each community and sector, as well as the patterns of interconnections among them, may then be regularly assessed according to techniques of 'ecological foot-printing' (Wackernagel and Rees, 1996; Chambers, Simmons and Wackernagel, 2000) where the environmental carrying capacity of regions are measured and deficits democratically addressed.

In applying the metric for economic viability to the tri-sector socialist model, it is evident that with the severing and rehabilitation of local community economic life from the ravages of global markets, geospatial reconnecting of production and consumption, instituting of collective ownership, and adopting of varying forms of economic reciprocity and LETS markets as core economic principles, the demand for basic goods within qualitative use-value sectors will be met with minimal difficulty and misallocation of social resources. Surpluses may then be traded for both services and quantitative sector use-values. In the quantitative state sector, socialist enterprises may effectively transmit economic information through iterative participatory plans and compete, as do successful publicly owned companies today (Roemer, 1994). Demand for basic goods will be met in both the state and administrative sectors by qualitative sector supply and potential auxiliary production established in those sectors as with guerrilla gardening in urban settings today.

The tri-sector model sketched here follows Marx in institutionally configuring socialism out of the current existing economy. In much of the developed highly urbanized industrial world, the sectors will not be separated geospatially, but rather the tri-sector format will create vehicles for the instatement of forms of direct political empowerment of publics as well as for the optimal functioning of modes of socio-material communication best geared to use-value economic concerns. In less developed economies and less urbanized areas of developed states, the tri-sector format offers a benchmark for revitalizing community economic life torn asunder by globalization's siphoning off resources (including the very livelihood of communities themselves) toward its urban sprawls and slums. This model also sets socialism on the track of realizing its promise of offering humanity socio-material betterment. The alienation of direct producers in pre-capitalist society deriving from extra-economic compulsions for work and that of capitalism flowing from its commodity-economic compulsion for work will be overcome in the qualitative communities as habits of *self-motivation* for work are engendered among collective owners working for themselves. The quantitative use-value sector will be able to offset the impact of work alienation through increasing automation of work and the democratic rotation of labour forces from qualitative and administrative sectors. This process will also serve to fulfill Marx's belief in socialism enhancing the multidimensionality of human beings in their work lives and to erode divides between mental and manual labour and town and country. Regularizing cooperative relations among sectors will contribute to a 'withering away' of the state. Such a system could be extended within a wider socialist commonwealth facilitating open emigration and immigration in efforts to overcome the apartheids, political, economic and environmental, that mark the current global era.

Conclusion

While it is not yet clear what constellation of class forces will spark socialist revolutionary change, questions of the contours of the future society can longer be avoided. To be sure, it will certainly take at least a few generations to efface the residues of the capitalist commodity economy and reverse much of the damage that this economy has hitherto inflicted upon human beings, the life-world, and earth. Some of the work however can begin immediately at the level of community life, as the global proliferation of community currencies and community based environmental movements display. The socialist *plan* must be to disentangle our economic existence from capitalism and its deleterious practices. This chapter demonstrates that Marx's political economic research agenda contains a wealth of untapped knowledge on economic viability and satisfying of the general norms of economic life and potential for an eco-sustainable socialism. Only by developing these insights will our endeavours for the future overcome the disappointments of the past.

Notes

1. The literature is immense, however benchmark monographs include, Altvater (1993); Burkett (1999); Kovel (2002).
2. Uno (1980) is an English translation of an abridged version of a two volume treatise both available only in Japanese.
3. The defining English language monograph of the Uno approach to Marx's *Capital* is Sekine (1997). The article literature is constantly growing, however for an accessible comparative treatment of the approach see Westra (1999). Westra (2001; 2002; 2004a) represent recent work on the Uno approach to socialism.
4. Simply put, socio-material betterment is the progressive transformation of structures of motivation for work, economic empowerment and quality of human material life in all its multidimensionality from that existing in pre-capitalist and capitalist societies.
5. Postone (1996, p.156) captures this aptly with the notion of capital assuming a position akin to that of the 'Absolute Subject'.
6. As put by Albritton (1999, p. 35), 'We can carry out this theoretical practice because we are objectified by capital but still have the potential cognitively to become knowing subjects capable of theoretically grasping what is happening to us. We can know capital as a subjectified object because we are objectified subjects'.
7. The *theory of a purely capitalist society* derives from Marx's three volumes of *Capital* but arguably completes that project which Marx left unfinished and does so in the modern language of economics and includes debate with neoclassical adversaries.
8. On dialectical logic in Marxian economic theory see Kourkoulakos (2003).
9. This argument is pursued in Westra (2003b; 2006).
10. The Japanese Uno approach argues against utilizing abstract theory directly to 'model' historical outcomes. It argues rather, that political economic study of capitalism requires three levels of analysis where the movement in thought from the abstract TPCS to what Unoists refer to as *historical-empirical analysis* is 'mediated' by a stage theory of capitalist development. Albritton (1991) is the defining Unoist English monograph on stage theory. Albritton, Itoh, Westra and Zuege (2001) are an anthology of competing views on the topic. Westra (2003a; 2006) constitute recent development and operationalizing of Uno's stage theory.

References

Albert, M. and Hahnel, R. 1991. *Looking Forward: Participatory Economics for the Twentieth Century*. Boston: South End Press.
Albritton, R. 1991. *A Japanese Approach to Stages of Capitalist Development*. Basingstoke: Macmillan Press.
—. 1999. *Dialectics and Deconstruction in Political Economy*. Basingstoke: Macmillan Press.
Albritton, R., Itoh, M., Westra, R. and Zuege, A. (eds.), 2001. *Phases of Capitalist Development: Booms, Crises and Globalizations*. Basingstoke: Palgrave.
Altvater, E. 1993. *The Future of the Market: An Essay on the Regulation of Money and Nature after the Collapse of 'Actually Existing Socialism'*. London: Verso.
Burkett, P. 1999. *Marx and Nature*. New York: St. Martin's Press.
Chambers, N., Simmons, C. and Wackernagel, M. 2000. *Sharing Nature's Interest: Ecological Footprints as an Indicator of Sustainability*. London: Earthscan.

Cockshott, W. P. and Cottrell, A. F. 1997. 'Value, Markets and Socialism', *Science & Society*, 61, 3.
—. 2003. 'Economic Planning, Computers and Labor Values'. Paper presented at the International Conference on the Work of Karl Marx and Challenges for the XXI Century, Havana, Cuba, May 5–8.
Gough, J. and Eisenschitz, A. 1997. 'The Division of Labour, Capitalism and Socialism: An Alternative to Sayer', *International Journal of Urban and Regional Research*, 21, 1.
Kourkoulakos, S. 2003. 'The Specificity of Dialectical Reason' in Albritton, R. and Simoulidis, J. (eds.), *New Dialectics and Political Economy*. Basingstoke: Palgrave.
Kovel, J. 2002. *The Enemy of Nature: The End of Capitalism or the End of the World*. London: Zed Books.
Lipietz, A. 2004. 'Kyoto, Johannesburg, Baghdad', *International Journal of Political Economy*, 34, 1.
Pepper, D. 1993. *Eco-Socialism*, London: Routledge.
Postone, M. 1996 *Time, Labor and Social Domination*. Cambridge: Cambridge University Press.
Roemer, J. E. 1994. *A Future for Socialism*. Cambridge, Mass.: Harvard University Press.
Schumacher, E. F. 1999 [1973]. *Small is Beautiful*. Vancouver, BC: Hartley and Marks.
Schweickart, D. 1998. 'Market Socialism: A Defense' in Ollman, B. (ed.), *Market Socialism: The Debate among Socialists*. London: Routledge.
Sekine, T. 1990. 'Socialism as a Living Idea', in Flakierski, H. and Sekine, T. (eds.), *Socialist Dilemmas, East and West*. New York: M E Sharp.
—. 2004. 'Socialism Beyond Market and Productivism' in Albritton, R., Bell, S., Bell, J. and Westra, R. (eds.), *New Socialisms: Futures Beyond Globalization*. Innis Centenary Series: Governance and Change in the Global Era. London: Routledge.
Uno, K. 1980. *Principles of Political Economy*. New Jersey: Humanities Press.
Wackernagel, M. and Rees, W. 1995. *Our Ecological Footprint: Reducing Human Impact on Earth*. Gabriola Island, B C.: New Society Publishers.
Webber, M. J and Rigby, D. L. 2001. 'Growth and Change in the World Economy Since 1950' in Albritton, R., Itoh, M., Westra, R. and Zuege, A. (eds.), *Phases of Capitalist Development: Booms, Crises and Globalizations*. Basingstoke: Palgrave.
Westra, R. 1999. 'A Japanese Contribution to the Critique of Rational Choice Marxism', *Social Theory and Practice*, 25, 3.
—. 2001. 'Phases of Capitalism and Post-Capitalist Social Change' in Albritton, R., Itoh, M., Westra, R. and Zuege, A. (eds.), *Phases of Capitalist Development: Booms, Crises and Globalizations*. Basingstoke: Palgrave.
—. 2002. 'Marxian Economic Theory and an Ontology of Socialism: A Japanese Intervention', *Capital & Class*, 78.
—. 2003a. 'Phases of Capitalism, Globalizations and the Japanese Economic Crisis' in Busumtwi-Sam, J. and Dobuzinskis, L. (eds.), *Turbulence and New Directions in Global Political Economy*. Basingstoke: Palgrave.
—. 2003b. 'Globalization: The Retreat of Capital to the 'Interstices' of the World?' in Westra, R. and Zuege, A. (eds.), *Value and the World Economy Today: Production, Finance and Globalization*. Basingstoke: Palgrave.
—. 2004a. 'The 'Impasse' Debate and Socialist Development' in Albritton, R., Bell, S., Bell, J. and Westra, R. (eds.), *New Socialisms: Futures Beyond Globalization*, Innis Centenary Series: Governance and Change in the Global Era. London: Routledge.
—. 2004b. 'Globalization and the Pathway to Socio-material Betterment', *Review of Radical Political Economics*, 36, 3.
—. 2006. 'The Capitalist Stage of Consumerism and South Korean Development', *Journal of Contemporary Asia*, 36, 1.

INDEX

A

accumulation 73, 78, 90, 93, 98, 100, 103, 112, 165, 203, 225
   by dispossession 4, 36, 85, 135–7, 146
   flexible 19
   logic of 209–10
   over 36, 38–9, 128, 133–4
addiction 45, 48, 57, 60, 61
administrative sector 231
adulteration 45
advertising 57, 60, 61
agriculture 53, 55
acquired immune deficiency disorders (AIDS) 28, 136, 150
Albritton, R. 4, 224
American food regime 61
American dollar 129–30, 142–3
American hegemony 14, 15, 67, 82–3, 86, 92–4
Antrobus, P. 148–9
Arrighi, G. 3, 7, 13–19, 37, 133
asset price volatility 134; *see also* housing bubble
austerity 94–5

B

balance of payments 92, 99, 129
bankruptcy 140
barter 231
beef industry 54
Bergson, Henri 48
biopiracy 138
Bond, Patrick 123
bourgeois-democratic state 163–4
Brandt, Barbara 124, 177–8
Braudel, Fernand 13-16, 37

Brennan, Teresa 48
Brenner, Robert 3, 7, 9, 17–19, 133
Bretton Woods System 90, 92, 112, 145, 215
bribes 56, 168
Buchanan, Alan 26
business confidence 164
business cycles 9, 10, 14, 16, 17, 21, 48, 49, 50, 72, 221
   see also crises

C

cadre radicalization 201–7, 210, 214
Callinicos, Alex 39
capital 12, 16, 30, 44–5, 167
capitalism 15, 21–2, 32, 38, 52, 68–9, 75, 160–2, 202, 220, 221–6
capitalist discipline, *see* capitalist hegemony
capitalist hegemony 14, 15, 20, 206, 216
capitalist property rights 163–4
carbon dioxide 53, 138
Carter, J. 165–6
central bank independence 90, 97, 105–113, 169
centralization/concentration 50, 55, 59, 208
Channel One 57
chemicals 53, 58–9, 61
China 38, 52, 56, 62, 143
chocolate 62
citizen rights 91
class 30, 48, 49, 92, 103, 124, 125, 183, 187, 192, 202–4, 222
class struggle 18, 44, 45, 50, 94, 104, 132

climate change xiv, xv, 128
Clinton, W. 165–6
Cold War xv, 80, 91
combining 193–4
commodity 12, 43, 44, 49, 57, 72
    fictitious 14, 16
commodification/decommodification 55, 123, 127, 131, 136, 150, 228
    of labour-power 50, 58, 136, 222, 224, 227
competition 11, 27, 35, 50–1
conjuncture 71
constant capital 16
consumerism 225–6
consumption 29, 31, 32, 48–9, 54, 56, 62, 225
    conspicuous 49
contingency 8, 21
contradiction 17, 43, 124
cooperatives 211
corporation 59, 188
corruption 167
credit policy 91
crises 2, 14, 72, 95, 97, 99, 104, 123, 127, 129, 132–4, 140, 145, 177, 202, 211; *see also* business cycles
critical theory of capital 8–9, 11, 18–19
culture 19, 20
currency
    collapse 92
    instability 142

D

debt/credit 46, 56, 61, 127, 129, 130, 139, 144
deep structure 19–21, 44, 221

deficit
    current account 141
    spending 139, 142
demand 48, 62, 225–6
democracy 104, 111, 125, 151, 216, 228, 231
    democratic socialism 46, 63
deregulation 101, 104, 137, 165
derivatives 75
desertification 55; *see also* land
desire 57
deskill 32
diabetes 52, 57
discernment 191–3
diversification 195–7
divide and rule 45
domination 74, 184; *see also* hegemony
dot.com bubble 140
dumping toxic waste 138–9

E

East Asia 15, 28, 129, 141
eating habits 60
ecology 51, 77, 83, 86, 132, 137, 138, 203, 212, 219–20, 223, 225–7, 229, 231–2
ecological dominance 74–86
economics 27, 33, 221
economic growth 26, 27, 29
economic policy 89
economic planning 227
economies of scale 53, 231
economic scale 228–9
education 162, 170–2
efficiency 101, 163
egalitarian universalism 27, 31
emancipation 22
employment 99, 100, 104, 114, 136
endogenous change 27, 30–1, 35, 70

enterprise resource planning 209
equilibrium 221–3, 228
equality 26, 41, 187–9; *see also* egalitarian universalism and inequality
euro-dollar market 93
exchange rate
  fixed 91–2, 94–5
  floating 90, 97, 99, 113
  instability 92
exploitation 58, 104, 138–9
externalities 225, 226–7
extra-economic factors/forces 73

F

fall in the profit rate 9, 10, 16, 17, 18, 36, 94, 134
families 136, 161–2, 169–71, 190
fast food 52–60, 169
fat 57, 58, 59
Felix, D. 131
feminism 193–4
financial crises 110, 145; *see also* crises
financial system 91
financialization 13–14, 18, 67, 70, 72–3, 84–5 93, 97, 102–3, 128, 132, 134, 211
fiscal policy 165, 172
  austerity 94, 99
  expansionary 91
fixed capital 9–10
Folbre, N. 190
food regime 4, 51
fordism 10, 21, 68, 73, 204
foreign direct investment (FDI) 28, 91–2, 143, 209
fossil fuels 53
four cycles 14, 37
freedom 49

Friedman, M. 98
Fukuyama, F. xv

G

gender 124, 136, 192–3
genetically modified organism (GM) 53, 61
Germany 91, 100
Gindin, S. 132
golden age 89
gold standard 94, 97
global capitalism 3, 26, 32
global commons 131
global governance 215
global justice 3, 28, 35, 123, 128, 147
global socialism 219
global slums 38
globalization 28, 40, 62, 68, 70, 72, 81, 101, 128, 175–6, 201–2, 209–10, 211, 214, 225–6, 230, 233
green society 227
gross domestic product (GDP) 100, 128–9, 132, 165

H

Habermas, J. 26
Harvey, D. 3, 7, 18–22, 133
Hayek, F. 98, 202, 207
health 51–2, 54–5, 57–61
hedge funds 143, 145
hegemonic
  capital 94, 103
  policy 90
  state 14
Held, D. 26
Hierarchical Polarization Paradigm 177–197

historical specificity 11–13, 18, 20, 68, 70
Hobbes, T. 49
homogenization 47, 54, 55, 61
housing bubble 130, 140
human flourishing 3, 4, 27–8, 31, 39
hunger 51–2

I

identity 49
identity politics 2, 189
ideology 22, 25, 35, 49, 94, 100, 123, 147, 202, 216
idleness 47
illegal aliens 62
industrial reserve army 50
inequality xiv–v, 52, 62 104, 112, 127, 131 180–2
inflation 93–4, 99, 100, 105, 111
   targeting 90, 105–8, 111–13
informal sector 136
insecurity 50
instability 97, 104, 111, 114, 132
integration 91, 102, 190–1, 202
intellectual property rights 38, 151
Internal Revenue Service 166
intensification 32, 54
interest rate 50, 91, 102, 109, 128, 132, 143
International Monetary Fund (IMF) 55, 103, 108, 130–1, 214
international monetary system 97
Ivory Coast 62

J

Japan 10, 91, 93
Jessop, R. 4, 67
justice 26; *see also* global justice

K

Keynes, J. M. 48
Keynesianism 2, 89–97, 100, 113, 139, 165, 202, 206–7
King, M. L. 189, 197
Kotz, D. 123, 159
Kyoto Accord xv

L

labour 19, 30–2, 59, 101, 104, 137; *see also* class, class struggle
land 47, 54
   degradation 212
law 163
large-scale historical patterns 8
legalism 58
legal subject 48–51, 57–8
legitimacy 3, 25, 113, 132
levels of analysis 43–4, 60, 224
Levine, D. 177
liability 58
local exchange and trading systems (LETS) 230–1
Luxemburg, R. 135

M

Malthus, T. 16
Marx, K. 16, 18, 30, 31, 33, 43, 50, 69–70, 80–1, 160, 161, 174n, 183, 211, 219, 220, 221, 226, 229, 230, 232, 234
   and 'new growth theory' 29–33
   critical theory of 8
   theory of the falling rate of profit of 17–18
   value theory of 12, 16–17

Marxism
    orthodox 73
    political economic analysis of 129, 132, 133, 201, 223, 224
Matthaei, J. 124
McDonalds fast food 55, 58, 59, 173
Millennium Development Goals (MDGs) 147, 148–49
modes of regulation 69
monetarism 98–100
monetary policy 112–14
Multilateral Agreement on Investment (MAI) 213

N

National Organization for Women 194
necessary labour 30
neoclassical economics 39n, 221, 223
neocon American xiv
neoconservatism xv, 147
neo-liberalism xiv, 4, 5, 20, 67, 68, 70–3, 81, 83–4, 85–6, 89–90, 100–104, 109, 130, 131–32, 137, 147, 165, 202, 211, 212, 215, 216, 225
    'disciplinary' 137, 216
    ideology 226
    mature 106
'new growth theory' 3, 25, 27–29, 33
New International Economic Order (NIEO) 207, 208
'new monetary policy consensus' (NMPC) 90, 102, 105, 109–10, 113–14
new wars 137

O

'old growth theory' 26
Organization for Economic Cooperation and Development (OECD) 108, 209

P

Panitch, L. 132, 133
participatory planning 227–28
'perfect competition' 35–6
Phillips curve 98
Polanyi, K. 13, 14, 16, 50, 220, 221
postmodernism 22, 23, 177
Postone, M. 3, 234n
Post-Washington Consensus 147
purchasing power parity (PPP) 142

Q

quantity theory of money (QTM) 98–9

R

Regulation School 11, 23n
regimes of accumulation 69
Resurgent Right-wing 147
Ricardo, D. 16
Rio Earth Summit xv
Romer, P. 27, 30, 35
Russia 82

S

Saad-Filho, A. 5
Schumacher, E. F.
    'small is beautiful' argument of 228, 229

Sekine, T. 43, 221
Smith, A. 16
Smith, T. 3
socialism 147, 220, 229, 233
   tri-sector model of 232–33
socialization
   globalized market 210
   market 205
   planned 205, 206
socio-material betterment 220
socio-material communication 230
Solow, R. 26
South Africa 91, 136–37
South Korea 80, 91, 93
Soviet Union (USSR) 202, 207, 208
   environmental record of 227
   economic planning by 227–28
spatio-temporal fix 69, 135
stage theory 224, 234n
state 79, 160, 165–69, 203, 212, 213
   capitalist 83, 163, 164
   capacity 37
   centric theory 18
   imperialist policies 177
   Keynesian 95
   post-Soviet Russian 168–69
   regulation 93
   spending 28
   system 13
   welfare 166
   'welfare-nationalist' 204
surplus labour 30
surplus profit 33
surplus value 30
'systemic cycles of accumulation' 14, 37

T

Taiwan 80, 93
technological dynamism 27, 30
theory of a purely capitalist society (TPCS) 221–22, 223, 234n
'Third Way' 83–4
Third World 127, 134, 144, 150, 206, 207
   debt crisis 140, 145
   Nationalism 147
   super-exploitation of 138
'transformative processes' 184–87
transhistorical logic 20–1
transnational production chains 209, 210
Trilateral Commission 204

U

'underconsumption' 56
uneven development 33, 34, 35
Union for Radical Political Economics 194
United Nations (UN) 101, 147, 206, 207
   Security Council 147
United States (US)
   corporations 134, 188
   corrupt officials and politicians of 167
   education system 170–73
   defeat in Vietnam 94
   families 169–70
   hegemony 14, 15, 67, 80, 93, 98, 103–104
   history 180
   financial system 140
   monetary policy 99
   poverty xiv–xv

regulated form of capitalism in 165–6
trade/budget deficits 129–30, 139
Uno, K. 219, 220, 224
use-value 31, 38, 44, 46, 47, 72, 225
　indifference of capital to 45, 52, 60–1

V

value
　self-valorizing 43
　law of 222
value theory 12
'valuing the devalued' 189
　processes 189–94
van der Pijl, K. 125
'varieties of capitalism' 68–9
Volker shock 99–100, 132, 133

W

'war on terrorism' 83, 84
　and 9/11 xii–iv, 80, 213
'Washington Consensus' 139, 147
Westra, R. 125–6
world market 68, 70, 81
World Social Forum 197
World Trade Organization (WTO) 101, 149, 194, 213, 216, 226

Y

Yum! Brand fast food 55, 59

Z

Zapatismo 146, 196

Printed in Great Britain
by Amazon